MY SECRET LIFE IN VICTORIAN BRITAIN;
A SOCIAL & PSYCHOSEXUAL HISTORY

I0423916

Mark Guy Valerius Tyson

ISBN: 1534883088
ISBN-13: 978-1534883086

OTHER BOOKS AVAILABLE FROM
MARK GUY VALERIUS TYSON

ISRAEL IN BRITAIN
RICHARD TRENCH ON THE STUDY
OF WORDS
HOW TO BE RICH QUICK

AVAILABLE TO BUY NOW ON
AMAZON

CONTENTS

FOREWORD

This work is commonly misunderstood as an erotic novel, however, it is not. It is a true account into not only the social life in Victorian Britain, but of the psychosexual development of the author. Its frank discussion of sexual matters and other hidden aspects of Victorian life make it a rare and valuable social document with the presence of much mundane detail, the writer's inclusion of incidents that do him little personal credit, and the lack of intrinsically improbable circumstances (in contrast to most Victorian erotica) lend it considerable credibility as a resource for any therapist or social scientist. One particularly interesting observation is that a great majority of the author's sexual conquests are either prostitutes, servants or working class women. This would appear to reflect the realities of his time. We also see how his fetishes develop, how experiences in his early life help him develop his confidence with women, in this manner, the author's experience is very much aligned to the kings of old, who's hunger and ability developed in much the same way.

The most frequently cited likely author is Henry Spencer Ashbee, a book collector, writer, and bibliographer notable as an early authority on erotic literature. If Ashbee was not the actual author, he may well have been the compiler of the work's lengthy, detailed, and disorganized index, and have provided other editorial assistance and help in getting the book into print. He is notable for his massive, clandestine three-volume bibliography of erotic literature written under the pseudonym of Pisanus Fraxi. Ashbee was born in Southwark, London. He was by occupation a textile trader, the senior partner in the London branch of the firm of Charles Lavy & Co. He travelled extensively during his life, including Europe, Japan, and San Francisco, collaborating with the American politician Alexander Graham on Travels in Tunisia, published in 1887.

Ashbee married Elisabeth Lavy in Hamburg, Germany in 1862. They had one son, Charles (the designer Charles Robert Ashbee, born 1863), and three daughters. His family life grew unhappier as he aged, as he became more conservative, his family followed the progressive movement of the era. The excessive education of his daughters irritated him, his Jewish wife's pro-suffragism infuriated him, and he became estranged from his socialist homosexual son, Charles. Henry and Elisabeth separated in 1893. Henry Spencer Ashbee is buried in Kensal Green Cemetery. He was an avid book collector, with perhaps the world's most extensive collections of Cervantes and erotica. Influenced by a friendship with the Belgian diplomat Joseph Octave Delepierre, his erotica collecting proceeded with purchases in Amsterdam, Brussels and Paris.

Ashbee was a part of a loose intellectual fraternity of English gentlemen who discussed sexual matters with a freedom that was at odds with Victorian mores; this fraternity included Richard Francis Burton, Richard Monckton Milnes, Algernon Charles Swinburne, and others. He also amassed thousands of volumes of pornography in several languages. He wrote on sex under the pseudonyms "Fraxinus" (Ash) and "Apis" (Bee), and sometimes combined them as "Pisanus Fraxi".

Ashbee's will left his entire collection to the British Museum, with the condition that the erotic works had to be accepted along with the conventional items. Because the trustees wanted the materials related to Cervantes, they decided to accept the bequest. The trustees were allowed to destroy any of the books if they had a duplicate, but in practice went much further and destroyed six boxes "of offensive matter which is of no value or interest" including cheaply produced Victorian erotica. The remainder of the works formed the core of the Private Case which were kept hidden from readers in the British Library for many years; they include a work by William Simpson Potter. MG

INTRODUCTION

In 18-- my oldest friend died. We had been at school and college together, and our intimacy had never been broken. I was trustee for his wife and executor at his death. He died of a lingering illness, during which his hopes of living were alternately raised, and depressed. Two years before he died, he gave me a huge parcel carefully tied up and sealed. Take care of, but don't open this he said: if I get better, return it to me, if I die, let no mortal eye but yours see it, and burn it.

His widow died a year after him. I had well nigh forgotten this packet which I had had full three years, when looking for some title deeds I came cross it, and opened it, as it was my duty to do. Its contents astonished me. The more I read it, the more marvellous it seemed. I pondered long on the meaning of his instructions when he gave it to me, and kept the manuscript some years, hesitating what to do with it.

At length I came to the conclusion knowing his idiosyncracy well, that his fear was only lest any one should know who the writer was; and feeling that it would be sinful to destroy such a history, I copied the manuscript and destroyed the original. He died relationless.

No one now can trace the author, no names are mentioned in the book, though they were given freely in the margin of his manuscript, and I alone know to whom the initials refer. If I have done harm in printing it, I have done none to him, have indeed only carried out his evident intention, and given to a few a secret history, which bears the impress of truth on every page, a contribution to psychology.

PREFACE

I began these memoirs when about twenty-five years old, having from youth kept a diary of some sort, which perhaps from habit made me think of recording my inner and secret life.

When I began it, I had scarcely read a baudy book, none of which excepting "Fanny Hill" appeared to me to be truthful, that did, and it does so still; the others telling of recherché eroticisms, or of inordinate copulative powers, of the strange twists, tricks, and fancies, of matured voluptuousness, and philosophical lewdness, seemed to my comparative ignorance, as baudy imaginings, or lying inventions, not worthy of belief; although I now know by experience, that they may be true enough, however eccentric, and improbable, they may appear to the uninitiated.

Fanny Hill was a woman's experience. Written perhaps by a woman, where was a man's, written with equal truth? That book has no baudy word in it; but baudy acts need the baudy ejaculations; the erotic, full flavoured expressions, which even the chastest indulge in, when lust, or love, is in its full tide of performance. So I determined to write my private life freely as to fact, and in the spirit of the lustful acts done by me, or witnessed; it is written therefore with absolute truth, and without any regard whatever for what the world calls decency. Decency and voluptuousness in its fullest acceptance, cannot exist together, one would kill the other; the poetry of copulation I have only experienced with a few women, which however neither prevented them, nor me from calling a spade, a spade.

I began it for my amusement; when many years had been chronicled I tired of it and ceased. Some ten years afterwards I met a woman, with whom, or with those she helped me do; I did, said, saw, and heard, well nigh everything a man and woman could do with their genitals, and began to narrate those events, when quite fresh in my memory, a great variety of incidents extending over four years or more. Then I lost sight of her, and my amorous amusements for a while were simpler, but that part of my history was complete.

After a little while, I set to work to describe the events of the intervening years of my youth, and early middle age; which included most of my gallant intrigues and adventures of a frisky order; but not the more lascivious ones of later years. Then an illness caused me to think seriously of burning the whole. But not liking to destroy my labor, I laid it aside again for a couple of years. Then another illness gave me long uninterrupted leisure; I read my manuscript, and filled in some occurrences which I had forgotten, but which my diary enabled me to place in their proper order. This will account for the difference in style in places, which I now observe; and a very needless repetition, of voluptuous descriptions, which I had forgotten, had been before described; that however is inevitable, for human copulation, vary the incidents leading up to it as you may, is, and must be, at all times, much the same affair.

Then for the first time, I thought I would print my work that had been commenced more than twenty years before, but hesitated. I then had entered my maturity, and on to the most lascivious portion of my life, the events were disjointed, and fragmentary and my amusement was to describe them just after they occurred. Most frequently the next day I wrote all down with much prolixity, since, I have much abbreviated it.

I had from youth an excellent memory, but about sexual matters a wonderful one. Women were the pleasure of my life. I loved cunt, but also she who had it; I like the woman I fucked and not simply the cunt I fucked, and therein is a great difference. I recollect even now in a degree which astonishes me, the face, colour, stature, thighs, backside, and cunt, of well nigh every woman I have had, who was not a mere casual; and even of some who were. The clothes they wore, the houses and rooms in which I had them, were before me mentally, as I wrote, the way the bed, and furniture were placed, the side of the room the windows were on, I remembered perfectly; and all the important events I can fix as to time, sufficiently nearly by reference to my diary, in which the contemporaneous circumstances of my life are recorded.

I recollect also largely what we said, and did, and generally our bawdy amusements. Where I fail to have done so, I have left description blank, rather than attempt to make a story coherent by inserting what was merely probable. I could not now account for my course of action, nor why I did this, or said that, my conduct seems strange, foolish, absurd, very frequently, that of some women, equally so, but I can but state what did occur.

In a few cases, I have for what even seems to me very strange, suggested reasons, or causes, but only where the facts seem by themselves to be very improbable, but have not exaggerated anything willingly. When I have named the number of times I have fucked a woman in my youth, I may occasionally be in error, it is difficult to be quite accurate on such points after a lapse of time. But as before said in many cases the incidents were written down a few weeks and often within a few days after they occurred. I do not attempt to pose as a Hercules in copulation, there are quite sufficient braggarts on that head, much intercourse with gay women, and doctors, makes me doubt the wonderful feats in coition, some men tell of.

I have one fear about publicity, it is that of having done a few things by curiosity and impulse (temporary abberations), which even professed libertines may cry fie on. There are plenty who will cry fie who have done all and worse than I have and habitually, but crying out at the sins of others was always a way of hiding one's own iniquity. Yet from that cause perhaps no mortal eye but mine, will see this history. The Christian name of the servants mentioned are generally the true ones, the other names mostly false, the phonetically resembling the true ones. Initials nearly always the true ones. In most cases the woman they represent are dead or lost to me. Streets and baudy houses named are nearly always correct. Most of the houses named are now closed or pulled down; but any middle aged man about town would recognize them. Where a road, house, room, or garden is described, the description is exactly true; even to the situation of a tree, chair, bed, sofa, pisspot. The district is sometimes given wrongly; but it matters little whether Brompton be substituted for Hackney, or Camden Town for Walworth. Where however owing to the incidents it is needful, the places of amusement are given correctly. The Tower, and Argyle rooms, for example. All this is done to prevent giving pain to some, perhaps still living, for I have no malice to gratify.

I have mystified family affairs, but if I say I had ten cousins, when I had but six, or that one aunt's house was in Surrey instead of Kent, or in Lancashire; it breaks the clue and cannot matter to the reader.

But my doings with man and woman are as true as

gospel. If I say that I saw, or did, that with a cousin male, or female, it was with a cousin and no mere acquaintance; if with a servant, it was with a servant; if with a casual acquaintance, it is equally true. Nor if I say I had that woman, and did this or that with her, or felt or did aught else with a man, is there a word of untruth excepting as to the place at which the incidents occurred. But even those are mostly correctly given, this is intended to be a true history, and not a lie.

SECOND PREFACE

Some years have passed away since I penned the foregoing, and it is not printed. I have since gone through abnormal phases of amatory life, have done and seen things, had tastes and letches which years ago I thought were the dreams of erotic mad-men; these are all described, the manuscript has grown into unmanageable bulk, shall it, can it be printed? What will be said or thought of me, what become of the manuscript if found when I am dead, better to destroy the whole, it has fulfilled its purpose in amusing me, now let it go to the flames!

I have read my manuscript, through what reminiscences I had actually forgotten some of the early ones; how true the detail strikes me as I read of my early experiences; had it not been written then, it never could have been written now, has anybody but myself faithfully made such a record? It would be a sin to burn all this, whatever society may say it is but a narrative of human life, perhaps the every day life of thousands, if the confession could be had.

What strikes me as curious in reading it, is the monotony of the course I have pursued toward women who were not of the gay class; it has been as similar, and repetitive as fucking itself; do all men act so, does every man kiss, coax, hint smuttily, then talk baudily, snatch a feel, smell his fingers, assault, and win, exactly as I have done? Is every woman offended, say no, then oh! blush, be angry, refuse, close her thighs, after a struggle open them, and yield to her lust as mine have done? A conclave of whores telling the truth, and of Romish Priests, could alone settle the point. Have all men had the strange letches which late in life have enraptured me, though in early days the idea of them revolted me? I can never know this, my experience if printed may enable others to compare as I cannot.

Shall it be burnt or printed? How many years have passed in this indecision, why fear; it is for others' good and not my own if preserved.

CHAPTER I.

Earliest recollections.--An erotic nurse-maid.--Ladies
abed.--My cock.--A frisky governess.--Cousin Fred.--Thoughts
on pudend.--A female pedler.--Baudy pictures.--A naked
baby.

My earliest recollections of things sexual are of what I think must have occurred some time between my age of

13

five, and eight years. I tell of them just as I recollect them, without attempt to fill in what seems probable.

She was I suppose my nursemaid. I recollect that she sometimes held my little prick when I piddled, was it needful to do so? I don't know. She attempted to pull my prepuce back, when, and how often I know not. But I am clear at seeing the prick tip show, of feeling pain, of yelling out, of her soothing me, and of this occurring more than once. She comes to my memory as a shortish, fattish young female and that she often felt my prick.

One day, it must have been late in the afternoon, for the sun was low, but shining--how strange I should recollect that so clearly--but I have always recollected sunshine.--I had been walking out with her, toys had been bought me, we were both carrying them, she stopped and talked to some men, one caught hold of her and kissed her, I felt frightened, it was near a coach stand, for hackney coaches were there, cabs were not then known, she put what toys she had on to my hands, and went into a house with a man. What house? I don't know. Probably a public-house, for there was one not far from a coach stand, and not far from our house. She came out and we went home.

Then I was in our house in a carpeted room with her; it could not have been the nursery I know, sitting on the floor with my toys, so was she; she played with me and the toys, we rolled over each other on the floor in fun, I have a recollection of having done that with others, and of my father and mother, being in that room at times with me playing.

She kissed me, got out my cock, and played with it, took one of my hands and put it underneath her clothes. It felt rough there, that's all, she moved my little hand violently there then she felt my cock and again hurt me, I recollect seeing the red tip appear as she pulled down the prepuce, and my crying out, and her quieting me.

Then of her being on her back, of my striding across or between her legs, and her heaving me up and down, and my riding cock-horse and that it was not the first time I had done so; then I fell flat on her, she heaved me up and down and squeezed me till I cried. I scrambled off of her, and in doing so, my hand, or foot went through a drum, I had been drumming on, at which I cried.

As I sat crying on the floor besides her, I recollect her naked legs, and one of her hands shaking violently beneath her petticoats, and of my having some vague notion that the woman was ill, I felt timid. All was for a moment quiet, her hand ceased, still she lay on her back, and I saw her thighs, then turning round she drew me to her, kissed me and tranquillised me. As she turned round I saw one side of her backside, I leant over it and laid my face on it, crying about my broken drum, the evening sunbeams made it all bright, it had at some time been raining I recollect.

I expect I must have seen her cunt, as I sat beside her naked thigh. Looking towards her and crying about my broken drum, and when I saw her hand moving no doubt she was frigging. Yet I have not the slightest recollection of her cunt, nor of anything more than I have told. But of having seen her naked thighs, I am certain, I seem often to have seen them, but cannot feel certain of that.

The oddest thing is, that whilst I early recollected more or less clearly what took place two or three years later on, and ever afterwards, on sexual matters; and what I said, heard, and did, and nearly consecutively, this my first recollection of cock, and cunt, escaped my memory for full twenty years.

Then one day talking with the husband of one of my cousins, about infantine incidents he told me something which had occurred to him in his childhood; and suddenly, almost as quickly as a magic lantern throws a picture on to a wall, this which had occurred to me came into my mind. I have since thought over it a hundred times, but cannot recollect one circumstance relating to the adventure more than I have told.

My mother had been giving advice to my cousin about nursemaids. They were not to be trusted. "When Walter was a little fellow, she had dismissed a filthy creature, whom she had detected in abominable practices with one of her children," what they were my mother never disclosed. She hated indelicacies of any sort, and usually cut short allusion to them by saying, "It's not a subject to talk about, let's talk of something else." My cousin told her husband, and when we were together he told me, and his own experiences, and then all the circumstances came into my mind, just as I have told here.

I could not, as the reader will hear, thoroughly uncover my prick tip without pain, till I was sixteen years old nor well then when quite stiff unless it went up a cunt. My nursemaid I expect thought this curious, and tried to remedy the error in my make, and hurt me. My mother, by her extremely delicate feeling, shut herself off from much knowledge of the world, which was the reason why she had such implicit belief in my virtue, until I had seen twenty-two years, and kept, or nearly so, a French harlot.

I imagine I must have slept with this nurse-maid, and certainly I did with some female, in a room called the Chinese room, on account of the colour of the wall papers. I recollect a female being there in bed with me, that I awoke one morning feeling very hot, and stifled, and that my head was against flesh; that flesh was all about me, my mouth and nose being embedded in hair, or some thing scrubby, which had a hot peculiar odour. I have a recollection of a pair of hands suddenly clutching, and dragging me up on to the pillow, and of daylight then. I have no recollection of a word being uttered. This incident I could not long have forgotten, having told my cousin Fred, of it before my father died. He used to say it was the governess. I suppose, I must have slipped down in my sleep, till my head laid against her belly, and cunt.

Some years afterwards when I got the smell of another woman's cunt on my fingers, it at once reminded me of the smell I had under my nose in the bed; and I knew at a flash, that I had smelt cunt before, and recollected where, but no more.

How long after, I have no idea, but it seems like two or three years, there was a dance in our house, several relations were to stop the night with us, the house was full, here was bustle, the shifting of beds, the governess going into a servant's room to sleep, and so on. Some female cousins were amongst those stopping with us; going into the drawing-room suddenly, I heard my mother saying to one of my aunts: "Walter is after all but a child, and its only for one night." Hish-hish both said, as they saw me, then my mother sent me out of the room, wondering why they were talking about me, and feeling curious, and annoyed at being sent away.

I had been in the habit then of sleeping in a room, either with another bed in it, or close to a room leading out of it, with another bed, I cannot recollect which; I used to call out to whoever might have been there when I was in bed: for being timid, the door was kept open for me. It could not have been a man who slept there, for the men

17

servants slept on the ground-floor, I have seen their beds there.

The night I speak of, my bed was taken out, and put into the Chinese paper room, one of the maids who helped to move it, sat on the pot and piddled; I heard the rattle, and as far as I can recollect it was the first time I noticed anything of the sort, tho I recollect well seeing women putting on their stockings and feeling the thigh of one of them just above her knee. I was kneeling on the floor at the time, and had a trumpet, which she took angrily out of my hand soon afterwards, because I made a noise.

I recollect the dance, that I danced with a tall lady, that my mother contrary to custom as it seems to me, put me to bed herself, and that it was before the dance was over, for I felt angry and tearful at being put to bed so early. My mother closed the curtains quite tightly all round a small four post bed, and told me, I was to lie quietly, and not get up till she came to me in the morning; not to speak, nor undo my curtains, nor to get out of bed, or I should disturb Mr. and Mrs. ------ who were to sleep in the big bed; that it would make them angry if I did. I am almost certain she named a lady and her husband, who were going to stay with us; but can't be sure. A man then frightened me more than a woman, my mother I dare say knew that.

I dare say, for it was the same the greater part of my life, that I went to sleep directly I laid down, usually never awaking till the morning. Certainly I must have gone fast asleep that night; perhaps I had had a little wine given me, who knows; I have a sudden consciousness of a light, and hear some one say, he is fast asleep, don't make a noise; it seemed like my mother's voice. I rouse myself and listen, the circumstances are strange, the room strange, it excites me, and I rise on my knees, I don't know whether naturally, or cautiously, or how; perhaps cautiously, because I fear angering my mother, and the gentleman, perhaps a sexual instinct makes me curious, though that is not probable. I have not in fact the slightest conception of the actuating motive, but I sat up and listened. There were two females talking, laughing quietly, and moving about, I heard a rattling in the pot, then a rest, then again a rattle and knew the sound of piddling. How long I listened, I don't know, I might have dozed and awakened again, I saw lights moved about; then I crawled on my knees, with fear that I was doing wrong, and pushed a little aside the curtains where they met at the bottom of the bed. I recollect their being quite tight by the tucking in and that I could not easily make an opening to peep through.

There was a girl, or young woman with her back to me, brushing her hair, another was standing by her, one took a night gown off the chair, shook it out, and dropped it over her head, after drawing off her chemise. As this was done I saw some black at the bottom of her belly, a fear came over me, that I was doing wrong and should be punished if found looking, and I laid down wondering at it all, I fancy I again slept.

Then there was a shuffling about, and again it seems as if I heard a noise like piddling, the light was put out, I felt agitated, I heard the women kiss, one say hish! you will wake that brat, then one said listen, then I heard kisses and breathing like some one sighing, I thought some one must be ill and felt alarmed and must then have fallen asleep. I do not know who the women were, they must have been my cousins, or young ladies who had come to the dance. That was the first time I recollect seeing the hair of a cunt, though I must have seen it before, for I recollect at times a female (most likely a nursemaid) stand naked, but don't recollect noticing anything black between her thighs, nor did I think about it at all afterwards.

In the morning my mother came and took me up to her room, where she dressed me, as she left the room, she said to the females in bed, they were not to hurry up, she had only fetched Wattie.

But all this only came vividly to my mind when, a few years after, I began to talk about women with my cousin, and we told each other all we had seen, and heard, about females.

Until I was about twelve years old I never went to school, there was a governess in the house who instructed me, and the other children, my father was nearly always at home. I was carefully kept from the grooms and other men servants; once I recollect getting to the stable yard and seeing a stallion mount a mare, his prick go right out of sight in what appeared to me to be the mares bottom, of father appearing and calling out "What does that boy do there," and my being hustled away. I had scarcely a boy acquaintance excepting among my cousins, and therefore did not learn as much about sexual matters, as boys early do at schools. I did not know what the stallion was doing. I could have had no notion of it then, nor did I think about it.

The next thing I clearly recollected, was one of my male cousins stopping with us, we walked out and when piddling together against a hedge, his saying: "show me your cock, Walter, and I will show you mine." We stood and examined each others cocks, and for the first time, I became conscious, that I could not get my foreskin easily back, like other boys. I pulled his backwards and forwards. He hurt me, laughed and sneered at me, another boy came and I think another, we all compared cocks, and mine was the only one which would not unskin, they jeered me, I burst into tears, and went away, thinking there was something wrong with me, and was ashamed to show my cock again, then I set to work earnestly to try to pull the foreskin back, but always desisted fearing the pain, for I was very sensitive.

My cousin then told me that girls had no cock, but only a hole they piddled out of, we were always talking about them, but I don't recollect the word cunt, nor that I attached any lewd idea to a girl's piddling hole, or to their cocks being flat, an expression heard I think at the same period. It remained only in my mind that my cock and the girl's hole were to piddle out of, and nothing more, I cannot be certain about my age at this time.

Afterwards I went to that uncle's house often, my cousin Fred was to be put to school, and we talked a great deal more about girls' cocks which began to interest me much. He had never seen one he said, but he knew that they had two holes, one for bogging and the other to piddle from. They sit down to piddle said he, they don't piddle against a wall as we do, but that I must have known already, afterwards I felt very curious about the matter.

One day, one of his sisters left the room where we were sitting, she is going to piddle, he said to me. We sneaked into a bed room of one of them one day, and gravely looked into the pot to see what piddle was in it. Whether we expected to find anything different from what there was in our own chamber pot, I do not know. When talking about these things my cousin would twiddle his cock. We wondered how the piddle came out, if they wetted their legs and if the hole was near the bum hole, or where; one day Fred and I pissed against each others cocks, and thought it excellent fun.

I recollect being very curious indeed about the way girls piddled after this, and seeing them piddle became a taste I have kept all my life. I would listen at the bed room doors, if I could get near them unobserved, when my mother, sister, the governess, or a servant went in, hoping to hear the rattle and often succeeded: it was accompanied by no sexual desire, or idea, as far as I can recollect; I had no cockstand, and am sure, that I then did not know that the women had a hole called a cunt, and used it for fucking. I can recall no idea of the sort, it was simple curiosity to know something about those, whom I instinctively felt were made differently from myself. What sort of a hole could it be I wondered. Was it large? Was it round? Why did they squat instead of stand up, like men, my curiosity became intense.

How long after this the following took place, I can't say, but my cock was bigger. I have that impression very distinctly.

One day, there were people in one of the sitting rooms, where my mother and father were I don't know; they were not in the room, and were most likely out. There were one or two of my cousins, some youths, my big sister and one brother, besides others, our governess, and her sister, who was stopping with us, and sleeping in the same room with her. I recollect both going into the bed room together, it was next to mine. It was evening, we had sweet wine, cake, and snap-dragon, and played at something, at which all sat in a circle on the floor. I was very ticklish, it nearly sent me into fits, we tickled each other on the floor. There was much fun, and noise, the governess tickled me, and I tickled her. She said as I was taken to bed, or rather went, as I then did by myself, "I'll go and tickle you." Now at that time when in bed, a servant, or my mother, or the governess took away the light, and closed the door; for I was still frightened to get into bed in the dark, and used to call out, "Mamma, I'm going to get into bed." Then they fetched the light, they wished to stop this timidity, often scolded me about it, and made me undress myself, by myself, to cure me of it.

I expect the other children had been put to bed. My mother keeping all the younger ones in the room near her. The nursery was also upstairs, my room, as said, was next to the governess.

When in bed, I called out for some one to put out the light, up came the governess and her sister. She began to tickle me, so did her sister, I laughed, screeched, and tried to tickle them. One of them closed the door and then came back to tickle me. I kicked all the clothes off, and was nearly naked, I begged them to desist, felt their hands on my naked flesh, and am quite sure, that one of them touched my prick more than once, though it might have been done accidentally. At last I wriggled off the bed, my night-gown up to my armpits, and dropped with my naked bum on to the floor, whilst they tickled me still, and laughed at my wriggling about, and yelling.

Then what induced me, heaven alone knows; it may have been what I had heard about the piddling-hole of a woman, or curiosity, or instinct, I don't know; but I caught hold of the governess' leg as she was trying to get me up on to the bed again, saying, "that will do, my dear boy, get into bed, and let me take away the light." I would not; the other lady helped to lift me, I pushed my hands up the petticoats of the governess, felt the hair of her cunt, and that there was something warm, and moist, between her thighs. She let me drop on to the floor, and jumped away from me. I must have been clinging to her thigh, with both hands up her petticoats, and one between her thighs, she cried out loudly--oh!

Then slap-slap-slap, in quick succession, came her hand against my head, "You...rude...bad...boy," said she slapping me at each word, "I've a good mind to tell your mamma, get into bed this instant," and into bed I got without a word. She blew out the light, and left the room with her sister, leaving me in a dreadful funk. I scarcely knew that I had done wrong, yet had some vague notion, that feeling about her thighs was punishable; the soft hairy place my hand had touched, impressed me with wonder, I kept thinking there was no cock there, and felt a sort of delight at what I had done.

I heard them then talking, and laughing loudly, thru the partition. "They are talking about me, oh if they tell mamma, oh! what did I do it for?" Trembling with fear, I jumped out of bed, opened my door, and went to theirs listening; theirs was ajar,--heard: "right up between my thighs, felt it! he must have felt it; ah! ah! ah! would you ever have thought the little beast would have done such a thing." They both laughed heartily. "Did you see his little thing?" said one. "Shut the door, it's not shut;"--breathless I got back to my room, and into bed, and laying there, heard them through the partition roaring with laughter again.

That is the first time in my life, I recollect passing an all but sleepless night. The dread of being told about, and dread at what I had done, kept me awake. I heard the two women talking for a long time. Mixed with my dread was a wonder at the hair, and the soft, moist feel, I had had for an instant, on some part of my hand. I knew I had felt the hidden part of a female, where the piddle came from, and that is all I did think about it, that I know of, I have no recollection of a lewd sensation, but of a curious sort of delight only.

It must have been from this time, that my curiosity about the female form strengthened, but there was nothing sensual in it. I was fond of kissing, for my mother remarked it; when a female cousin, or any female kissed me, I would throw my arms round them, and keep on kissing. My aunts used to laugh, my mother corrected me, and told me it was rude. I used to say to the servants, kiss me. One day I heard my godfather say: "Walter knows a pretty girl from an ugly one doesn't he?"

I had a dread of meeting the governess, at breakfast, watched her, and saw her laugh at her sister, I watched my mother for some days after, and at length said to the governess, who had punished me for something. "Don't tell mamma." "I have nothing to tell about, Walter," she replied, "and don't know what you mean." I began to tell her what was on my mind. "What's the child talking about, you are dreaming, some stupid boy has been putting things into your head, your papa will thrash you, if you talk like that." "Why you came and tickled me," said I. "I tickled you a little when I put your light out," said she, "be quiet." I felt stupified, and suppose the affair must have passed away from my mind for a time, but I told my cousin Fred about it afterwards. He thought I must have been dreaming, and I began to wonder if it really had occurred, I never thought much about it until I began to recall my childhood for this history.

I must have been twelve years old, when I went to an uncle's in Surrey, and became a close friend of my cousin Fred, a very devil from his cradle, and of whom much more will be told: before then I had only seen him at intervals. We were then allowed, and it seems to me not before that time, to go out by ourselves. We talked boyish baudiness. "Ain't you green," said he, "a girl's hole isn't called a cock, it's a cunt, they fuck with it," and then he told me all he knew. I don't think I had heard that before, but can't be sure.

From that time a new train of ideas came into my head. I had a vague idea, though not a belief, that a cock and cunt, were not made for pissing only. Fred treated me as a simpleton in these matters, and was always calling me an ass; I have quite a painful recollection of my inferiority to him, in such things, and of begging him to instruct me. "They make children that way," said Fred. "You come up and we will ask the old nurse, where children come from, and she'll say 'out of the parsley-bed,' but it's all a lie." We went and asked her in a casual sort of way. She replied, "the parsley-bed," and laughed. The nurse at my house told me the same, when I asked afterwards about my mother's last baby. "Ain't they liars?" Fred remarked to me, "it comes out of their cunts, and it's made by fucking."

We both desired to see women piddling, though both must have before seen them at it often enough. Walking near the market-town with him just at the outskirts, and looking up a side-road, we saw a pedler woman squat down and piss. We stopped short and looked at her: she was a short-petticoated, thick-legged, middle-aged woman; the piss ran off in a copious stream, and there we stood grinning. "Be off, be off, what are you standing grinning at, yer dam'd young fools," cried the woman, "be off, or I'll heave a stone at yer," and she pissed on. We moved a few steps back, but keeping our face towards her, Fred stooped, and put his head down. "I can see it coming," said he jeeringly. He was rude from his infancy, bold in baudiness to the utmost, had the impudence of the devil. The stream ceased, the woman rose up swearing, took up a big flint and threw it at us. "I'll tell on yer," she cried. "I know yer, wait till I see yer again." She had a large basket of crockery for sale, it was put down in the main-road at the angle; she had just turned round into the side lane to piss. We ran off, and when well away, turned round and shouted at her, "I saw your cunt," Fred bawled out;--she flung another stone. Fred took up one, threw it, and it crashed into the crockery, the woman began to chase us, off we bolted across the fields home. She could not follow us that way; it was an eventful day for us. I recollect feeling full of envy at Fred's having seen her cunt. Though writing now, and having in my mind's eye, exactly how the woman squatted, and the way her petticoats hung, I am sure he never did see it; it was brag when he said he had, but we were always talking about girls' cunts, the desire to see one was great, and I then believed that he had seen the pedlar woman's.

Then one of Fred's companions showed us a bawdy picture, it was coloured. I wondered at the cunt being a long sort of gash, I had an idea that it was round, like an arse-hole. Fred told his friend I was an ass, but I could not get the idea of a cunt, not being a round hole quite out of my head, until I had fucked a woman. We were all anxious to get the picture, and tossed up for it, but neither I nor Fred got it, some other boy did.

Soon after that, Fred came to stop with us and our talk was always about women's privates, our curiosity became intense. I had a little sister about nine months old, who was in the nursery. Fred incited me to look at her cunt, if I could manage it. The two nurses came down in turns, to the servants dinner. I was often in the nursery, and soon after Fred's suggestion, was there one day, when the oldest nurse said: "Stop here, master Walter, while I go downstairs, for a couple of minutes, Mary (the other nurse) will be up directly, and don't make a noise." My little sister was lying on the bed asleep. "Yes, I'll wait." Down went nurse, leaving the door open; quick as lightning, I threw up the infant's clothes, saw her little slit, and put my finger quite gently on it, she was laying on her back most conveniently. I pulled one leg away to see better, the child awakened and began crying, I heard footsteps and had barely time to pull down her clothes, when the under nursemaid came in. I only had a momentary glimpse, of the outside of the little quim, for I was not a minute in the room with the child by myself altogether, and was fearful of being caught all the time I was looking.

There must have been something in my face, for the nursemaid said: "What it the matter, what have you been doing to the baby?" Nothing. "Yes, you are colouring up, now tell me." "Nothing. I have done nothing." "You wakened your sister." "No, I have not." The girl laid hold of me, and gave me a little shake. "I'll tell your mamma if you don't tell me, what is it now?" "No, I have done nothing, I was looking out of the window when she began to cry." "You're telling a story, I see you are," said the nursemaid; and off I went, after being impudent to her.

I told Fred and he tried the same dodge, but don't recollect whether he succeeded or not. His sisters were somewhat older, and we began to scheme how to see their cunts, when I was on a visit to his mother's (my aunt) which was to come off in the holidays. The look of the little child's cunt, as I described it, convinced him that the picture was correct, and that a cunt was a long slit, and not a round hole. That cast doubt on males putting their pricks into them, and we clung somehow to the idea of a round hole, and we quarrelled about it.

It must have been about this time, that I was walking with my father, and read something that was written with chalk, on the walls. I asked him what it meant. He said he did not know, that none but low people, and blackguards wrote on walls; and it was not worth while noticing such things. I was conscious that I had done wrong somehow, but did not know exactly what. When I went out, which I was now allowed to do for short distances by myself, I copied what was on the walls, to tell Fred, it was foul, baudy language of some sort, but the only thing we understood at all, was the word cunt.

Just then, being out with some boys, we saw two dogs fucking. I have no recollection of seeing dogs doing that before. We closed round them, yelling with delight as they stuck rump to rump, then one boy said that was what men and women did, and I asked, did they stick together so, a boy replied that they did; others denied it, and all the remainder of the day, some of us discussed this; the impression left on my mind is, that it appeared to be very nasty; but it seemed at the same time to confirm me in the belief, that men put their pricks up into women's holes, about which I seemed at that time to have grave doubts.

After this time my recollection of events is clearer, and I can tell not only what took place, but better what I heard, said, and thought.

CHAPTER II.

My godfather.--At Hampton-Court.--My aunt's backside.--
Public baths.--My cousins' cunts.--Haymaking frolics.--
Family difficulties.--School amusements.--A masturbating
relative.--Romance and sentiment.

My godfather (whose fortune I afterwards inherited) was very fond of me; somewhere about this time he used perpetually to be saying, "When you get to school, don't you follow any of the tricks yourself, that other boys do, or you will die in a mad-house; lots of boys do." And he told me some horrible tales; it was done in a mysterious way. I felt there was a hidden meaning, and not having knowledge of what it was, asked him. I should know fast enough, said he, but mark his words. He repeated this so often, that it sunk deeply into my mind, and made me uneasy, something was to happen to me, if I did something--I did not know what--it was intended as a caution against frigging, and it had good effect on me I am sure in various ways in the after time.

One day talking with Fred, I recollected what I had done to the governess. I had kept it to myself all along for fear. "What a lie," said he. "I did really." "Oh! ain't you a liar," he reiterated, "I'll ask Miss Granger." The same governess was with us then.

At this remark of his, an absolute terror came over me, the dread was something so terrible, that the recollection of it is now painful. "Oh don't, pray don't, Fred," I said, "oh if Papa should hear!" He kept on saying he would. I was too young to see the improbability of his doing anything of the sort. "If you do, I'll tell him what we did when the pedler woman piddled." He did not care. "Now, it's a lie, isn't it, you did not feel her cunt?" In fear, I confessed it was a lie. "I know it was," said Fred. He had kept me in a state of terror about the affair for days, till I told a lie, to get quit of the subject.

I was evidently always secret, even then, about anything amorous, excepting with Fred (as will be seen) and have continued so all my life. I rarely bragged, or told anyone of my doings; perhaps this little affair with the governess, was a lesson to me, and confirmed me in a habit natural to me from my infancy. I have kept to myself everything I did with the opposite sex.

We now frequently examined our pricks, and Fred jeered me so about my prepuce being tight, that I resolved that no other boy should see it; and though I did not keep strictly to that intention, it left a deep-seated mortification on me. I used to look at my prick with a sense of shame, and pull the prepuce up and down, as far as I could constantly, to loosen it, and would treat other boys' cocks in the same way, if they would let me, without expecting me to make a return; but the time was approaching when I was to learn much more.

One of my uncles, who lived in London, took a house in the country for the summer near Hampton-Court Palace. Fred and I went to stay there with them. There were several daughters and sons, the sons quite young. People then came down from London in vans, carts, and carriages of all sorts, to see the Palace and grounds (there was no railway), they were principally of the small middle classes, and used to picnic, or else dine at the taverns when they arrived; then full, and frisky, after their early meal, go into the parks and gardens. They do so still, but times were different then, so few people went there comparatively; fewer park-keepers to look after them, and less of what is called delicacy, amongst visitors of the class named.

Our family party used to go into the grounds daily, and all day long nearly, if we were not on the river banks. Fred winked at me one day, "let's lose Bob," said he, "and we'll have such a lark." Bob was one of our little cousins, generally given into our charge. We lost Bob purposely. Said Fred, "if you dodge the gardiners, creep up there, and lay on your belly quietly, some girls will be sure to come, and piss, you'll see them pull their clothes up as they turn round, I saw some before you came to stay with us." So we went pushing our way among shrubs, and evergreens, till a gardiner, who had seen us, called out, "You there, come back, if I catch you going off the walks, you'll be put outside." We were in such a funk, Fred cut off one way, I another, but it only stopped us for that day. Fred so excited me about the girls' arses, as he called them, that we never lost an opportunity of trying for a sight, but were generally baulked. Once or twice only we saw a female squat down, but nothing more, till my mother and Fred's came to stop with us.

Fred's mother, mine, the girls, Fred and I went into the Park gardens, one day after luncheon. A very hot day, for we kept in the shady walks, one of which led to the place where women hid themselves to piss. My aunt said, "Why don't you boys go and play, you don't mind the sun," so off we went, but when about to leave the walk, turned round and saw the women had turned back. Said Fred, "I'm sure they are going to piss, that's why they want to get rid of us." We evaded the gardiners, scrambled through shrubs, on our knees, and at last on our bellies up a little bank, on the other side of which was the vacant place on which dead leaves and sweepings were shot down. As we got there, pushing aside the leaves, we saw the big backside of a woman, who was half standing, half squatting, a stream of piss falling in front of her, and a big hairy gash, as it seemed, under her arse; but only for a second, she had just finished as we got the peep, let her clothes fall, tucked them between her legs, and half turned round. We saw it was Fred's mother, my aunt. Off aunt went. "Isn't it a wopper," said Fred, "lay still, more of them will come."

Two or three did, one said, "you watch if anyone is coming," squatted and piddled, we could not see her cunt, but only part of her legs, and the piddle splashing in front of her. Then came the second, she had her arse towards us, sat so low, that we could not even see the tips of her buttocks. Fred thought it a pity they did not stand half up like his mother. On other occasions, we went to the same place, but though I recollect seeing some females' legs, don't recollect seeing any more. Nevertheless the sights were very delightful to us, and we used to discuss his mother's "wopper" and the hair, and the look of the gash, but I thought there must be some mistake, for it was not the idea I had formed of a cunt.

Fred soon after stopped with us in town, we had been forbidden to go out together, without permission, but we did, and met a boy bigger than either of us, who was going to bathe. "Come and see them bathing," he said. My father had refused to take me to the public baths. Disregarding this, Fred and I paid our six pence each, and in we went with our friend; we did not bathe, but amused ourselves with seeing others, and the pricks of the men. None, as far as I can recollect, wore drawers in those days, they used to walk about hiding their prides generally, with their hands, but not always. I was astonished at the size of some of them, and at the dark hair about them, and on other parts of their bodies. I wondered also at seeing one or two, with the red tip showing fully, so different from mine. All this was much talked over by us afterwards, it was to me an insight into the male make and form. Fred told me, he had often seen men's pricks in their fields, and in those days, living in the country as he did, I dare say it was true, but I don't recollect ever having seen the pricks of full grown men, or a naked man before in my life.

It must have been in the summer of that same year, that I went after this to spend some days at my aunt's at H...ds...e..., Fred's mother. We slept in the some room, and sometimes got up quite at daybreak to go fishing. One morning Fred had left something, in one of his sisters' rooms and went to fetch it, though forbidden to go into the girls' bedrooms. The room in question was opposite to ours. He was only partly dressed, and came back in a second, his face grinning. "Oh! come Wat, come softly, Lucy and Mary are quite naked, you can see their cunts, Lucy has some black hair on hers." I was only half dressed, and much excited by the idea of seeing my cousins' nudity.

We both took off our slippers, and crept along through the door half open, then went on our knees! But why we did so, to this day I don't understand, and so crept to the foot of the bed, then raising ourselves, we both looked over the footboard.

Lucy, fifteen years old, was laying half on her side, naked from her knees to her waist, the bed-clothes kicked off (I suppose through heat), were dragging across her feet and partly laying on the floor; we saw her split, till lost in the closed thighs, she had a little dark short hair over the top of her cunt, and that is all I can recollect about it.

Mary-Ann by the side of her, a year younger only, laid on her back, nacked up to her navel, just above which was her night-gown in a heap and ruck; she had scarcely a sign of hair on her cunt, but a vermillion line, lay right through her crack. Projecting more towards the top, where her cunt began, she had what I now know was a strongly developed clitoris; she was a lovely girl and had long chestnut hair.

Whilst we looked she moved one leg up in a restless manner, and we bobbed down, thinking she was awaking; when we looked again, her limbs were more open, and we saw the cunt till it was pinched up, by the closing of her buttocks. In fear of being caught, we soon crept out, closed the door ajar, and regained our bedroom, so delighted that we danced with joy, as we talked about the look of the two cunts; of which, after all, we had only had a most partial, rapid glimpse.

Lucy was a very plain girl, and was so as a woman. She had, I recollect, a very red bloated looking face as she lay (it was so hot); she it was, who in afterlife my mother cautioned about leaving her infant son to a nursemaid.

Mary-Ann was lovely. I used afterwards to look and

talk with her, thinking to myself: "Ah! you have but little idea, that I have seen your cunt." She was unfortunate; married a cavalry officer, went to India with him, was left at a station unavoidably by her husband, who was sent on a campaign, for a whole year; could not bear being deprived of cock, and was caught in the act of fucking with a drummer boy, a mere lad. She was separated from him, came back to England, and drank herself to death. She was a salacious young woman, I think from what I recollect of her, and am told, was afterwards fucked by a lot of men; but it was a sore point with the family, and all about her was kept quiet.

One of Lucy's sons, in after years, I saw fucking a maid in a summer-house: both standing up against a big table; I was on the roof. Many years before that, I fucked a nurse-maid, she laying on that table, in the very same summer-house, as I shall presently tell.

Fred and I used to discuss the look of his sisters' and mother's cunts, as if they had belonged to strangers. The redness of the line in Mary-Ann's quim astonished us. I do not recollect having even then, formed any definite notion of what a girl's cunt was, though we had seen the splits, but had still, and till much further on, the notion that the hole was round, and close to where the clitoris is, having no idea then of what a clitoris was, though we had got an Aristotle and used to read it greedily; the glimpse of the two cunts were but momentary, and our excitement confused our recollections.

Fred and I then formed a plot to look at another girl's cunt; who the girl was, I don't know, it may have been another of Fred's sisters, or a cousin by another of my aunts, but I think not; at all events she was stopping in aunt's house, and from her height, which was less than that of Fred and myself, I should think a girl of about eleven or

35

twelve years of age. I scrupulously avoid stating anything positively, unless quite certain. Some years afterwards when we were very young men, we did the same thing with a female cousin (but not his sister), as I shall tell.

There was haymaking. We romped with the girl, buried each other in hay, pulled each other out, and so on. I was buried in the hay and dragged out by my legs by Fred and the girl. Then Fred was: then we buried the girl, and as Fred pulled her out he threw up her clothes, I lay over her head, which was covered with hay. Fred saw, winked and nodded. It came to my turn again to be buried, and then hers; I laid hold of her legs and pulling them from under the hay, saw her thighs, I pushed her knees up, and had a glimpse of the slit, which was quite hairless. My aunt and others were in the very field, but had no idea of the game we were playing, the girl romping with us, had no idea, that we were looking at her cunt, and an instantaneous peep only it was.

What effect sensuously, these glimpses of cunt, had on me, I don't know; but have no recollection of sexual desire, nor of mine nor Fred's cock being stiff. I expect that what with games, and our studies, that after all the time we devoted to thinking about women, was not long, and curiosity our sole motive in doing what we did. I clearly recollect our talking at that time about fucking, and wondering if it were true or a lie. We could repeat what we had read, and heard, but it still seemed improbable to me that a cock should go up a cunt, and the result be a child.

Then a passionate liking for females came over me; I fell in sort of love with a lady who must have been forty, and had a sad feeling about her, that is all I recollect. Then I began to follow servants about, on the hope of seeing their legs, or seeing them piddle, or for some undefined object: but that I was always looking after them, I know very well.

Then (I know now) my father got into difficulties, we moved into a smaller house, the governess went away, I was sent to another school, one of my brothers and sisters died; my father went abroad to look after some plantations, and after a year's absence came back and died, leaving my mother, in what compared with our former condition, were poor circumstances, but this in due course will be more fully told.

I think I went to school, though not long before what I am going to tell of happened, but am not certain, if so, I must have seen boys frigging; yet as far as I can arrange in my mind the order of events, I first saw a boy doing that, in my own bed-room at home.

I was somewhere, I suppose, about thirteen years of age, when a distant relative came from the country, to stay with us, until he was put to some great school. He was the son of a clergyman, and must have been fifteen, or perhaps sixteen years old, and was strongly pitted with the small-pox. I had never seen him before, and took a strong dislike to him; the family were poor, this boy was intended for a clergyman. I was excessively annoyed, that he was to sleep with me, but in our small house, there was just then no other place for him.

How many nights he slept in my bed, I don't recollect, it can have been but few; One evening in bed he felt my prick; repulsing him at first, I nevertheless afterwards felt his, and recollect our hands crossing each other and our thighs being close together. Awaking one morning, I felt his belly up against my rump, and his feeling or pushing his prick against my arse, putting my hand back, I pushed him away; then I found it pushing quickly backwards and forwards between my thighs, and his hand, passed over my hips, was grasping my cock. Turning round, I faced him; he asked me to turn round again, and said I might do it to him afterwards, but nothing more was done. An unpleasant feeling about sleeping with him is in my memory, but as said, I disliked him.

The next night undressing, he showed me his prick, stiff, as he sat naked on a chair; it was an exceedingly long, but thin article; he told me about frigging, and said he would frig me, if I would frig him. He commenced moving his hand quickly up and down, on his prick, which got stiffer and stiffer, he jerked up one leg, then the other, shut his eyes and altogether looked so strange, that I thought he was going to have a fit; then out spurted little pasty lumps, whilst he snorted, as some people do in their sleep, and fell back in the chair with his eyes closed; then I saw stuff running thinner over his knuckles. I was strangely fascinated as I looked at him, and at what was on the carpet, but half thought he was ill; he then told me it was great pleasure, and was eloquent about it. Even now, as it did then, the evening seemed to me a nasty unpleasant one, yet I let him get hold of my prick and frig it, but had no sensation of pleasure, he said, "your skin won't come off, what a funny prick;" that annoyed me, and I would not let him do more; we talked till our candle burnt out; he stamped out the sperm on the carpet, saying the servants would think we had been spitting. Then we got into bed.

Afterwards he frigged himself several times before me, and at his request I frigged him, wondering at the result, and amused, yet at the same time much disgusted. When frigging him one day; he said it was lovely to do it in an arse-hole, that he and his brother took it in turns that way: it was lovely, heavenly! would I let him do it to me. In my innocence I told him, it was impossible and that I thought him a liar. He soon left us and went to college. I saw him once or twice after this, in later years, but at a very early age he drowned himself. I told my cousin Fred about this when I saw him; Fred believed in the frigging, but thought him a liar about the arse-hole business, just as I did. This was the first time I ever saw frigging and male semen, and it opened my eyes.

Though now at a public school, I was shy, and reserved, but greedily listened to all the lewd talk, of which I did not believe a great deal. I became one of a group of boys of the same tastes as myself. One day some of them coaxed me into a privy, and there, in spite of me, pulled out my cock, threw me down, held me, and each one spat upon it, and that initiated me into their society. They had what they called cocks-all-round: anyone admitted to the set, was entitled to feel the others' cocks. I felt theirs, but again to my mortification, the tightness of my prepuce caused jeering at me; I was glad to hear that there was another boy at the school in the same predicament, though I never saw his. This confirmed me in avoiding my companions, when they were playing at cocks-all-round; being a day scholar only, I was not forced at all times into their intimacy, as I should have been had I been a boarder.

We had a very large playground; beyond it were fields, orchards and walks of large extent reserved for the use of the two head-masters' families, many of whom were girls. On Saturday half-holidays only, if the fruit was not ripe, we were allowed to range certain fields, and the long bough-covered paths, which surrounded them. Two or three boys of my set told me mysteriously one afternoon, that when the others had gone ahead, we were to meet in the play-ground privy, in which were seats for three boys of a row, and I was to be initiated into a secret without my asking. I was surprised at what took place, there was usually an usher in the play-ground in play-hours, and if boys were too long at the privy, he went there, and made them come out. On the Saturdays, he went out with the boys into the fields: there was no door to the privy, I should add, it was a largish building.

One by one, from different directions, some dodging among trees which bordered one side of the playground, appeared boys. I think there were five or six together in the privy, then it was cocks-all-round, and every boy frigged himself. I would not, at first. Why? I don't know. At length incited, I tried, my cock would not stand, and vexed and mortified, I withdrew, after swearing not to split on them, on pain of being kicked and cut. I don't think I was one of the party again, though I saw each of the same boys frig himself in the privy when alone with me, at some time or another.

After this a boy asked me to come to a privy with him in school time, and he would show me how to do it. Only two boys were allowed to go to those closets at the same time, during school time. There were two wooden legs with keys hung up on the wall by string: a boy if he wanted to ease himself looked to see if a log and key was hanging up, and if there was, stood out in the centre of the room; by that the master understood what he wanted. If he nodded, the boy took the key and went to the bog-house (no water-closets then), and when he returned, he hung up the log in its place. Those privies were close together, and separate, there were but two of them.

"You wait till there are two logs hanging up, and directly I get one, you get up and come after me." Soon we were both in one privy together. "Let's frig," said he; we were only allowed to be away five minutes. Out he pulled his prick, then out I pulled mine; he tried to pull my skin back, and could only half do it, he frigged himself successfully, but I could not. He had a very small prick compared with mine. How I envied him the ease with which he covered and uncovered the red tip. I frigged that boy one day, but finding my cock was becoming a talk among our set, I shrunk from going to their frigging parties, which I have seen even take place in a field, boys sitting at the edge of a ditch, whilst one stood up to watch if anyone approached. When they were frigging in the privy, a boy always stood in the open door on the watch, and his time for frigging came afterwards.

With this set I began to look through the Bible, and study all the carnal passages; no book ever gave us perhaps such prolonged, studious, baudy amusement; we could not understand much, but guessed a good deal.

Before I had seen anyone frig, I had been permitted to read novels, not a moment of my time when not at studies was I without one. My father used to select them for me at first, but soon left me to myself, and now he was dead, I devoured what books I liked, hunting for the love passages, thinking of the beauty of the women, reading over and over again, the description of their charms, and envying their love meetings. I used to stop at print-shop windows and gaze with delight at the portraits of pretty women, and bought some at six pence each, and stuck them into a scrap-book. Although a big fellow for my age, I would sit on the lap of any woman who would let me, and kiss her. My mother in her innocence called me a great girl, but she neverthless forbid it. I was passionately fond of dancing and annoyed when they indicated a girl of my own age, or younger, to dance with.

These feelings got intensified, when I thought of my aunt's backside, and the cunts of my cousins, but when I thought of the heroines, it seemed strange that such beautiful creatures should have any. The cunt which seemed to have affected my imagination, was that of my aunt, which appeared more like a great parting, or division of her body, than a cunt as I then understood it; as if her buttock parting was continued round towards her belly, and as unlike the young cunts I had seen as possible. Those seemed to be but little indents. That the delicate ladies of the novels should have such divisions seemed curious, ugly, and unromantic. My sensuous temperament was developing, I saw females in all their poetry and beauty, but suppose that my physical forces had not kept pace with my brain, for I have no recollection of a cock-stand, when thinking about ladies; and fucking never entered into my mind, either when I read novels, or kissed women, though the pleasure I had when my lips met theirs, or touched their smooth, soft cheeks was great. I recollect the delight it gave me perfectly.

After having seen frigging, it set me reflecting, but it still seemed to me impossible, that delicate, handsome ladies, should allow pricks to be thrust up them, and nasty stuff ejected into them. I read Aristotle, tried to understand it, and thought I did, with the help of much talk with my schoolfellows; yet I only half believed it. Dogs fucking were pointed out to me; then cocks treading hens, and at last a fuller belief came.

I began then, I recollect, to think of their cunts when I kissed women, and then of my aunt's; I could not keep my eyes off of her, for thinking of her large backside and the gap between her thighs; it was the same with my cousins. Then I began to have cock-stands and suppose a pleasurable feeling about the machine, though I do not recollect that. I then found out that servants were fair game, and soon there was not one in the house whom I had not kissed. I had a soft voice and have heard, an insinuating way, was timorous, feared repulse, and above all being found out; yet I succeeded. Some of the servants must have liked it, who called me a foolish boy at first; for they would stop with me on a landing, or in a room, when we were alone, and let me kiss them for a minute together.

There was one, I recollect, who rubbed her lips into mine, till I felt them on my teeth, but of what she was like, I have no recollection, and I did not like her doing that to me.

My curiosity became stronger, I got bolder, told servants I meant to see them wash themselves, and used to wait inside by bed-room, till I heard one of them come up to dress. I knew the time each usually went to her bedroom for that purpose, the person most in my way was the nurse: she after a time left, and mother nursed her own children. "Let's see your neck; do, there is a dear," I would say. "Nonsense, what next?" "Do, dear, there is no harm; I only want to see as much as ladies show at balls." I wheedled one to stand at the door in her petticoats and show her neck across the bedroom lobby. The stays were high and queerly made in those days, the chemises pulled over the top of them like flaps. One or two let me kiss their necks, a girl one day said to my entreaties, "Well, only for a minute," and easing up one breast, she showed me the nipple, I threw my arms around her, buried my face in her neck and kissed it. "I like the smell of your breast and flesh," said I. She was a biggish woman, and I dare say I smelt breasts and armpits together; but whatever the compound, it was delicious to me, it seemed to enervate me. The same woman, when I kissed her on the sly afterwards, let me put my nose down her neck to smell her. We were interrupted. "There is someone coming," said she, moving away.

"What makes ladies smell so nice?" said I to my mother one day. My mother put down her work and laughed to herself. "I don't know that they smell nice."

"Yes, they do, and particularly when they have low dresses on." "Ladies," said mother, "use patchouli and other perfumes." I supposed so, but felt convinced from mother's manner, that I had asked a question which embarrassed her.

I used to lean over the backs of the chairs of ladies, get my face as near to their necks as I could, quietly inhale their odours, and talk all the time. Not every woman smelt nice to me, and when they did, it was not patchouli, for I got patchouli, which I liked, and perfumed myself with it. This delicate sense of smell of a woman I have had throughout life, it was ravishing to me afterwards, when I embraced the naked body of a fresh, healthy young woman.

From about this time of my life, I recollect striking events much more clearly, yet the circumstances which led up to them or succeeded them I often cannot. One day, Miss Granger, our former governess, came to see us. I kissed her. Mother said: "Wattie, you must not kiss ladies in that way, you are too big." I sat Miss Granger on my lap in fun (my mother then in the room), and romped with her. Mother left us in the room, and then seating Miss Granger on my lap again, I pulled her closely to me. "Kiss me, she's gone," I said. "Oh! what a boy," and she kissed me, saying, "let me go now--your mamma is coming." It came into my mind that I had had my hand up her clothes, and had felt hair between her legs. My prick stiffening in thinking of a women. I clutched her hard, put one hand on to her and did something I know not what. She said: "You are rude, Wattie." Then I pinched her and said: "Oh! what a big bosom you have." "Hish! hish!" said she. She was a tallish woman with brown hair; I have heard my mother say she was about thirty years of age.

A memorable episode then occurred. There were two sisters, with other female servants, in our house. My father was abroad at that time; I was growing so rapidly, that every month they could see a difference in my height, but was very weak. My godfather used to look at me, and severely ask if I was up to tricks with the boys. I guessed then what he meant, but always said I did not know what he meant. "Yes, you do; yes, you do," he would say, staring hard at me, "you take care, or you'll die in a mad-house, if you do, and I shall know by your face, not a farthing more will I give you." He had been a surgeon-major in the Army, and gave me much pocket-money. I could not bear his looking at me so; he would ask me why I turned down my eyes.

About this time, I had had a fever, had not been to school for a long time, and used to lie on the sofa reading novels all day. Miss Granger had come to stop with my mother. One day I put my hand up her clothes, nearly to her knees; that offended her, and she left off kissing me. One of my little sisters slept with her, in a room adjoining my mother's room; I slept now on the servants floor, at the top of the house. Again I recollect my cock standing when near Miss Granger, but recollect nothing else.

I was then ordered by my mother to cease speaking to the servants, excepting when I wanted anything, though I am sure my mother never suspected my kissing one. I obeyed her hypocritically, and was even at times reprimanded for speaking to them, in too imperious a tone. She told me to speak to servants respectfully. For all that I was after them, my curiosity was unsatiable, I know the time each went up to dress, or for other purposes, and if at home, would get into the lobby, or near the staircase, to see their legs, as they went upstairs. I would listen at their door, trying to hear them piss, and began for the first time to peep through keyholes at them.

CHAPTER III.

A big servant.--Two sisters.--Armpits.--A quiet feel.-
-

Baudy reveries.--Felt by a woman.--Erections.--My prepuce.--

Seeing and feeling.--Aunt and cousin.--A servant's thighs.--

Not man enough.

A big servant, of whom I shall say much, had most of my attention; she went to her room usually when my mother was taking a nap in the afternoon; or when out with my sisters and brother. When I was ill in bed, this big woman usually brought me beef-tea, I used to make her kiss me, and felt so fond of her, would throw my arms around her, and hold her to me, keeping my lips to hers, and saying how I should like to see her breasts; to all which she replied in the softest voice, as if I were a baby. I wonder now if my homage gave the big woman pleasure, or my amatory pressures made her ever feel randy. She was engaged to be married, but I only heard that at a later day, when my mother talked about her; her sister was also with us, as already said.

The sister was handsome, according to my notions then (I now begin to remember faces clearly); both had bright, clear complexions. I kissed both, each used to say, "Don't tell my sister," and ask, "Have you kissed my sister?" I was naturally cunning about women, and my mother said, she must get rid of them.

The youngest was often dancing my little sister round in the room, then swinging herself round, and making cheeses with her petticoats. As I got better, I would lay on the rug with a pillow, and my back to the light reading, and say it rested me better, to be on the floor, but in hope of seeing her legs as she made cheeses. I often did, and have no doubt now that she meant me to do so, for she would swing round, quite close to my head, so that I could see to her knees, and make her petticoat's edge as she squatted, just over my head, immediately snatching her petticoats back and saying: "Oh! you'll see more than is good for you."

It used to excite me. One day as she did it, and squatted, I put out my hand and pulled her clothes, she rolled on to her back, threw up her legs quite high, and for a second I saw her thighs; she recovered herself, laughing. "I saw your thighs," said I. "That you didn't." One day she let me put my hand into her bosom; I sniffed. "What's there to smell?" said she. I have some idea that she used to watch me closely, when I was with her sister, as she was always looking after her, and before she kissed me, would open the door suddenly or go out of the room, and then return. I've seen the other sister just outside the door of the room, when suddenly opened.

The big sister must have been five feet nine high, and large in proportion; the impression on my mind, is that she was two and twenty: that age dwells in my recollection, and that my mother remarked it. She had brown hair and eyes, I recollect well the features of the woman. Her lower lip was like a cherry, having a distinct cut down the middle, caused she said by the bite of a parrot, which nearly severed her lip when a girl. This feature I recollect more clearly than anything else. My mother remarked that though so big, she was lighter in tread, than anyone in the house, her voice was so soft, it was like a whisper or a flute; her name was I think Betsy.

I had none of the dash, and determination towards females, which I had in after life; was hesitating, fearful of being repulsed, or found out, but was coaxing and wheedling. Betsy used to take charge of my two little sisters (there was no regular nursery then), and used to sit with them in a room adjoining our dining room; it had a settee, and a large sofa in it, we usually breakfasted there. She waited also at table, and did miscellaneous work. I am pretty certain that we had then no man in the house. I used to lie down on the sofa in this room. One day I talked with her about her lip, put my head up and said: "Do let me kiss it." She put her lips to mine, and soon after if I was not kissing her sister, I was kissing her regularly, when my mother was out of the way.

One day when she went up to her bed-room, I went softly after her, as I often did, hoping to hear her piddling. Her door was ajar, one of my little sisters was in the room with her, I expect I must have had incipient randiness on me. She taught the child to walk up stairs in front of her, holding her up, and in stooping to do so, I had glimpses of her fat calves. At the door, I could not see her wash, that was done at the other side of the room, but I heard the splash of water, and to my delight, the pot moved, and her piddle rattle. The looking-glass was near the window. Then she moved to the glass, and brushed her hair, her gown off, and now I saw her legs, and most of her breast, which looked to me enormous.

Then I noticed hair in her armpits; it must have been the first time I noticed any thing of the sort, for I told a boy afterwards, that grown women had hair under their armpits; he said every fool knew that. When she had done brushing, she turned round, and passing the door, shut it: she had not seen me.

I fell in love with this woman, an undefined want took possession of me, I was always kissing her, and she returned it without hesitation. "Hush! your mamma's coming"; then she would work, or do something with the children if there, as demurely as possible. I declare positively as I write this, that I believe I gave that woman a lewd pleasure in kissing me, her kisses were so much like those I have had from women, I have fucked in after years, so long, and soft, and squeezing.

One day, I was in the sitting-room laying on the sofa reading, she sitting and working; where the children were, where my mother was, I can't say: they must have been out, why this servant was in the room with me alone, I don't know. On a table was something the doctor had ordered me to sip, from time to time. "Come and sit near me, I like to touch you, dear" (I used to say dear to her). She drew her chair to the sofa, so that her thighs were near my head, she handed me my medicine, I turned on one side, put my head on her lap, and then my hand on her knee. "Kiss me." "I can't." I moved my head up and she bent forward and kissed. "Keep your face to mine, I want to tell you something." Then I told her I had seen her brushing her hair, her breasts, her armpits. "Oh! you sly boy! you naughty boy! you must not do it again, will you?" "Won't I, if I get the chance; put your head down, I've something more to tell you." "What?" "I can't if you look at me; put your ear to my mouth."

I was longing to tell her, and could not do it whilst she looked at me. I recollect my bashfulness perfectly, and more than that, my fear of saying what I wanted to say.

She bent her ear to my mouth. "I heard you piddle." "Oh! you naughty!" and she burst into a quiet laugh. "I'll take care to shut the door in future." I let my hand drop by the side of the sofa, laid hold of her ankle, then the calve of her leg (without resistance); then up I slid it gently, and gradually above her garter, and felt the flesh; she was threading a needle. As I touched the thigh, she pressed both hands down on to her thighs, barring further investigation. "Now, Wattie, you're taking too much liberty, because I've let you feel my ankles." I whined, I moaned. "Oh do dear, do, kiss me dear; only for a minute." I tried very gently to push my hand (it was my left hand) further. "What do you want?" "I want to feel it, oh! kiss me--let me,--do,--Betsy, do," and I raised my head.

Sitting bent forward towards me as I lay, until she was nearly double, she put her lips to mine and kissing me said: "What a rude, boy you are, what do you expect to find?" "I know what it's called, and it's hairy, isn't it, dear?" Her hands relaxed, she laughed, my left hand slid up, until I felt the bottom of her belly. I could only twiddle my fingers in the hair, could feel no split, or hole, was too excited to think, too ignorant of the nature of the female article; but oh the intense delight I felt at the touch of the warm thighs, and the hair, which now I knew was outside the cunt, somewhere, I recollect my delight perfectly.

She kept on kissing me, saying in a whisper, "what a rude boy you are." Then I whispered modestly, all I had read, told of the Aristotle I had hidden in my cupboard, and she asked me to lend her the book. I touched nothing but hair, her thighs must have been quite closed, and a big stay-bone dug into my hand and hurt it, as I moved it about. I have felt that obstacle to my enterprise in years later on, with other women.

Then came over me a voluptuous sensation, as if I was fainting with pleasure, I seem to have a dream of her lips meeting mine, of her saying oh! for shame I of the tips of my fingers entangling in hair, of the warmth of the flesh of her thighs upon my hand, of a sense of moisture on it, but I recollect nothing more distinctly.

Afterwards she seems to have absorbed me. I ceased

speaking to her sister, and could think of nothing but her neck, legs and the hair at the bottom of her belly. I was several times in the same room with her, and was permitted the same liberties, but no others. I lent her Aristotle, which I had borrowed, and one day recollect my prick stiffening, and a strange overwhelming, utterly indescribable feeling coming over me, of my desire to say to her "cunt," and to make her feel me, and at the same time a fear and a dread overtook me, that my cock was not like other cocks, and that she might laugh at me. After that, I used to pull the skin down violently every day, I bled, but succeeded; it became slightly easier to do so, yet I have no recollection of having a desire to fuck that woman, all that I recollect of my sensations I have here described.

I was still ill, for there was brought me to my bed at nights, a cup of arrowroot. My mother usually did this, but sometimes the big woman did, I was so glad, when my mother did not. Then I would kiss her as if I never wanted to part with her, put my hand out of bed, scramble it up her clothes, till I could feel the hair. Then she would jut her bum back, so that I could not touch more. One night my prick stood, "Take the light outside," I said, "I've something to say to you." The door was half open when she had complied; the gleam of the light struck across the room, my bed was in the shade, "do let me feel you further, dear and kiss me." "You naughty boy!" but we kissed. Again I felt her thighs, belly and hair. "What good does it do you, doing that," she said. I took hold of her hand, and put it under the bed-clothes on to my prick. She bent over me, kissing and saying "naughty boy," but feeling the cock, and all round it, how long, I can't say, "oh! I'd like to feel your hole," I said. "Hish!" said she, going out of the room, and closing the door.

She felt me several times afterwards. When my mother

brought me the arrowroot, she having an idea, that I liked her to do so, I would not take it, saying it was too hot. She said, "I can't wait, Wattie, while it cools." "Don't care, mamma, I don't want it." "But you must take it." "Put it down then." "Well, don't go to sleep, and I'll send Betsy up with it in a few minutes." Up Betsy would come, and quickly and voluptuously kissing, keeping her lips on mine for two or three minutes at a time, she would glide her hand down and feel my cock, whilst my fingers were on her motte, her thighs closed, then she would glide out of the room. I never got my hand between her thighs, I am sure.

I used to long to talk to her about all I had heard, but don't think I ever did more than I have told, for I had a fear about using baudy words to a woman, though I already used them freely enough among boys.

I used to talk only of her hole, my thing, of doing it, and so forth; but what made her laugh was my calling it pudendum, a word I had got out of Aristotle and my latin dictionary. In spite of all this, and of the voluptuous sensations, which used to creep over me, I have no clear, defined, recollection of wishing to fuck her, nor did I ever say anything smutty, if I could see her face.

I got better. Then she refused either to feel me, or let me feel her, on account of my boldness. One day, just at dusk, she was closing the dining-room shutters, I went behind her, and after pulling her head back to kiss me, stooped and pulled up her clothes to her waist; it exposed her entire backside. Oh how white and huge it seemed to me. She moved quickly round not hollowing out, but saying quietly: "What are you doing? don't, now!" As she turned round, so did I, gloating over her bum, then laid both hands on it, slid them round her thighs, and rapidly kneeling down, put my lips on to the flesh, her petticoats fell over my head. She dislodged me, saying she would never speak with me again. She never either felt me, or permitted me, any liberties afterwards, and soon left. One or two years after that, she came to see my mother with her baby. She smiled at me. I don't recollect what became of her sister, but think she soon left us also.

My physique could not then have been strong, nor my sexual organs in finished condition, because I am sure that up to that time, I had not had a spend; perhaps my growing fast and the fever, may have had something to do with it. My father came home broken hearted I have heard, and ill. Soon after we only kept two female servants, a man outside the house, and a gardener. Father was ordered to the sea-side, my mother went with him, taking the children and one servant (all went by coach then). One of father's sisters, my aunt, a widow, came to take charge of our new house, and brought her daughter, a fair, slim girl, about 16 years old.

I remained at home, so as to go to school; the servant left in the house was a pleasant, plump young woman, dark haired, and was always laughing; she was to do all the work. My godfather who lived a mile or two away from us, and whose maiden sister kept house for him, was to see me frequently, and did so till I was sick of him. Every half-holiday, he made me spend with him in walking, and riding; he insisted on my boating, cricketting and keeping at athletic games, when not at my studies. The old doctor I expect guessed my temperament, and thought by thoroughly occupying, and fatiguing me, to prevent erotic thoughts. He wanted me to stay at his house, but I refused, and it being a longer way from my school, it was not persisted in.

My aunt slept in my parents bed-room, my cousin in the next room. I was taken down, during my parents' absence, from the upper floor, to sleep on the same floor as my aunt. They had not been in the house a week before I had heard my cousin piddle, and stood listening outside her bed-room door, night after night, in my bed-gown, trying to get a glimpse of her charms through the key-hole, but was not successful.

I made up to the servant, beginning when she was kneeling, by putting myself on her back. It made her laugh, she gave her back a buck up, and threw me over; then I kissed her, and she kissed me. She and my aunt quarrelled, my aunt was very poor and proud, and wanted a hot dinner at seven o'clock, I my dinner in the middle of the day. The servant said she could not do it all. The girl said quietly to me, "I'll cook for you, don't you go without, let her do without anything hot at night." She did not like her. My aunt said she was saucy and would write to my mother and complain that she wasted her time with the gardener. Godfather then renewed his offer for me to stay with him, but I would not, for I was getting on very comfortably with the servant in kissing, and things settled themselves somehow. I learnt the ways of my aunt, and tried to get home when she was out, so as to be alone with the servant; but to escape both aunt and godfather was difficult. I did so at times by saying I was going out with the boys somewhere, on my half-holidays, or something of the sort, but was rarely successful.

The servant went to her bed-room, one afternoon; with palpitating heart I followed her, and pushed her on to the bed. She was a cheeky, chaffing, woman, and I guess knew better than I did, what I was about. I recollect her falling back on to the bed, and showing to her knees. "Oh I what legs!" said I, "Nothing to be ashamed of," said she. Whatever my wishes or intentions might have been, I went no further. My relations were of course cut.

Another day we romped, and pelted each other with the pillows from her bed, she stood on the landing, I half way down the stairs, and kept when I could, my head just level with the top of the landing on which she was, so that as she whisked backwards and forwards, picking up the pillows to heave at me, I saw up to her knees. She knew what she was about, though I thought myself very cunning to manage to get such glimpses. On the landing I grappled with her for a pillow, and we rolled on the floor. I got my hand up her clothes, to her thighs, and felt the hair. "That's your thing," said I with a burst of courage. "Oh! oh!" she laughed, "what did you say?" "Your thing!" "My thing! what's that?" "The hole at the bottom of your belly," said I, ashamed at what I uttered. "What do you mean? who told you that? I've no hole." It is strange but a fact, that I had no courage to say any more, but left off playing, and went down stairs.

On occasions afterwards, I played more roughly with her, and felt her thighs; but fear prevented me from going further up. She gave me lots of opportunities, which my timidity, prevented me from availing myself of. One day she said: "you are not game for much, although you are so big," and then kissed me long and furiously, but I never saw her wants, nor my chances that I know of, though I see now plainly enough, that boy as I was, she wanted me to mount her.

About that time,--how I got it, I know not,--I had a book describing the diseases caused by sacrificing to Venus. The illustrations in the book, of faces covered with scabs, blotches, and eruptions, took such hold of my mind, that for twenty years afterwards, the fear was not quite eradicated. I showed them to some friends, and we all got scared. I had no definite idea of what syphilis, and gonorrhea were, but that both were something awful, we all made up our minds. My godfather also used to hint now to me about ailments men got, by acquaintance with loose, bad, women; perhaps he put the book in my way. Frigging also was treated of, and the terrible accounts of people dying through it, and being put into straight waistcoats, etc., I have no doubt was useful to me. Several of us boys were days in finding out what the book meant, by masturbation, ononism, or whatever, the language may have been. We used dictionaries and other books to help us, and at last one of the biggest boys explained the meaning to us.

One evening my aunt being out (it was not I think any plan on my part), I had something to eat, and then went into the kitchen, where the servant was sitting at needle-work by candle-light. I talked, kissed, coaxed her, began to pull up her clothes, and it ended in her running round the kitchen, and my chasing her; both laughing, stopping at intervals, to hear if my aunt knocked. "I'll go and lock the outer gate," said she, "then your aunt must ring, if she comes up to the door, she will hear us, for you make such a noise." She locked it and came back again.

The kitchen was on the ground-floor, separated from the body of the house by a short passage. I got her on to my knees, I was now a big fellow, and though but a boy, my voice was changing, she chaffed me about that; then my hand went up her petticoats, and she gave me such a violent pinch on my cock (outside the clothes), that I yelled. Whenever I was getting the better of her in our amatory struggles, she said "oh! hush! there is your aunt knocking," and frightened me away, but at last she was sitting on my knees, my hand touching her thighs, she feeling my prick, she felt all round it and under. "You have no hair," she said. That annoyed me, for I had just a little growing. Then how it came about I don't recollect, but she consented to go into the parlor with me, after we had sat together feeling each other for a time, if mine could be called feeling, when my lingers only touched the top of the notch. I took up the candle. "I won't go if you bring a light," said she, so I put down the candle, and holding her by the arm, we walked through the passage across the little hall, to the front parlour; she closed the door, and we were in the dark. And now I only recollect generally what took place, it seems as if it all could but have occupied a minute, or two, though experience tells me it must have been longer.

We sat on a settee or sofa, she had hold of my prick, and I her cunt, for she now sat with thighs quite wide open. It was my first real feel of a woman, and she meant me to feel well. How large and hairy, and wet it seemed; its size overwhelmed me with astonishment, I did not find the hole, don't recollect feeling for that, am sure I never put my finger in it, all seemed cunt below her belly, wet, and warm, and slippery. "Make haste, your aunt will be in soon," said she softly, but I was engrossed with the cunt, in twiddling it and feeling it in delighted wonder at its size, and other qualities. "Your aunt will be in," and leaving off feeling my cock, she laid half on, half off the settee. "No, no, not so," I recollect the words, but what I was doing, know not; then I was standing by her side, my cock stiff, and still feeling her cunt in bewilderment. "I can't... stop..., get on to the sofa." I laid half over her, my prick touched something--her cunt of course. Whether it went in or not, God knows, I pushed, it felt smooth to my prick, then suddenly came over me, a fear of some horrible disease, and I ceased whatever I was doing. "Go on, go on," said she, moving her belly up. I could not, said nothing, but sat down by her side, she rose up, "You're not man enough," said she, laying hold of my prick. It was not stiff, I put my hand down, and again the great size--as it seemed to me--of her cunt, made me wonder.

What then she did with me, I know not, she may have

frigged it, I think she did, but can't say, a sense of disgrace had come over me, as she said I was not man enough, disgrace mixed with fear of disease. "Let me try," said I; again she laid back, I have a faint recollection of my finger going in somewhere deep, again of my prick touching her thighs and rubbing in something smooth, but nothing more. "You're not man enough" said she again. A ring... "Hark! it's your aunt, go!" and it was.

I went into the adjoining room, where my books were and a lamp, she went to the street-door. My aunt and cousin came in, and went up to their bed-rooms, I sat smelling my fingers; the full smell of cunt that I had for the first time. I smelt and smelt almost out of my senses, sat poring over a book, seeming to read, but with my fingers to my nose and thinking of cunt, its wonderful size and smell. Aunt came down. "Have you got a cold, Wattie?" "No, aunt." "Your eyes look quite inflamed, child." Soon after again, she said: "You have a cold." "No, aunt." "Why are you sniffing so, and holding your hand to your mouth?" Suddenly the fear of the pox came over me, I went up to the bedroom, soaped and washed my prick, and had a terrible fear on me.

I was overwhelmed with a mixed feeling of pride, at having had my prick either touch or go up a cunt, fear that I had caught disease, and shame at not being man enough. Instinct told me, I had lost, in the eyes of the woman; and my pride was hurt in a woeful manner. I tried to avoid seeing her, instead of as before getting excitedly into a room, where she was likely to be alone for a minute. I did that for three days, then fear of disease vanished, and my hopes of feeling her cunt again, or of poking--I don't know which--impelled me towards her.

During those three days, I washed my prick at every possible opportunity, and thought of nothing else but the incident; all seemed to me hurry, confusion, impossible, I wondered, and wonder still, whether my prick went into her or not; but above all, the largeness of the cunt filled me with wonder; for though I had had rapid glimpses of cunts as told, and had now seen a few pictures of the long slit, I never could realise that that was only the outside of the cunt, until I had had a woman. My fingers had no doubt slipped over the surface of hers, from clitoris to arse-hole; the space my hand covered filled me with astonishment, as well as the smell it left on my fingers, I thought of that more than anything else. This seems to me now laughable, but it was a marvel to me then.

When I sneaked into the kitchen again, I was ashamed to look at her, and left almost directly, but one day I felt her again, laughing she put her hand outside my trousers, gave my doodle a gentle pinch and kissed me. "Let's do it!" I said. "Lor! you ain't man enough," and again I slunk away ashamed.

CHAPTER IV.

My first frig.--My godfather.--Meditations on copulation.--
Male and female aromas.--Maid and gardener.--My father
dies.--A wet dream.--Bilked by a whore.

The frequency of my cock-stands, up to this time I don't know. Voluptuous sensation, I have no clear recollection of; but no doubt during that half swooning delight, which I had when big Betsy allowed me to lay my head on her lap and feel her limbs, that impulse towards the woman was accompanied by sensuous pleasure, though I don't recollect the fact, but soon my manhood was to declare itself.

Some time after I had felt this servant's quim, I noticed a strong smelling, whitish stuff inside my foreskin, making the underside of the tip of the prick sore. At first I thought it disease, then pulling the foreskin up, I made it into a sort of cup, dropped warm water into it, and working it about, washed all round the nut, and let the randy smelling infusion escape. This marked my need for a woman, I did not know what the exudation was, it made me in a funk at first. One day I had been toying with the girl, had a cockstand, and felt again my prick sore, and was washing it with warm water, when it swelled up. I rubbed it through my hand, which gave me unusual pleasure, then a voluptuous sensation came over me quickly so thrilling and all pervading that I shall never forget it. I sunk on to a chair, feeling my cock gently, the next instant spunk jotted out in large drops, a full yard in front of me, and a thinner liquid rolled over my knuckles. I had frigged myself, without intending it.

Then came astonishment, mingled with disgust, I examined the viscid gruelly fluid with the greatest curiosity, smelt it, and I think tasted it. Then came fear of my godfather, and of being found out; for all that, after wiping up my sperm from the floor, I went up to my bed-room, and locking the door, frigged myself until I could do it no more from exhaustion.

I wanted a confidant and told two schoolfellows who were brothers, I could not keep it to myself, and was indeed proud though ashamed to speak of the pleasure. They both had bigger pricks than mine, and never had jeered at me because I could not retract my prepuce easily.

Soon after they came to see me, we all went into the garden, each pulled my prepuce back, I theirs, and then we all frigged ourselves in an out-house.

Then I wrote to Fred, who was at a large public school, about my frigging. He replied that some fellows at his school had been caught at it, and flogged; that a big boy just going to Oxford had had a woman and got the pox badly. He begged me to burn his letter, or throw it down the shit-house directly I had read it, adding that he was in such a funk for he had lost mine; and that I was never to write to him such things at the school, because the master opened every day indiscriminately one or two letters of the boys. He knew my mother was away and so did not mind writing to me. When I heard that he had lost my letter, I also was in a funk; the letter never was found. Whether the master got it, or sent it to my godfather, or not, I can't say, but it is certain that just after I had one night exhausted myself by masturbation, my godfather came to see me.

He stared hard at me. "You look ill." "No, I'm not." "Yes, you are, look me full in the face, you've been frigging yourself," said he just in so many words. He had never used an improper word to me before. I denied it. He raved out, "No denial, sir, no lies, you have sir; don't add lying to your bestiality, you've been at that filthy trick, I can see it in your face, you'll die in a mad-house, or of consumption, you shall never have a farthing more pocket-money from me, and I won't buy your commission, nor leave you any money at my death." I kept denying it, brazening it out. "Hold your tongue, you young beast, or I'll write to your mother." That reduced me to a sullen state, only at times perking out: "I haven't!" He put on his hat angrily, and left me in a very uncomfortable state of mind.

I knew that my father was not so well off as he had been, my mother always impressed upon me not to offend my godfather, and now I had done it. I wrote Fred all about it, he said the old beggar was a doctor, and it was very unfortunate; he wondered if he really did see any signs in my face, or whether it was a bounce; that I was not to be a fool, and give in, and still say I hadn't, but had better leave off frigging.

From that time my godfather was always at my heels, he waited for me at the schooldoor, spent my half-holidays with me, sat with me and my aunt of an evening till bed-time, made me ride and drive out with him, stopped giving me pocket-money altogether, and no one else did; so that I was not very happy.

The pleasure of frigging, now I had tasted it (and not before), opened my eyes more fully to the mystery of the sexes, I seemed at once to understand why women and men got together, and yet was full of wonder about it. Spunking seemed a nasty business, the smell of cunt an extraordinary thing in a woman, whose odour generally to me was so sweet and intoxicating. I read novels harder than ever, liked being near females and to look at them more than ever, and whether young or old, common or gentle, was always looking at them and thinking that they had cunts which had a strong odour, and wondering if they had been fucked; I used to stare at aunt and cousins, and wonder the same. It seemed to me scarcely possible, that the sweet, well dressed, smooth-spoken ladies who came to our house, could let men put the spunk up their cunts. Then came the wonder if, and how, women spent; what pleasure they had in fucking, and so on; in all ways was I wondering about copulation, the oddity of the gruelly, close smelling sperm being ejected into the hole between a woman's thighs so astonished me. I often thought the whole business must be a dream of mine; then that there could be no doubt about it. Among other doubts, was whether the servant's quim, which had made by fingers smell, was diseased, or not. Fear of detection perhaps kept me from frigging, but I was weak and growing fast, and have no recollection of much desire, though mad to better understand a cunt. It does not dwell in my mind now that I had a desire to fuck one, but to see it, and above all, to smell it; the recollection of its aroma seems to have had a strange effect on me. I did not like it much, yet yearned to smell it again. Watching my opportunity one day, I managed to feel the servant; it was dusk, she stood with her back up against the wall, and felt my prick whilst I felt her; it was an affair of a second or two, and again we were scared. I went to the sitting-room, and passed the evening in smelling my fingers and looking at my cousin. This occurred once again, and I think now, that the servant must just have been on the point of letting me fuck her, for she had been feeling my prick and in a jeering way saying, "You are not man enough if I let you," I emboldened, blurted out that I had spent, I recollect her saying "oh! you story," and then something put us to flight, I don't now know what. I certainly was not up to my opportunities, that I see now plainly.

I had a taste for chemistry, which served my purpose, as will be seen further on, and used to experimentalize in what was called a washhouse, just outside the kitchen, with my acids and alkalis; that enabled me to slip into the kitchen on the sly, but the plan of the house rendered it easy, for my aunt to come suddenly into the kitchen.

My bed-room window overlooked the kitchen yard, in which was this wash-house, a knife-house and a servant's privy, etc., etc., the whole surrounded by a wall, with a door in it, leading into the garden. Just outside on the garden side, was a gardener's shed; the servant in the morning, used to let the gardener in at the kitchen entrance; and he passed through this kitchen yard into the garden. I was pissing in the pot in my bedroom early one morning, and peeping through the blind, when I saw the servant's head just coming out of the gardener's shed, she passed through the kitchen yard into the kitchen in great haste, looking up at the house, as if to see if anyone was at the windows. Then it occurred to me, that if I got quite early to the kitchen, I could play my little baudy tricks without fear, for my relatives never went down till half-past eight to breakfast, whilst the servant went down at six.

The next morning, I went down early to the kitchen, did not see the wench, and thinking she might be in the privy in the kitchen yard, waited. The shutters were not down, after some minutes delay, in she came; she started. "Hulloh! what are you up for?" I don't think I spoke, but making a dash, got my hand up her clothes and on to her cunt. She pushed me away, then caught hold of the hand with which I had touched her cunt, and squeezed it hard with a rubbing motion, looking at me as I recollected (but long afterwards), in a funny way. "Hish! hish! here is the old woman," said she. "It is not." "I'm sure I heard the wires of her bell," and sure enough there came a ring. Up I went without shoes, like a shot to my bedroom, began to smell my fingers, found they were sticky, and the smell not the same. I recollect thinking it strange that her cunt should be so sticky, I had heard of dirty cunts,--it was a joke among us boys, and thought hers must have been so, which was the cause, that the smell and feel were different.

Two or three days afterwards my mother came to town by herself, there was a row with the servant, I was told to leave the room; the servant and gardener were both turned off that day and hour, a char-woman was had in, a temporary gardener got, and my mother went back to my sick father. Years passed away, and when I had greater experience and thought of all this, concluded that my aunt had found the gardener and the servant amusing themselves too freely, had had them dismissed, and that the morning I found my fingers sticky, the girl had just come in from fucking in the gardener's shed.

With all the opportunities I had, both with big Betsy and with this woman, I was still virgin.

When I saw Fred next, he told me he had felt the cunt of one of their servants. I told him partly what I had done, but kept to myself how I had failed to poke when I had the opportunity, fearing his jeers; and as I was obliged to name some woman, mentioned one of my godfather's servants. He went there to try his chances of groping her as well, but got his head slapped. We talked much about the smell of cunt, and he told me that one day after he had felt their servant, he went into the room where his sisters were, and said, "oh what a funny smell there is on my fingers, what can it be, smell them." Two of his sisters smelt, said they could not tell what it was, but it was not nice. Fred used to say, that he thought they knew it was like the smell of a cunt, because they coloured up so.

I had noticed a strong smell on my prick, whenever the curdy exudation had to be washed out. Fred's talk made me imitative, so I saturated my fingers with the masculine essence one evening, and going to my female cousin, "oh what a queer smell there is on my fingers," said I, "smell them." The girl did. "It's nasty, you've got it from your chemicals," said she. "I don't think I have, smell them again, I can't think what it can be, what's it like?" "I don't think it's like anything I ever smelt, but it is not so nasty, if you smell it close, it's like southern wood," she replied. I wonder if that young lady when she married, ever smelt it afterwards, and recognized it. I did this more than once, it gave me great delight to think my slim cousin had smelt my prick, through smelling my fingers; what innate lubricity comes out early in the male.

Misfortunes of all sort came upon us, the family came back to town, another brother died, then my father who had been long ill, died, and was found to be nearly bankrupt; then my godfather died, and left me a fortune, all was trouble and change, but I only mention these family matters briefly.

My physique still could not have been strong, for though more than ever intensely romantic, and passionately fond of female society, I don't recollect being much troubled with cock-standings, and think I should, had I been so. My two intimate school-friends left off frigging, the elder brother, who had a very long red nose, having come to the conclusion with me, that frigging made people mad, and worse, prevented them afterwards from fucking and having a family. Fred, my favourite cousin, arrived at the same conclusion--by what mental process, we all arrived at it, I don't know.

When I was approaching my sixteenth year, I awakened one night with a voluptuous dream, and found my night-shirt saturated with semen, it was my first wet-dream; that set me frigging again for a time, but I either restrained myself, or did not naturally require much spending at that time, for I certainly did not often do so.

But our talk was always about cunt and woman, I was always trying to smell their flesh, look up their petticoats, watch to see them going to piddle; and the wonder to me now is, that I did not frig myself incessantly; and can only account for it on the grounds, that though my imagination was very ripe, my body was not. The fact of hair under the arms of women had a secret charm for me about that time. I don't recollect thinking much about it before, though it had astonished me when I first saw it; and why it came to my imagination so much now, do not know, but it did. I have told of the woman under whose arms I first saw hair.

One afternoon after my father's death, and that of my godfather, Fred was with me, we went to the house of a friend, and were to return home about nine o'clock. It was dark, we saw a woman standing by a wall. "She is a whore," said Fred, "and will let us feel her if we pay her." "You go and ask her." "No, you." "I don't like to." "How much money have you got?" We ascertained what we had, and after a little hesitation, walked on, passed her, then turned round and stopped. "What are you staring at, kiddy," said the woman. I was timid, and walked away, Fred stopped with her. "Wattie, come here," said he in a half whisper. I walked back. "How much have you got?" the woman said. We both gave her money. "You'll let us both feel?" said Fred. "Why of course, have you felt a woman before?" Both of us said we had, feeling bolder. "Was it a woman about here?" "No." "Did you both feel the same woman?" "No." "Give me another shilling then, you shall both feel my cunt well, I've such a lot of hair on it." We gave what he had, and then she walked off without letting us. "I'll tell your mothers, if you come after me," she cried out.

We were sold; I was once sold again in a similar manner afterwards, when by myself.

These are the principal baudy incidents of my early youth, which I recollect, and have not told to friends; many other amusing incidents told them, are omitted here, for the authorship would be disclosed, if I did. One or two were peculiar and most amusing, yet I dare not narrate them; but all show how soon sexual desires developed in me, and what pleasure early in life even these gave me and others.

I now had arrived at the age of puberty, when male nature asserts itself in the most timid, and finds means of getting its legitimate pleasure with women. I did, and then my recollection of things became more perfect, not only as to the consummations, but of what led to them; yet nothing seems to me so remarkable as the way I recollect matters which occurred when I was almost an infant.

CHAPTER V.

Our house.--Charlotte and brother Tom.--Kissing and

groping.--Both in rut.--My first fuck.--A virginity taken.--

At a baudy house.--In a privy.--Tribulations.--Charlotte

leaves.--My despair.

After father's death, our circumstances were further reduced, at the time I am going to speak of, we had come to a small house nearer London; one sister went to boarding-school, an aunt (I had many) took another, I went to a neighboring great school or college, as it was termed, my little brother Tom was at home; but reference henceforth to members of my family will be but slight, for they had but little to do with the incidents of this private life, and unless they were part actors in it, none will be mentioned.

Our house had on the ground-floor a dining-room, a drawing-room, and a small room called the garden parlor, with steps leading into a large garden. On the first floor my mother's bed-room and two others; above were the servants' room, mine, and another much used as a lumber-room; the kitchens were in the basement, beside them a long covered way led to a servants' privy, and close to it a flight of stairs leading up into the garden; at the top of the stairs was a garden-door leading into the fore-court, on to which opened the street-door of the house. This description of plan is needful to understand what follows.

I was about sixteen years old, tall, with slight whiskers and moustache, altogether manly and looking seventeen or eighteen, yet my mother thought me a mere child, and most innocent; she told our friends so. I had developed without her having noticed it, love of women, and the intensest desire to understand the secrets of their nature had taken possession of me; the incessant talk of fucking with which the youths I knew beguiled their leisure, the stories they told of having seen their servants, or other girls half, or quite naked, the tricks by which they managed this, the dodges they were up to, inflamed me, sharpened my instinctive acuteness in such matters, and set me seeking every opportunity to know women naked, and sexually. Frigging was now hateful to me; I had never done so more than the times related, that is as far as I now can recollect, frightened as said, by my godfather telling me, that it sent men mad, and made them hateful to women. So although boiling with sensuality, I was still all but a virgin, and actually so in fucking.

A housemaid arrived just as I came home from college, the cook stood at the door, she was a lovely woman about twenty-five or six years old, fresh as a daisy, her name was Mary. The housemaid was in a cart, driven by her father, a small market gardener living a few miles from us. I saw a fresh, comely girl about seventeen years old in the fore-court, turned round to look, she was getting down, the horse moved, she hesitated. "Get down," said her father angrily. Down she stepped, her clothes caught on the edge of the cart, or step, or somehow; and I saw rapidly appear white stockings, garters, thighs, and a patch of dark hair between them by her belly; it was instantaneous, and down the clothes came, hiding all. I stood fascinated, knowing I had seen her cunt hair. She, without any idea of having been exposed, helped down with her box, I went into the parlor ashamed of having as I thought, been seen looking.

I could think of nothing else, and when she brought in tea, could not take my eyes off her, it was the same at supper (we lead a simple life, dining early and having supper). In the evening my mother remarked, "that girl will do," I recollect feeling glad at heart.

I went to bed, thinking of what I had seen, and stared whenever I saw her the next day, until by a sort of fascination, she used to stare at me; in a day or two I fancied myself desperately in love with her, and indeed was. I recollect now her features, as if I had only seen her yesterday, and after the scores and scores of women I have fucked since, recollect every circumstance attending my having her, as distinctly, as if it only occurred last week; yet very many years have passed away.

She was a little over seventeen years, had ruddy lips, beautiful teeth, darkish hair, hazel eyes, and a slightly turn-up nose, large shoulders and breast, was plump, generally of fair height, and looked eighteen or nineteen, her name was Charlotte.

I soon spoke to her kindly, by degrees became free in manner, at length chucked her under her chin, pincher her arm, and used the familiarities which nature teaches a man to use towards a woman. It was her business to open the door, and help me off with my coat and boots if needful; one day as she did so, her bum projecting upset me so, that as she rose from stooping I caught and pinched her. All this was done with risk, for my mother was then nearly always at home, and the house being small, a noise was easily heard.

I was soon kissing her constantly. In a few days got a kiss in return, that drove me wild, her cunt came constantly into my mind, all sorts of wants, notions, and vague possibilities came across me; girls do let fellows feel them I said to myself, I had already succeeded in that. What if I tell that I have seen it outside? Will she tell my mother? Will she let me feel her? What madness! Yet girls do let men, girls like it so all my friends say. Wild with hopes and anticipations, coming in doors one day, I caught her tightly in my arms, pulled her belly close to mine, rubbed up against hers saying, "Charlotte, what would I give, if you would..." it was all I dare say. Then I heard my mother's bed-room door open, and I stopped.

Hugging and kissing a woman never stopped there, I told her I loved her, which she said was nonsense. We now used regularly to kiss each other when we got the chance; little by little I grasped her closer to me, put my hands round her waist, then cunningly round to her bum, then my prick used to stand and I was mad to say more to her, but had not the courage. I knew not how to set to work, indeed scarce knew what my desires lead me to hope, and think at that time, putting my hand on to her cunt, and seeing it, was perhaps the utmost; fucking her seemed a hopelessly mad idea, if I had the expectation of doing so at all very clearly.

I told a friend one or two years older than myself how matters stood, carefully avoiding telling him who the girl was. His advice was short. Tell her you have seen her cunt, and make a snatch up her petticoats when no one is near; keep at it, and you will be sure to get a feel, and some day, pull out your prick, say straight you want to fuck her, girls like to see a prick, she will look, even if she turns her head away. This advice he dinned into my ears continually, but for a long time, I was not bold enough to put it into practice.

One day, my mother was out, the cook upstairs dressing, we had kissed in the garden parlour, I put my hand round her bum, and sliding my face over her shoulder half ashamed, said, "I wish my prick was against your naked belly, instead of outside your clothes." She with an effort disengaged herself, stood amazed, and said, "I never will speak to you again."

I had committed myself, but went on, though in fear, prompted by love or lust. My friend's advice was in my ears. "I saw your cunt as you got down from your father's cart," said I, "look at my prick (pulling it out), how stiff it is, it's longing to go into you, 'cock and cunt will come together'." It was part of a smutty chorus the fellows sang at my college; she stared, turned round, went out of the room, through the garden, and down to the kitchen by the garden stairs, without uttering a word.

The cook was at the top of the house, I went into the kitchen reckless, and repeated all I had said. She threatened to call the cook. "She must have seen your cunt, as well as me," said I; then she began to cry. Just as I was begging pardon, my friend's advice again rang in my ears, I stooped and swiftly ran both hands up her clothes, got one full on to her bum, the other on her motte; she gave a loud scream, and I rushed off upstairs in a fright.

The cook did not hear her, being up three pairs of stairs; down I went again, and found Charlotte crying, told her again all I had seen in the court yard, which made her cry more. She would ask the cook, and would tell my mother--then hearing the cook coming downstairs, I cut off through the passage up into the garden.

The ice was quite broken now, she could not avoid me, I promised not to repeat what I had said and done, was forgiven, we kissed, and the same day I broke my promise; this went on day after day, making promises and breaking them, talking smuttily as well as I knew how, getting a slap on my head, but no further, my chances were few. My friend, whom I made a half confidant of, was always taunting me with my want of success, and boasting of what he would have done, had he had my opportunities.

My mother just at that time began to resume her former habits, leaving the house frequently for walks and visits. One afternoon she being out for the remainder of the day, I went home unexpectedly; the cook was going out, I was to fetch my mother home in the evening; Charlotte laid the dinner for me; we had the usual kissing, I was unusually bold and smutty. Charlotte finding me not to be going out, seemed anxious. All the dinner things had been taken away, when out went the cook, and there were Charlotte, my little brother and I alone. It was her business to sit with him in the garden parlor when mother was out, so as to be able to open the street-door readily, as well as go into the garden if the weather was fine. It was a fine day of Autumn, she went into the parlor and was sitting on the huge old sofa, Tom playing on the floor, when I sat myself down by her side; we kissed and toyed, and then with heart beating, I began my talk and waited my opportunity.

The cook would be back in a few minutes, said she. I knew better, having heard mother tell cook she need not be home until eight o'clock. Although I knew this, I was fearful, but at length mustered courage to sing my cock and cunt song. She was angry, but it was made up. She went to give something to Tom, and stepping back put her foot on the lace of one boot which was loose, sat down on the sofa and put up one leg over the other, to relace it. I undertook to do it for her, saw her neat ankle, and a bit of a white stocking. "Snatch at her cunt," rang in my ears. I had never attempted it since the afternoon in the kitchen.

Lacing the boot, I managed to push the clothes up so as to see more of the leg, but resting as the foot did on one knee, the clothes tightly between, a snatch was useless: lust made me cunning, I praised the foot (though I knew not at that time how vain some women are of their feet). "What a nice ankle," I said putting my hand further on. She was off her guard; with my left arm, I pushed her violently back on to the large sofa, her foot came off her knee, at the same moment, my right hand went up between her thighs, on to her cunt; I felt the slit, the hair, the moisture.

She got up to a sitting posture, crying "you wretch, you beast, you blackguard," but still I kept my fingers on the cunt; she closed her legs, so as to shut my hand between her thighs, and keep it motionless, and tried to push me off; but I clung round her. "Take your hand away," said she, "or I will scream." "I shant!" Then followed two or three loud, very loud screams. "No one can hear," said I, which brought her to supplication. My friend's advice came again to me: pushing my right hand still between her thighs, with my left I pulled out my prick, as stiff as a poker. She could not do otherwise than see it; and then I drew my left hand round her neck, pulled her hand to me, and covered it with kisses.

She tried to get up and nearly dislodged my right hand, but I pushed her back, and got my hand still further on to the cunt. I never thought of pressing, under towards the bum, was in fact too ignorant of female anatomy to do it, but managed to get one of the lips with the hair between my fingers, and pinch it; then dropped on to my knees in front of her, and remained kneeling, preventing her getting back further on the sofa, as well as I could by holding her waist, or her clothes.

There was a pause from our struggles, then more entreaties, then more attempts to get my right hand away; suddenly she put out one hand, seized me by the hair of my head, and pushed me backwards by it. I thought my skull was coming off, but kept my hold and pinched or pulled the cunt lip till she yelled and called me a brute. I told her I would hurt her as much as I could, if she hurt me; so that game she gave up; the pain of pulling my hair made me savage, and more determined and brutal, than before.

We went on struggling at intervals, I kneeling with prick out, she crying, begging me to desist; I entreating her to let me see and feel her cunt, using all the persuasion, and all the baudy talk I could, little Tom sitting on the floor playing contentedly. I must have been half an hour on my knees, which became so painful, that I could scarcely bear it; we were both panting, I was sweating; an experienced man would perhaps have had her then; I was a boy inexperienced, and without her consent almost in words, would not have thought of attempting it; the novelty, the voluptuousness of my game was perhaps sufficient delight to me; at last I became conscious that my fingers on her cunt were getting wet; telling her so, she became furious and burst into such a flood of tears, that it alarmed me. It was impossible to remain on my knees longer, in rising, I knew I should be obliged to take my hand from her cunt, so withdrawing my left hand from her waist, I put it also suddenly up her clothes, and round her bum, and lifted them up, showing both her thighs, whilst I attempted to rise. She got up at the same instant, pushing down her clothes, I fell over on one side,--my knees were so stiff and painful--and she rushed out of the room upstairs.

It was getting dusk, I sat on the sofa in a state of pleasure, smelling my fingers. Tom began to howl, she came down and took him up to pacify him, I followed her down to the kitchen, she called me an insolent boy (an awful taunt to me then), threatened to tell my mother, to give notice and leave, and left the kitchen, followed by me about the house; talking baudily,

telling her how I liked the smell of my fingers, attempting to put my hand up her clothes, sometimes succeeding, pulling out my ballocks, and never ceasing until the cook came home, having been at this game for hours. In a sudden funk, I begged Charlotte to tell my mother, that I had only come home just before the cook, and had got to be unwell; she replying she would tell my mother the truth, and nothing else. I was in my bed-room before cook was let in.

Mother came home later, I was in a fright having laid in bed cooling down, and thinking of possible consequences; heard the street-door knocker, got out of bed, and in my night-shirt went half way downstairs listening. To my relief, I heard Charlotte in answer to my mother's enquiry, say I had come home about an hour before, and had gone to bed unwell. My mother came to my room, saying how sorry she was.

For a few days I was in fear, but it gradually wore off, as I found she had not told; our kissing recommenced, my boldness increased, my talk ran now freely on her legs, her bum, and her cunt, she ceased to notice it, beyond saying she hated such talk, and at length she smiled in spite of herself. Our kissing grew more fervid, she resisted improper action of my hand, but we used to stand with our lips close together for minutes at a time, when we got the chance, I holding her to me as close as wax. One day cook was upstairs, mother in her bed-room, I pushed

Charlotte up against the wall in the kitchen, and pulled up her clothes, scarcely with resistance; just then my mother rang, I skipped up into the garden, and got into the parlour that way, soon heard my mother calling to me to fetch water, Charlotte was in hysterics at the foot of the stairs-- after that, she frequently had hysterics, till a certain event occurred.

My chances were chiefly on Saturdays, a day I did not go to college; soon I was to cease going there, and was to prepare for the army.

I came home one day, when I knew Charlotte would be alone--the cook was upstairs--I got her on to the sofa in the garden parlour, knelt and put my hands between her thighs, with less resistance than before, she struggled slightly but made no noise. She kissed me as she asked me to take away my hand; I could move it more easily on her quim, which I did not fail to do; she was wonderfully quiet. Suddenly I became conscious that she was looking me full in the face, with a peculiar expression, her eyes very wide open, then shutting them. "Oho--oho," she said with a prolonged sigh, "do--oh take away--oh--your hand, Walter dear,--oh I shall be ill,--oho,--oho," then her head dropped down over my shoulder as I knelt in front of her; at the same moment, her thighs seemed to open slightly, then shut, then with a quivering, shuddering motion, as it then seemed to me, and then she was quite quiet.

I pushed my hand further in, or rather on, for although I thought I had it up the cunt, I really was only between the lips--I know that now. With a sudden start she rose up, pushed me off, snatched up Tom from the floor, and rushed upstairs. My fingers were quite wet. For two or three days afterwards, she avoided my eyes and looked bashful, I could not make it out, and it was only months afterwards, that I knew, that the movement of my fingers on her clitoris had made her spend. Without knowing indeed then that such a thing was possible, I had frigged her.

Although for about three months, I had been thus deliciously amusing myself, anxious to feel, and see her cunt, and though I had at last asked her to let me fuck her; I really don't think I had any definite expectation of doing it to her. I guessed now at its mutual pleasures, and so forth, yet my doing it to her appeared beyond me; but urged on by my love for the girl--for I did love her--as well as by sexual instinct, I determined to try. I also was quickened by my college friend, who had seen Charlotte at our house and not knowing it was the girl I had spoken to him about, said to me, "What a nice girl that maid of yours is, I mean to get over her, I shall wait for her after church next Sunday, she sits in your pew I know." I asked him some questions,--his opinion was that most girls would let a young fellow fuck them, if pressed and that she would (this youth was but about eighteen years old), and I left him fearing what he said was true, hating and jealous of him to excess. He set me thinking, why should not I do it if he could, and if what he said about girls was true,--so I determined to try it on, and by luck did so earlier than I expected.

About one hour's walk from us, was the town house of an aunt, the richest of our family, and one of my mother's sisters. She alone now supplied me with what money I had, my mother gave me next to nothing. I went to see aunt, who asked me to tell my mother, to come and spend a day with her, the next week, and named the day. I forgot this until three days afterwards, when hearing my mother tell the cook, she could go out for a whole holiday! I said, that my aunt particularly wished to see mother on that day. My mother scolded me for not having told her sooner, but wrote and arranged to go, forgetting the cook's holiday. To my intense joy, on that day she took brother Tom with her, saying to Charlotte, "You will have nothing to think of, but the house, shut it up early, and do not be frightened." I was as usual to fetch my mother home.

In what an agitated state I passed that morning at school, and in the afternoon went home, trembling at my intentions. Charlotte's eyes opened with astonishment at seeing me. Was I not going to fetch my mother? I was not going till night. There was no food in the house, and I had better go to my aunt's for dinner. I knew there was cold meat, and made her lay the cloth in the kitchen. To make sure, I asked if cook was out,--yes, she was, but would be home soon. I knew that she stopped out till ten o'clock on her holidays. The girl was agitated with some undefined idea of what might take place, we kissed and hugged, but she did not like even that, I saw.

I restrained myself whilst eating, she sat quietly beside me; when I had finished she began to remove the things, the food gave me courage, her moving about stimulated me, I began to feel her breasts, then got my hands on to her thighs, we had the usual struggles, but it seems to me as I now think of it, that her resistance was less, and that she prayed me to desist more lovingly than was usual. We had toyed for an hour, she had let a dish fall and smashed it, the baker rang, she took in the bread, and declared she would not shut the door unless I promised to leave off. I promised, and so soon as she had closed it, pulled her into the garden parlour, having been thinking when in the kitchen, how I could get her upstairs. Down tumbled the bread on the floor, on to the sofa, I pushed her, and after a struggle she was sitting down, I kissing her, one arm round her waist, one hand between her thighs, close up to her cunt. Then I told her I wanted to fuck her, said all in favour of it I knew, half ashamed, half frightened as I said it. She said she did not know what I meant, resisted less and less as I tried to pull her back on the sofa, when another ring came: it was the milkman.

I was obliged to let her go, and she ran down stairs with the milk. I followed, she went out, and slammed the door which led to the garden, in my face; for the instant, I thought she was going to the privy, but opened and followed on; she ran up the steps, into the garden, through the garden parlor, and upstairs to her bed-room just opposite to mine, closed and locked the door in my face, I begged her to let me in.

She said she would not come out, till she heard the knocker or bell ring; there was no one called usually after the milkman, so my game was up, but nothing makes man or woman so crafty as lust. In half an hour or so, in anger, I said I should go to my aunt's, went downstairs, moved noisily about, opened and slammed the street-door violently, as if I had gone out, then pulled off my boots, and crept quietly up to my bed-room.

There I sat expectantly a long time, had almost given up hope, began to think about consequences if she told my mother, when I heard the door softly open and she came to the edge of the stairs. "Wattie!" she said loudly, "Wattie!" much louder, "he has," said she in a subdued tone to herself, as much as to say that worry is over. I opened my door, she gave a loud shriek and retreated to her room, I close to her; in a few minutes more, hugging, kissing, begging, threatening, I know not how; she was partly on the bed, her clothes up in a heap, I on her with my prick in my hand, I saw the hair, I felt the slit, and not knowing then where the hole was or much about it, excepting that it was between her legs, shoved my prick there with all my might. "Oh! you hurt, I shall be ill," said she, "pray don't." Had she said she was dying, I should not have stopped. The next instant a delirium of my senses came, my prick throbbing and as if hot lead was jetting from it, at each throb; pleasure mingled with light pain in it, and my whole frame quivering with emotion; my sperm left me for a virgin cunt, but fell outside it, though on to it.

How long I was quiet I don't know; probably but a short time; for a first pleasure does not tranquillize at that age; I became conscious that she was pushing me off of her, and rose up, she with me, to a half-sitting posture; she began to laugh, then to cry, and fell back in hysterics, as I had seen her before.

I had seen my mother attend to her in those fits, but little did I then know, that sexual excitement causes them in women, and that probably in her I had been the cause. I got brandy and water, and made her drink a lot, helping myself at the same time, for I was frightened, and made her lay on the bed. Then ill as she was, frightened as I was, I yet took the opportunity her partial insensibility gave me, lifted her clothes quietly, and saw her cunt and spunk on it. Roused by that, she pushed her clothes half down feebly and got to the side of the bed. I loving, begging pardon, kissing her, told her of my pleasure, and asked about hers, all in snatches, for I thought I had done her. Not a word could I get, but she looked me in the face beseechingly, begging me to go. I had no such intention, my prick was again stiffened, I pulled it out, the sight of her cunt had stimulated me, she looked with languid eyes at me, her cap was off, her hair hanging about her head, her dress torn near her breast.

More so than she had ever looked, was she beautiful to me, success made me bold, on I went insisting, she seemed too weak to withstand me. "Don't, oh pray, don't," was all she said as pushing her well on the bed, I threw myself on her, and again put my doodle on to the slit now wet with my sperm. I was though cooler, stiff as a poker, but my sperm was not so ready to flow, as it was in after days, at a second poke, for I was very young; but nature did all for me; my prick went to the proper channel, there stopped by something it battered furiously. "Oh, you hurt, oh!" she cried aloud. The next instant something seemed to tighten round its knob, another furious thrust,--another,--a sharp cry of pain (resistance was gone), and my prick was buried up her, I felt that it was done, and that before I had spent outside of her. I looked at her, she was quiet, her cunt seemed to close on my prick, I put my hand down, and felt round. What rapture to find my machine buried; nothing but the balls to be touched, and her cunt hair wetted with my sperm, mingling and clinging to mine; in another minute nature urged a crisis, and I spent in a virgin cunt, my prick virgin also. Thus ended my first fuck.

My prick was still up her, when we heard a loud knock; both started up in terror, I was speechless. "My God; it is your mamma!" Another loud knock. What a relief, it was the postman. To rush downstairs, and open the door was the work of a minute. "I thought you were all out," said he angrily, "I have knocked three times." "We were in the garden," said I. He looked queerly at me and said, "With your boots off!" and grinning went away. I went up again, found her sitting on the side of the bed, and there we sat together. I told her what the postman had said, she was sure he would tell her mistress. For a short time, there never was a couple who had just fucked, in more of a foolish funk than we were; I have often thought of our not hearing the thundering knocks of a postman, whilst we were fucking, though the bed-room door was wide open; what engrossing work it is so to deafen people. Then after unsuccessfully struggling to see her cunt, and kissing, and feeling each others' genitals, and talking of our doings and our sensations for an hour, we fucked again.

It was getting dark, which brought us to reason, we

both helped to remake the bed, went downstairs, shut the shutters, lighted the fire which was out, and got lights. I then having nothing to do, began thinking of my doodle which was sticking to my shirt, and pulling it out to see its condition, found my shirt covered with sperm smears, and spots of blood, my prick was dreadfully sore. I said to her that she had been bleeding, she begged me to go out of the kitchen for a minute, I did, and almost directly she came out, and passed me saying, she must change her things before the cook came home. She would not let me stay in the room whilst she did it, nor did I see her chemise, though I had followed her upstairs; then the idea flashed across me that I had taken a virginity; that had never occurred to me before. She got hot water to wash herself. I did not know what to do with my shirt; we arranged I should wash it before I went to bed. We thought it best to say, I had not been home at all, and that I should go and fetch my mother. After much kissing, hugging, and tears on her part, off I went, hatching an excuse for not having fetched mother earlier, and we came home with Tom in my aunt's carriage I recollect.

Before going to bed, I ordered hot water for a footbath. How we looked at each other as I ordered it. I washed my shirt as well as I could, and looked sadly at my sore prick, I could not pull the skin back, so much as usual, it was torn, raw, and slightly bleeding.

Awake nearly all night, thinking of my pleasure and proud of my success; I rose early, and looking at my shirt, found stains still visible, and that I had so mucked it in washing, that an infant could have guessed what I had been doing. I knew that my mother who now did household duties herself, selected the things for the laundress; and in despair hit on a plan: I filled the chamber-pot with piss and soap-suds, making it as dirty as I could, put it near a chair and my shirt hanging over it carelessly, so as to look as if it had dropped into the pot by accident; left it there, and put on a clean shirt. After breakfast my mother who usually helped to make my bed, and her own as well, called out to me; up I went with my heart in my mouth, to hear her say, she hoped I would be a little more careful, and remember that we had no longer my poor father's purse. "Look," said she, "a disgraceful state you left your shirt in, I am ashamed to have it sent to the laundress, have been obliged to tell the housemaid to partly wash it first, you are getting very careless." Charlotte afterwards told me, that when mother gave her the shirt to rough wash, she felt as if she should faint.

I need not repeat about my prepuce, which as said I could now pull down with a little less difficulty. Lacerated and painful over night, it was much more swollen and sore the next morning, when I pissed it smarted, the thinking and smarting made me randy: risking all, whilst my mother was actually in the adjoining room, the poor girl in horrid fear and looking shockingly ill, I thrust my hand up her clothes and on to her split. She whispered, "What a wretch you are!" I went to college, came back at three o'clock, thinking always on the same subject; my prick got worse, I took it into my head, that Charlotte had given me some disease, and was in a dreadful state of mind. I washed it with warm water, and greased it, having eased it thus a little, got the skin down, then could not get it back again, it got stiff; as it did so sexual pleasures came into my mind, and worse got the pain. I greased it more, my pain grew less, I touched the tip with my finger, it gave a throb of pleasure, I went on without meaning, almost without knowing, the pleasure came and spunk shot out. I had frigged myself unintentionally again.

I watched my penis shrink, its tension lessen, its high colour go, then came the feeling of disgust at myself that I have always felt after frigging, a disgust not quite absent even when done by the little hands of fair friends, to whose quims I was paying similar delicate attentions. I was able to pull up the skin again, but the soreness got worse, I told the poor girl that my prick was very sore, and that I thought it strange. It did not wound her feelings, for she did not know my suspicions. The next morning being no better, I with much hesitation told a college friend, he looked at my prick, and thought it either clap or pox. Frightened to go to our own doctor, I at his advice went to a chemist, who did a little business in such matters; we dealt there, but my friend assured me that the man never opened his mouth to any one, if youths consulted him, and many he knew had.

With quaking I said to the chemist, that I had something the matter with my thing. "What?" said he. "I don't know." "Let me see it." I began to beg him not to mention it to my mother, or anyone. "Don't waste my time," said he, "show it to me, if you want my advice." Out I pulled it as small as could be, but still with the skin over it. "Have you been with a woman?" said he. "Yes." He looked at my shirt, there was no discharge, then he laid hold of my prick with both hands, and with force pulled the skin right down, I howled. He told me there was nothing the matter with me, that the skin was too tight, that a snip would set me to rights, and advised me soon to have it done, saying, "it will save you trouble and money if you do, and add to your pleasure." I declined. "Another day then." "No." He laughed and said, "Well, time will cure you, if you go on as you have began," gave me a lotion, and in three days I was pretty right: warm water I expect would have had the same effect. I had simply torn the skin in taking the virginity.

Of course I wanted Charlotte again, she seemed in no way to help me, and used to cry, still there was a wonderful difference between then, and before the happy consummation: she tried to prevent my hands going up her petticoats, but once up objections ceased, and my hands would rove about on the outside and inside of all, we stood and kissed at every opportunity. "When shall we do it again?" she replied "Never!" for she was sure it would bring punishment on us both.

I neglected my studies absolutely; all I thought about was her, and how to get at her, it must have been a week or more before I did. Ready for any risk, that day my mother was out, I came home, had the early dinner; the cook after that always went up to dress, or as she said, clean herself, and there she always was an hour. Waiting till I heard her go up, I went into the garden parlour, where as usual Charlotte was with my little brother. Going at her directly, I was refused, but now how different, once she would not rest until my hand was altogether away from her. Now I begged and besought her, with my hand up her clothes, my fingers on her quim. No--if we had not been found out before, we were fortunate, but never, never, would she do it again; was I mad? did I wish to ruin her? was not the cook upstairs? might she not come down, whilst we did it? how light the room was (the sun was coming in). I dropped the blinde, her resistance grew less, as her cunt felt my twiddling. "No--now no--oh what a plague you are; hush! it is the cook." I open the door, listen, there is no one stirring. "What will she think if she finds you here?" "What does it matter; now do--let me,--I'll bolt the door, if she comes I will get under the sofa, you say you don't know how it got bolted." Such was my innocent device, but it sufficed, for both were hot in lust. I bolted it. My prick is out, I pull her reluctant hand on to it, my hands are groping now, but too impatient for dallying, I push her down on the sofa--that dear cunt. "Don't hurt me so much again, oh don't push so hard." Oh! what delight! in a minute we are spending, together this time.

I unlock the door, go back to the dining-room, she strolls out into the garden, cook speaks to her out of the window. "Where is master Wattie?" "In the dining-room I suppose." Soon out I stroll into the garden, play with Tommy of course, she can scarcely look me in the face, she is blushing like a rose. "Was it not lovely, Charlotte, is not your thing wet?" In she rushes with Tom, soon I follow, cook is still upstairs. "Come, be quick." Again the bolt, again we fuck, she walks off into the garden with Tommy, and her cunt full, and cook and she chat from the window. How we laughed about it afterwards.

Modesty retired after this, we gave way to our inclinations, she refusing but always letting me if we got a chance! We were still green and timid, at the end of three weeks we only had done it a dozen times or so, always with the cook in the house, always with fear. I was longing for complete enjoyment of all my senses, had never yet seen her cunt, except for a minute at a time, was mad for "the naked limb entwined with limb," and all I had read of in amatory poetry. I had gained years in boldness and manhood, and although nervous, began to practice what I had heard.

I heard of accommodation houses, where people could have bed-rooms and no questions were asked; and found one not far from my aunt's, although she lived in the best quarter of London. Just before Charlotte's day out, I went to my aunt, complained of my mother's meanness, and she gave me a sovereign. On my way home, I loitered a full hour in the street with the baudy house, marked it so as to know it in the day, and saw couples go in, as my knowing friend who had told said I should. The next day instead of going to college, and risking discovery, I waited till Charlotte joined me, took a hackney coach to the street, and telling Charlotte it was a tavern walked to the door with her, to my astonishment it was closed. Disconcerted I nearly turned back, but rang the bell. Charlotte said she would not go in. The door opened, a woman said, "Why did you not push the door?" Oh! the shame I felt as I went into that baudy house with Charlotte; the woman seemed to hesitate, or so I fancied, before she gave us a room.

It was a gentleman's house, although the room cost but five shillings: red curtains, looking-glasses, wax lights, clean linen, a huge chair, a large bed, and a cheval-glass, large enough for the biggest couple to be reflected in, were all there. I examined all with the greatest curiosity, but my curiosity was greater for other things, of all the delicious voluptuous recollections, that day stands among the brightest; for the first time in my life I saw all a womans' charms, and exposed my own manhood to one; both of us knew but little of the opposite sex. With difficulty I got her to undress to her chemise, then with but my shirt on, how I revelled in her nakedness, feeling from her neck to her ankles, lingering with my fingers in every crack and cranny of her body; from armpits to cunt, all was new to me. With what fierce eyes after modest struggles, and objections to prevent, and I had forced open her reluctant thighs, did I gloat on her cunt; wondering at its hairy outer covering and lips, its red inner flaps, at the hole so closed up, and so much lower down and hidden, then I thought it to be; soon at its look and feel, impatience got the better of me; hurriedly I covered it with my body and shed my sperm in it. Then with what curiosity I paddled my fingers in it afterwards, again to stiffen, thrust, wriggle, and spend. All this I recollect as if it occurred but yesterday, I shall recollect it to the last day of my life, for it was a honeymoon of novelty, years afterwards I often thought of it when fucking other women.

We fell asleep, and must have been in the room some hours, when we awakened about 3 o'clock. We had eaten nothing that day, and both were hungry; she objected to wash before me, or to piddle; how charming it was to overcome that needless modesty, what a treat to me to see that simple operation. We dressed and left, went to a quietish public-house, and had some simple food and beer, which set me up, I was ready to do all over again, and so was she. We went back to the house and again to bed, the woman smiled when she saw us, the feeling, looking, tittillating, baudy inciting and kissing recommenced. With what pleasure she felt and handled my prick, nor did she make objection to my investigations into her privates, though saying she would not let me. Her thighs opened, showing the red-lipped, hairy slit, I kissed it, she kissed my cock, nature taught us both what to do. Again we fucked, I found it a longish operation, and when I tried later again, was surprised to find that it would not stiffen for more than a minute, and an insertion failed. I found out that day that there were limits to my powers. Both tired out, our day's pleasure over, we rose and took a hackney coach towards home, I went in first, she a quarter of an hour afterwards, and everything passed off as I could have wished.

From that day lust seized us both; we laid our plans to have each other frequently, but it was difficult: my mother was mostly at home, the cook nearly always at home if mother was out; but quite twice a week we managed to copulate, and sometimes oftener. We arranged signals. If when she opened the door, she gave a shake of the head, I knew mother was in; if she smiled and pointed down with her fingers, mother was out, but cook downstairs; if it pointed up, cook was upstairs; in the latter case, to go into the garden parlour and fuck, all this was done off hand. If cook was known to be going out, Charlotte told me beforehand, and if mother was to be out, I got home, letting college and tutors go to the devil. Then there was lip kissing, cunt kissing, feeling and looking, tickling and rubbing each others articles, all the preliminary delights of copulation, and but one danger in the way: my little brother could talk in a broken way, we used to give him some favourite toy, and put him on the floor, whilst we indulged voluptuously. On the sofa one day, I had just spent in her, when I felt a little hand tickling between our bellies, and Tommy who had tottered up to us said, "Don'ty hurt Lotty, der's a good Wattie." We settled that Tom was too young to notice or recollect, what he saw, but I now think differently.

Winter was coming on, she used to be sent to a circulating library to fetch books, the shop was some distance off, a few houses, long garden-walls and hedges were on the road. I used to keep out, or go out just before she went, and we fucked up against the walls. I took to going to church in the evening also, to the intense delight of my mother, but it was to fuck on the road home. One day hot in lust, we fucked standing on the lobby near my bed-room, my mother being in the room below, the cook in the kitchen. We got bold, reckless, and whenever we met alone, if only for an instant, we felt each others genitals.

At last we found the servant's privy one of the best places. I have described its situation near to a flight of steps, at the end of a covered passage, which could be seen from one point only in the garden; down there, anyone standing was out of sight. If all was clear I used to ring the parlour bell, ask for something, and make a sign; when she thought it safe, there she would go, I into the garden, to where I could see into the passage by the side of the garden stairs. If I saw her, or heard "ahem," down I went into the privy, and was up her cunt in a second, standing against the wall, and shoving to get our spent over, as if my life depended on it; this was uncomfortable, but it had its charm. We left off doing it in the privy, being nearly caught one day there.

We thought cook was upstairs mother was out, I was fucking her, when the cook knocked saying, "make haste Charlotte, I want to come." We had just spent, she was so frightened I thought she was fainting, but she managed to say "I cannot." "Do," said cook, "I am ill." "So am I," said Charlotte. Said cook, "I can sit on the little seat." "Go to misses's closet, she's out." Off cook went, out we came, and never fucked in that place again; one day I did her on the kitchen table, and several times on the dining-room table.

We in fact did it everywhere else, and often enough for my health, for I was young, weak and growing, and it was the same with her. The risks we ran were awful, but we loved each other with all our souls. Both young, both new at the work, both liking it, it was rarely we got more than just time to get our fucking over, and clothes arranged before we had to separate, for her to get to her duties. Many times I have seen her about the house, cunt full and with the heightened colour, and brilliant eyes, of a woman who had just been satisfied. I used to feel pleasure in knowing she was bringing in the dinner, or tea, with my spunk in her cunt; not having had the opportunity to wash, or piddle it out.

When she had another holiday, we went to the baudy house, and stayed so long in it, that we had a scare; just asleep, we heard a knocking at the door. My first idea was that my mother had found me out, and although I ruled her in one way, I was in great subjection to her, from not having any money. She thought her father was after her. What a relief it was to hear a voice say: "Shall you be long sir, we want the room." I was having too much accommodation for my money. That night we walked home, for I had no money for a coach, and barely enough to get us a glass of beer and a biscuit; we were famished and fucked out, my mother had refused to give me money, and another aunt whom I had asked, said I was asking too often, and refused also.

Although we went to this baudy house, I always felt as if I was going to be hanged when I did, and it was with difficulty I could make her go; she called it a bad house, and it cost money. Something then occurred which helped me, penniless as I was.

At the extreme end of our village were a few little houses, one stood with its side entrance up a road only partially formed, and without thoroughfare; its owner was a pew-opener, her daughter a dressmaker, who worked for servants and such like; they cut out things for servants, who in those days largely made their own dresses. Charlotte had things made there. At a fair held every year near us of which I shall have to tell more, my fast friend, who had put me up to so much, and whom I forgot to say tried to get hold of Charlotte, I saw with the dressmaker's daughter. Said he, talking to me next day, "She is jolly ugly, but she's good enough for a feel, I felt her cunt last night, and think she has been fucked (he thought that of every girl), her mother's a rum old gal too, she will let you meet a girl at her cottage, not whores, you know, but if they are respectable." "Is it a baudy house?" I asked. "Oh no, it's quite respectable, but if you walk in with a lady, she leaves you in the room together, and when you come out, if you just give her half a crown, she drops a curtesy, just as she does when she opens the pew-doors and anyone gives her six pence, but she is quite respectable--the clergyman goes to see her sometimes."

Charlotte asked to go out to a dressmaker, I met her as if by chance at the door, the old pew-opener asked if I would like to walk in and wait. I did. Charlotte came in after she had arranged about her dress. There was a sofa in the room, and she was soon on it; we left together, I have two or three shillings (money went much further then), and the pew-opener said, "You can always wait here when your young lady comes to see my daughter."

When we went a second time, she asked me if I went to St. Mary's Chapel (her Chapel). We went to her house in the day that time. When going away she said, "Perhaps you wont mind always going out first, for neighbours are so ill-natured." The old woman was really a pew-opener, her daughter really a dressmaker, but she was glad to earn a few shillings, by letting her house be used for assignations of a quiet sort; she would not have let gay women in, from what I heard.

She had lived for years in the parish, and was thought respectable. She had not much use of her house in that way, wealthy people going to town for their frolics,--town only being an hour's journey--and no gay women being in the village that I know of.

At this house, I spent Charlotte's third holiday with her, in a comfortable bed-room. We stopped from eleven in the morning, till nine at night, having mutton chops and ale, and being as jolly as we could be. We did nothing the whole day long, but look at each other's privates, kiss, fuck and sleep outside the bed. It was there she expressed curiosity about male emissions. I told her how the sperm spurted out, then discussing women's, she told me of the pleasure I had given her when fingering her in the manner described already; we completed our explanations by my frigging myself to show her, and then my doing the same to her with my finger. I bungled at that, and think I hear her now saying, "No, just where you were is nicest." "Does it give you pleasure?" "Oh yes, but I don't like it that way, oh!--oh!--I am doing it--oh!" I had no money that day, Charlotte had her wages, and paid for everything, giving me her money to do so.

One day we laughed at having nearly been caught fucking in the privy. "She must have a big bum, must Mary," said I, "to sit on that little seat at the privy." Said Charlotte, "She is a big woman, twice as big as me, her bottom would cover the whole seat." This set us talking about the cook, and as what I then heard affected me much at a future day, I will tell all Charlotte said as nearly as I can recollect.

"Of course I have seen her naked bit by bit--when two women are together they can't help it, why should they mind--if you sit down to pee, you show your legs, and if you put on your stockings you show your thighs, then we both wash down to our waists, and if you slip off your chemise or night-gown you show yourself all over. Mary's beautiful from head to foot, one morning in the summer, we sleeping in the same bed, were very hot. I got out to pee, we had kicked all the clothes off, Mary was laying on her back with night-clothes above her waist fast asleep, I could not help looking at her thighs, which were so large and white--white as snow." "Had she much hair on her cunt?" said I. "What's that to you?" said she laughing, but went on: "Oh! twice as much as I have, and of a light brown." "I suppose her cunt is bigger than yours?" said I reflectively. "Well, perhaps it is," said Charlotte, "she is a much bigger woman than me, what do you think?" I inclined to the opinion it must be, but had no experience to guide me; on the whole we agreed that it was likely to be bigger.

"Then," said she, "I suppose some men have smaller things than yours?" I told her that as far as I knew they varied slightly, but only had knowledge of youthful pricks, and could not be certain whether they varied much when full grown or not. We went on about Mary. "I know I should like to be such a big, fine woman." "But" said I, "I don't like light hair, I like dark hair on a cunt, light hair can't look well, I should think." "I like her," said Charlotte, "she is a nice woman, but often dull, she has no relatives in London, never says anything about them or herself, she used to have letters, and then often cried, she has none now; the other night she took me in her arms, gave me a squeeze and said, 'Oh! if you were a nice young man now', then laughed and said, 'perhaps we would put our things together and make babies.' I was frightened to say anything, for fear she would find out I knew too much; I think she has been crossed in love."

I was twiddling Charlotte's quim as I was never tired of doing, something in the sensation I suppose reminded her, for laughing she went on: "You know what you did to me the other night." "What?" said I not recollecting. "You know, with your finger." "Oh! frig." "Yes, well Mary does that; I was awake one night, and was quite quiet, when I heard Mary breathing hard, and felt her elbow go jog, jog, just touching my side, then she gave a sigh, and all was quiet. I went to sleep, and have only just thought of it." She had heard or felt this jog from the cook before, so we both concluded, that she frigged herself, Charlotte knew what frigging was.

"Do you recollect your mamma's birthday?" said Charlotte, "she sent us down a bottle of sherry, the gardener was to have some, but did not; so we were both a little fuddled when we went to bed. When Mary was undressed she pulled up her clothes to her hips, and looking at herself said, 'my legs are twice as big as yours.' Then we made a bet on it and measured; she lost, but her thigh was half as big again round as mine; then she thew herself on her back and cocked up her legs, opening them for a minute. I said 'Lor, Mary, what ever are you doing?' 'Ah I' said she, 'women's legs were made to open', and there it ended. I never heard her before say or do anything improper, she is most particular." If Charlotte had been older or wiser, she would not have extolled the naked beauties of a fellow servant to her lover, for the description of the big bum, white thighs and hairy belly bottom, the jog, jog, of the elbow, and all the other particulars sunk deep into my mind.

We fucked more than ever, recklessly--it is a wonder we were not found out, for one evening, it being dark, I fucked her in the forecourt, outside our street-door; but troubles were coming.

Her father wrote to know why she had not been home at her holidays, she got an extra holiday to go and pacify him; then we had a fright because her courses stopped, but they came on all right again. One of my sisters came home, and diminished our opportunities, still we managed to fuck somehow, most of the times they were uprighters. The next holiday she went home by coach (the only way), I met her on the return, and we fucked up against the garden wall of our house. A month slipped away, again we spent her holiday at the pew-opener's; no man and woman could have liked each other more, or more enjoyed each other's bodies, without thinking of the rest of the world. I disguised nothing from her, she told me all she knew of herself, the liking she took for me, her pleasure yet fear and shame when first I felt her cunt, the shock of delight and confusion when on my twiddling it, she had spent; how she made up her mind to run out of the house when the milkman came, the hysterical faint when I first laid my prick between her slit and spent, the sensation of relief when I had not done, an instinct told her I should, in spending outside, the sort of feeling of "poor fellow, he wants me, he may do as he likes," which she had; I told my sensations. All these we told each other over and over again, and never tired of the conversation; we were an innocent, reckless, randy couple.

We had satisfied our lusts in simple variety, but I, never put my tongue in her mouth, nor do I know that I had heard of that form of lovemaking--but more of that hereafter. I did her on her belly, and something incited me to do it to her dog fashion, but it was never repeated; we examined as said each others appendages, but once satisfied, having seen mine get from flaccid to stiff, the piddle issue, the spunk squirt, she never wanted to see it again, and could not understand my insatiable curiosity about hers. She knew I think less than most girls of her age about the males, having never I recollect nursed male children, and I don't think she had brothers.

How is it that scarcely any woman will let you willingly look at her cunt after fucking, till it is washed; most say it is beastly, gay or quiet, it is the same. Is it more beastly to have it spurted up, to turn and go to sleep with the spunk oosing on to a thigh, or an hour afterwards to let a man paddle in what has not dried? They don't mind that, but won't let you look at it after your operations, willingly--why?

A modest girl lays quietly after fucking, and does not wash till you are away. A young girl who has let you see her cunt and take her virginity, won't wash it at all, until you point out the necessity. A gay woman often tries to shove back her bum just as you spend, gets the discharge near the outlet, uncunts you quickly and at once washes and pisses at the same time. A quiet young girl wipes her cunt on the outside only. A working man's wife does the same. I have fucked several, and not one washed before me. I incline to the opinion that poor women rarely wash their cunts inside, their piddle does all the washing. "What's the good of washing it?" said a poor, but not a gay girl to me, "it's always clean, and feels just the same an hour afterwards, whether washed or not." Is the unwashed cunt less healthy than one often soaped and syringed? I doubt it. An old roue said to me he would not give a damn to fuck a cunt at night, which has been washed since the morning.

About sexual matters each of us knew about as much as the other, and we had much to learn. A girl however in the sphere of life of Charlotte usually knows more about a man's sex, than a youth of the same age does of a woman's; they have nursed children, and know what a cock is; a girl is never thought too young to nurse a male child, no one would trust a boy after ten years of age to nurse a female child; but she had never nursed. From Charlotte I had my first knowledge of menstruation, and of other mysteries of her sex. Ah! that menstruation was a wonder to me, it was marvellous, but all was really a wonder to me then.

After Christmas my sister went back to school, our chances seemed improving, we spent another holiday at the pew-opener's. I had got money, and we were indiscreet enough to go to see some wax-works. Next day her father came to see her; he ordered her to tell where she had been. She refused, he got angry, and made such a noise, that mother rang to know what it was. He asked to see her, apologized, and said his daughter had been out several holidays, without his knowing where she had been. My mother said it was very improper, and that he ought. A friend was with us in the room, and I sat there reading and trembling. My mother remarked to the lady, "I hope that girl is not going wrong, she is very good looking." Mother asked me to go out of the room, then had Charlotte up, and lectured her; afterwards Charlotte told me for the first time, that her father was annoyed because she would not marry a young man.

A young man had called at our house several times to see her; she saw him once and evaded doing so afterwards. He was the son of a well-to-do baker, a few miles from Charlotte's home, and wished to marry her; his father was not expected to live, and the young man said he would marry her directly the father died. Her mother was mad at her refusing such a chance. Charlotte showed me his letters, which then came, and we arranged together the replies.

She went home, and came back with eyes swollen with crying, some one had written anonymously, to say she had been seen at the wax-works with a young man, evidently of position above her, and had been seen walking with a young man. The mother threatened to have a doctor examine her to see if she had been doing anything wrong, no one seemed to have suspected me; her father would have her home, her mother had had suspicion of her for some time, "The sooner you marry young Brown the better, he will have a good business, and keeps a horse and chaise, you will never have such a chance again, and it will prevent you going wrong, even if you have not already gone wrong," said her mother.

It was a rainy night, I had met her on her return, and we both stood an hour under an umbrella, talking and crying, she saying, "I knew I should be ruined; if I marry he will find me out, if I don't they will lead me such a life; oh! what shall I do!" We fucked twice in the rain against a wall, putting down the umbrella to do it. Afterwards we met at the dressmaker's, talked over our misery and cried, and fucked, and cried again. Then it was nothing but worry, she crying at her future, I wondering if I should be found out; still with all our misery, we never failed to fuck if there was a clear five minutes before us. Then her mother wrote to say that old Brown was dead, and her father meant to take her away directly; she refused, the father came, saw my mother, and settled the affair by taking back Charlotte's box of clothes. I had not a farthing; at her age a father had absolute control, and nothing short of running away would have been of use. We talked of drowning ourselves, or of her taking work in the fields. I projected things equally absurd for myself. It ended in her agreeing to go home,--she could not help that,--but refusing to marry.

Charlotte wrote me almost directly after her return. My mother had reserved the right of opening my letters, although she had ceased to do so. That morning seeing she had one addressed to me, in fear I snatched it out of her hand. She insisted on having it back, I refused, and we had a row. "How dare you sir? give it me." "I won't, you shant open my letter." "I will, a boy like you!" "I am not a boy, I am a man, if you ever open a letter of mine, I will go for a common soldier, instead of being an officer." "I will tell your guardian." "I mean to tell him how shamefully short of money I am, uncle says it's a shame, so does aunt." my mother sunk down in tears, it was my first rebellion; she spoke to my guardian, never touched my letters again, and gave me five times the money I used to have; but to make sure, I had letters enclosed to a friend, and fetched them.

Charlotte was not allowed to go out alone, and was harassed in every way; for all that, I managed to meet her at a local school, one Saturday afternoon when it was empty; some friendly teacher let her in, and she let me in. We fucked on a hard form, in a nearly dark room, about the most difficult poke I ever had, it was a ridiculous posture. But our meeting was full of tears, despondency, and dread of being with child. She told me I had ruined her, even fucking did not cheer her. A week or so afterwards, having no money, I walked all the way to try to see her, and failed. Afterwards in her letters, she begged me never to tell anyone about what had passed between us. Her father sent her away to his brother's, where she was to help as a servant; for somehow it had got wind that she had met some one at the school-house. There she fell ill and was sent home again. Then she wrote that she should marry, or have no peace, wished I was older, and then she could marry me; she did not write much common sense, although it did not strike me so then. She was coming to London to buy things, would say she would call on my mother on the road, but would meet me instead. How she humbugged the young woman who came to town with her, I don't know, but we met at the baudy house, cried nearly the whole time, but fucked for all that till my cock would stand no longer; then vowing to see each other after she was married, we parted.

She married soon, my mother told me of it; she lived twelve miles from us, and did not write to me. I went there one day, but although I lingered long near their shop, I never saw her. I did that a second time, she saw me looking in, and staggered into a back room. I dared not go in for fear of injuring her. Afterwards came a letter not signed, breathing love, but praying me not to injure her, as might be if I was seen near her house. Money, distance, time was all against me; I felt all was over, took to frigging, which, added to my vexation, made me ill. What the doctor thought I don't know, he said I was suffering from nervous exhaustion, asked my mother if I was steady, and kept good hours. My mother said I was the quietest, and best of sons, as innocent as a child, and that I was suffering from severe study--she had long thought I should; the fact being that for four months I had scarcely looked at a book, excepting when she was near me, and had when not thinking of Charlotte, spent my time in writing baudy words, and sketching cunts and pricks with pen and ink.

Thus I lost my virginity, and took one, thus ended my

first love or lust; which will you call it? I call it love, for I was fond of the girl, and she of me. Some might call it a seduction, but thinking of it after this lapse of years, I do not. It was only the natural result of two people being thrown together, both young, full of hot blood, and eager to gratify their sexual curiosity; there was no blame to either, we were made to do it, and did but illustrate the truth of the old song, "Cock and cunt will come together, check them as you may," and point to the wisdom, of never leaving a young male and female alone together, if they were not wanted to copulate.

In all respects we were as much like man and wife as circumstances would let us be. We poked and poked, whenever we got a chance; we divided our money, if I had none, she spent her wages; when I had it, I paid for her boots and clothes--a present in the usually sense of the term I never gave her; our sexual pleasures were of the simplest, the old fashioned way was what we followed, and altogether it was a natural, virtuous, wholesome, connection, but the world will not agree with me on that point.

One thing strikes me as remarkable now: the audacity with which I went to a baudy house; all the rest seems to have began, and followed as naturally as possible. What a lovely recollection it is! nothing in my career since is so lovely as our life then was; scarce a trace of what may be called lasciviousness was in it, had the priest blest it by the bands of matrimony, it would have been called the chaste pleasure of love and affection--as the priest had nothing to do with it, it will be called I suppose beastly immorality. I have often wondered if her husband found out that she was not a virgin, and if not whether it was owing to some skill of hers, or to his ignorance; I heard afterwards that they lived happily.

CHAPTER VI.

Mary the cook.--A bloody nose and broken piss-pot.--An
involuntary spend.--A feel and a poke.--A new sensation.--At
a baudy house.--Mary's history.--She leaves.

As the certainty that all was finished between us came to me, I got better, my grief moderated, my prick expected occupation, I was horrified at having frigged myself, and ceased doing it. Then naturally I looked at the servants. The new housemaid was ugly as sin, so I turned to Mary the cook. I was then about seventeen years old.

She was now I think twenty-six or eight years old, big, stout, but as it seemed to me then, symmetrical; she had exquisite teeth, blue eyes, and a fine complexion--so fine that my mother remarked it. She was quiet in a remarkable degree, and treated me as a boy. Nine months before this I should as soon have dared to think of fucking my aunt, but experience had altered me. I thought of the light hair on her cunt, and of all I could not see, which Charlotte had innocently described to me; and the conclusions we had arrived at, that she frigged herself. Then I thought that after all, old as she was, and young as I was, she might like Charlotte, let me do her. I had once kissed her when Charlotte was with us, and she had taken it as if she was letting a child kiss her; I now tried it again, and got a quiet kiss in return; it was done with the air and manner of "There, there, you troublesome boy," which mortified me much.

I had now special tutors at home, and was at home when I liked, yet my chances with the cook were fewer than they had been with Charlotte, owing to her occupations. I was studying elementary chemistry, and when making some experiments in the garden parlour, burnt a table cover. My mother angry, said I had better experiment in the back kitchen again, so under that pretence, I managed to be downstairs frequently.

I used to watch Mary, slipping out into the outside passage leading to the servant's privy, and take pleasure in the idea of her piddling there. One day, I watched her coming back, she gave her clothes a tuck between her legs, and I knew it was to dry her cunt; opened the door just as she did it, she knew that I saw the action by my grin, and her face turned scarlet. I kissed her that day, asked her timidly if she had dried it properly that morning. "Dried what?" said she innocently. "What I saw you drying when you came from the closet." She turned away without saying a word.

A day or two after as she went upstairs to the parlour, I stopped, saw her legs, and told her she had jolly fat legs. She wished I would go upstairs, for I was in the way with my chemicals, and after that ceased talking to me. But it was difficult to avoid me, I got rude, would tuck my coat between my legs, laugh and make believe to stoop down to see her ankles, but she took no notice. Begging her to kiss me one day; she gave me two or three at once saying, "There now, go on with your chemicals," in such a motherly way, that it mortified me excessively; making me feel the difference in our ages, as a barrier to my hopes.

But if discouraged one day, I got courage the next; impelled by a cock-stand, and my mother being out, I said, "Should I not like to see your legs." For a wonder she answered, "Look at your own." "Oh!" I replied, "they are not the same, you have got a slit between them, I have got something hanging, and ready to put into the slit." "I wish you would go upstairs," said she, "you are always down here now." Then she told mother I was in her way,--I promised only to go to the back kitchen when it suited the cook, but did not keep my word.

She was alone one evening, I went home and downstairs, kissed and fondled, and would not be repulsed. At some time every woman is more yielding than at others, they always are if randy. Getting my courage up I said I wished she would let me feel her thing, then said, "Let me do you," in a whisper. It was quite dusk down there when I said it. She was speechless for a full minute, whilst I kept repeating my demand. At length she replied, "How dare a boy like you, speak like that to a woman like me." "I--am not a boy," said I in anger; "I have had many women, I know all about a woman's pleasure, I know where your thing is; I know why you tuck your hand outside your clothes after you have piddled." Then she pushed me out of the kitchen, but I thought she smiled.

Our family habits were much as they had been, but the weather getting finer, mother often took both Tom and the housemaid with her out for a walk; but not until the cook had dressed herself after our early dinner. Unless she took the housemaid out, I was worse off than ever. Yet my chances came.

Cook one day was alone in the kitchen darning a stocking; it was cold--the beginning of March--her feet were on the old fashioned iron fender, I sat myself down on the fender, and we talked, I laid my hand on her lap, and tried quietly without letting her know it, to feel where she gartered. I felt the knot distinctly above her knee, thought how near it was to the cunt I was burning to feel, then put my hand up her clothes, and felt her naked leg under the knee.

She told me to leave off, my prick was standing, "Have you not jolly big white thighs, I have heard of them," said I. "Heard?" said she. "Yes, and a good lot of hair between them." "Who, to look at you would believe you were such a liar, such a young monkey; get out of the kitchen." She arose, drew some water, took it in one hand, some clean clothes in the other, and went upstairs, taking no further notice of me. I followed her a few steps up, then pushed my hands up her clothes on to her thighs, just beneath her backside; round she swung facing me, and sat down on the stairs; in swinging round my hand came just into contact with the hair of her cunt; then with a push she sent me downstairs tumbling. As I got up she said quite quietly, "It's your fault if you are hurt; if you follow me, I will push you down again," "I am stronger than you." I sung out, "I don't care, so long as I can feel you." "If I was not so comfortable here in many ways, I would leave to-morrow," said she, continuing to go upstairs, and thinking she had settled me; but I followed, tried again, and she threw the whole jug of water over me. "Now tell your mamma," said she, "and I'll surprise her, she don't know her son," and again she pushed me down. That did not stop my tongue, for I had now got angry and reckless, sang out my wants, bawling out about her cunt, and said, "Did you ever sit on the little privy seat Mary, tell me." She went up, and locked herself in her bed-room, till I was tired of waiting.

I had been a month at this fun, and as in Charlotte's case seemed not getting on at all, my experience was confined to one woman, and naturally I used to compare everything taking place, with what had taken place with her. To my inexperienced mind, there was a difference between the two women which I could not understand: when I first got my hand up Charlotte's clothes, she was as quick as me, struggled, screeched, and got my hand away, seemed in dread and astonished. When I got my hand on Mary's flesh, which I did repeatedly afterwards, she would turn round quite quietly, remove my hand with force, look at me as if she were collecting her thoughts, did not seem at all alarmed, but gave me a lecture. When she kissed me afterwards, it seemed to be upon reflection, but she did it with force, looked me full in the face, then turned away. One day she said, "I would not leave a sister of mine here, if she were young, for five times my wages, but I am old enough to keep you in your place."

Soon after mother was one day out, I at home, housemaid and Tom in the garden; it was a clear, bright day, there was a fire in the garden parlour, the garden window-door was shut, and I bolted it; it was about half-past three o'clock, the cook was dressing, I burning with lust, went to my bed-room, opposite then to her door and listened. I heard the rattle of piddle, excitement got the better of my fears, I knocked. "It's not locked," she called out, thinking it was the housemaid; I opened the door, went in and closed it.

She was standing before the glass brushing her hair, with but stays on; over her chemise, I saw at a glance big white breasts, and big white legs up to her knees. She turned round, and seeing me, put her hands up to cover her breasts, stepped backwards till the bedstead stopped her, and said, "Go out, mister Walter," but I threw my arms round her, clasping her tightly and kissing her on her breasts before she could repeat her request, and said, "Oh! do Mary, do let me."

She did not answer, but disengaged herself from my arms. Crafty with lust and doubtless thinking of former experience, I dropped on my knees, in an instant had her chemise up, both hands round her great bum, and my mouth buried in the hair, kissing the outside of her cunt; she sat down nearly crushing my hands, between her bum and the bedstead, I withdrew them with a cry of pain.

She pushed me away; being on my knees, back I tumbled; as I did so, caught her chemise and lifted it; she put her hands down to prevent it; I kept my hold tightly, and it tore up with a noise, to where her stays stopped it from going further; but the rent disclosed thighs belly and motte simultaneously. She rose, tried to hide her nakedness, and stop the chemise going further, her legs got somehow entangled with mine, I fell back, and she fell clean over me. As I fell, my head struck the pot and overturned it, I felt the warm piddle round my neck and head, and at the same instant a heavy sort of blow on my nose, and hair on my lips--it was her naked belly and motte which struck me as she fell on me. We rolled over, and struggled for a second, I saw white thighs, a huge bum, and then we were both up. She opened the window and shouted out, "Eliza, Eliza, I want you."

Then she turned to me with her eyes wide open, her bosom palpitating, and said, "Get out, you are a nice young blackguard, I would not have believed it, had I not found you out." And in the same breath hurriedly, "Oh! my God, Wattie, what is the matter?" I felt a funny trickling sensation on my upper lip, and putting my hand up to feel, removed it covered with blood, the result of the blow of her motte on my nose, which was pouring down blood copiously, and dropping on to my shirt. The sight of blood always made me furious, "It's a blow from your belly," said I, "you did it purposely." She saw by that time it was not serious and said, "it serves you right, and directly your mamma comes in I will tell her." "Do," said I. She repeated, "You are a young blackguard."

In the excitement of opening the window, calling out,

and seeing my nose bleeding, she had forgotten her torn chemise; and I had thought about nothing but my bleeding nose. Standing by the table to open the window, her form had been hidden, but she moved, disclosed the torn chemise, partly one of her hips, thigh, leg, and partially the hair of her cunt. "I can see your cunt," said I staunching my nose. She snatched up the torn chemise, hiding herself with it. "Oh! go, go," said she, "oh! that mess, what shall I do!" and she stopped to set up the piss-pot which was laying on one side; I rushed forward, nose still bleeding, and tried to feel the half naked thigh. "For God's sake go," said she, "here is Eliza coming." I heard Tom lumping up step by step slowly, assisted by the housemaid, and bolted into my room.

I held the door ajar and listened. "Where is Master Walter?" said the housemaid as she got to the top landing. "I don't know," said Mary, "is he not in the drawing-room?" "I don't know," replied Eliza, "what do you want?" The door closed, I heard no more, but felt sure that Mary did not mean to tell. My nose left off bleeding, I washed it, and crept quietly downstairs.

Eliza and Tommy went down again into the garden; shortly afterwards down went cook into the kitchen, five minutes after down I went. It was always dullish in the afternoon there. I had thought that I might risk, and as I passed the door from the kitchen leading into the garden, shot the bolt so that, had the housemaid come down that way, she could not get in also.

Mary was sitting close to the fire. "No more nonsense I hope," said she. There was a kiss and forgiveness soon given me, in her tranquil way.

Again I sat down on the huge kitchen fender, and the next instant was thinking what I had best do. I had seen those wonderfully large, white thighs, seen the thicket of lightish hair between them, had felt no cunt fully for weeks, and was dying with lust. She was as serene as if nothing had happened, and kissed me, but in the usual motherly sort of way. She rose up saying, "I must begin to shut up; what is Eliza staying out so late in the garden with that child for?" That instant I thrust my hand up her clothes, got it on to the motte, and clutched the hair between my fingers; it was easy enough, for it was about the longest and thickest motte thatch I have yet felt. Down she sat, and tried to push me away, but I had firm hold of the hair, and as I did on a similar occasion with Charlotte, pulled and hurt her; she ceased to push me off, and there I stopped, my prick throbbing, and every fibre in me, palpitating with the lust of long continence. Then I pulled and hurt her again, threatening to hurt her more still unless she let me feel her; knowing the housemaid must knock before she could get in suddenly, I was bold.

She bore my tugs with a little flinching and never answered my entreaties. I had found my courage, and used the words cunt and fuck; it was getting dark; looking at me steadily, she said, "So young and yet so cruel, five minutes ago you were saying you were so fond of me, and now you are trying to hurt me; you promised you would not touch me again, now you are doing it; you are all alike, young and old, cruel and liars." I felt ashamed, but was mad with lust. "A youth like you, and so quiet as you look." "Youth! I am a man, have had women, feel me, let me feel you, oh! do feel me." I had my prick out. To get better at her, go from the fender on to my knees, and was pushing my hand between her thighs with energy. Pulling her bum back, she stooped, and her face came near mine. "Kiss me, feel me, and I will indeed leave off, I have seen your belly, let me feel it, and I will leave off." "You will break your word again," said she. "I swear not." She put her face to mine and kissed me, her right hand dropped, and gently laid hold of my prick, her thighs just so little opened that my fingers passed the hair and felt the smooth inner face of the lips; it was too much for me, for some hours my prick had been standing off and on, I had been pulling it about, longing and hoping to use it, and for a long time no emission had left it.

I felt my sperm coming, and could not stop it, my arse jogged and pushed my prick involuntarily between her fingers, pleasure suddenly overwhelmed me, and kissing her I spent in her hand--all the work of half a minute. Then burning shame came over me, I could kiss her no longer, dared not look her in the face, nor keep my hand between her thighs, but rose quickly and without a word rushed upstairs to my bed-room.

I have done for myself I thought, what a beast she will think me, I shall never dare to speak to her again, and was ready to cry; little knowing then that every step in baudiness, is a step towards the end, and that my spunk on her hand, would help me to shed some in her elsewhere.

Feeling so uncomfortable I went out; calling out to the housemaid, that I should be home about eight o'clock, went to a friend's, had dinner, but could not talk nor scarcely eat. My friend joked and asked if I was in love. My prick was standing again after I had eaten, I went home, making up my mind to go to bed early, preferring solitude and my own thoughts; it was about seven P. M., to my astonishment Mary opened the door. I felt my face hot, and could scarcely look at her; she was as tranquil as ever, nothing ever seemed to disturb that woman. This tranquility reassured me, the more so when I found mother was still out. The housemaid had gone out to make a few purchases, leaving Mary alone with Tommy, who she was just going to put to bed, and upstairs she went with him for that purpose, without speaking to me.

What a chance! oh! if I had not been such a beast. My prick rose stiff, the afternoon's spend was the first I had had for a long time, a stiff prick gives courage, and darkness helps. We are alone, she said nothing as I spent in her hand, indeed went on kissing me when spending, what if I ask her again? What an age she seemed putting Tommy to bed, at last I heard her say, "Go to sleep, mamma will be home soon," and she went up to her bed-room. She is going thought I to sit there till Eliza knocks, and did not dare go up, but stood listening in the hall, feeling my prick and longing; at last I heard her coming down with slow, measured steps. In the hall, I flung my arms around her, kissing and begging her to forgive me. "I could not help it," said I in a whisper, "you do not know how I longed for you." "Let me go downstairs," said she.

The garden parlour door was open. "Come in here and talk." I pulled her in with but little difficulty, pushed her down on the sofa, and put both arms round her. The door closed, leaving a small opening; there was no light, but the gleam which shot from the hall-lamp through the door ajar; I could barely see her face, and sat by her begging forgiveness and kissing, but got no reply. My prick was more than stiff, I put my hand down on her lap, on to her knees, then down to her feet, waiting a second at each advance--no movement. My hand slipped up bit by bit, it passed her ankle, her garter, and was on the flesh above-- still no movement. I hesitated and begged--no reply. Up further went my hand, the thighs were not closed, but let my hand slip between them, a long drawn sigh came from her as my fingers buried themselves in a fat, warm quim. I pushed her back gently, and put her hand on to my prick; she held it tight, and in a whisper said, "Will you never tell anyone?" By my body and soul I swore it; the thighs opened wider, her body fell back and disposed itself on the sofa, my hands roved over a large expanse of flesh, I could see the white mass only, the rest seemed dark. I kissed the hair on her cunt which I could not see, felt the smooth velvety haunches, and threw myself on one of the finest, whitest and broadest bellies I ever yet have had close to mine. The thighs opened to receive me, and the next moment my prick was gliding up her cunt--she was not a virgin.

What a heavenly sense of satisfaction at being up a cunt again. I could scarcely realize my success; my hands felt between the fat lips, to ensure my being in all right. I was conscious of a difference between her and Charlotte, the way she lay, the size of the thighs, the quantity of hair, and a quiescent manner, made her as different as possible from my former sweetheart. Novelty made me think this one more delicious, but nature would not postpone, and was impelling her as well as me; was tightening her cunt round my prick, her body was thrilling for a spend. I pushed as her cunt tightening, roused me, tighter was my prick grasped within her; her arms folded across me, drew me towards her like a vice; her belly moved up quite slowly to mine, as if to throw me off, then moved twice or thrice as if in a spasm--a sigh, and her belly sunk down as slowly as it had risen up, drawing my sperm into her, as she spent.

We lay without stirring, or uttering a word for a long time, supremely happy; my prick lingered as if it intended to stop permanently in its trap, she made no effort to dislodge it; at last it began to shrink, then curiosity began, down went my hand between our bellies, wet as if from a bath of gruel was my doodle and her quim. Then she spoke--the first words uttered--"No--no--." The feel had such an effect on me, that my prick began again to stiffen. I had with Charlotte failed ignominiously two or three times, in a third fuck on the same day, and feared a failure now. I kissed and felt her, as far as my hands and our clothes would let me, she moved her bum up gently to let my hand under it, but not a word could I get from her. "Can I do it again?" thought I, and began pushing--yes it was stiffening, and again was that cunt tightening. I push harder,--with a gentle heave the belly comes up, I am off on the ride without having withdrawn; was this the fist time I had ever been man enough to do it twice without uncunting? I think so.

The passage of privates was longer, I felt more movement in her buttocks, her sighs were stronger, her hand moved more restlessly over my back, our mouths got glued together. Her lips are wet, or it is mine which are getting wet? There is a new, voluptuous sensation I never experienced before, it delights me; I glued my lips tighter to hers, our heaves are quicker, our sighs shorter, I feel the least bit of her tongue touching my lips. I had never heard of that voluptuous accompaniment of fucking, and it was to me an inspiration; shooting out my tongue into her mouth,--hers comes out to meet it; they are exchanging liquids,--the delight spreads electrically through our bodies,--up comes her belly,--shorter are my shoves,--a quivering wriggle to get deeper up her--and we both spend together, as it seems with more pleasure than I ever did before. How strange I should recollect this all so clearly.

The delights of the wet kisses are new to me; although not able to see them, I thought of her exquisite teeth, and rolled my tongue over them. She kisses me, still holds me, again my hand goes down to feel the parts now separating, slobbered, and sticky with past joy; out comes my prick, and then she speaks. "No-no," she sits up, I by her side, my hand on her naked thighs for a minute. She gets up, gives me a long kiss, goes to her room, and soon after comes down, her eyes wet with crying, "Don't come near me, don't be unkind, let me alone," she says. Her manner was so commanding, that I let her go to the kitchen without following her. Shortly Eliza and then my mother came home.

Mad for her again, I took to my chemistry in the back kitchen constantly, you may be sure. When I got the chance, spoke of our pleasures and my hopes. "We ought," said she, "both to be ashamed of ourselves, but I especially who am so many years older than you, ought to have known better; if I am punished it will serve me right. Oh! if you don't hold your tongue! My risk is more than you have any idea of." All was said in a way as if she were preaching, and looking me full in the face.

She refused what I wanted and avoided me, but it was impossible for her altogether to escape me. Risking everything, emboldened by impunity with Charlotte, I used to clutch her knees, and put my head up her clothes, kissing and smelling her motte, I began to love the smell of it. She used to dislodge me, and neither made a noise, nor uttered a word in doing so--indeed she rarely spoke at any time. But it is difficult for a woman who has been fucked by a man to refuse him again; I watched my opportunities, my conversation broken as it was, and rarely but for a minute at a time, was one repetition of lustful wants and prayers; I used to pull my prick out, beg her to see and feel it. At length she did, saying, "May God forgive me for my weakness." That day I fucked her again standing in the kitchen, and a second time a few hours afterwards in the dusk, which experience began to show me was the time she was most accessible; the other servant was somewhere in the house at the time I recollect.

After that her manner changed, she ceased to resist; but when I asked her to go to a house with me, she said, "No, no, I am not coming to that." Now, though tranquil, she was more capricious, sometimes letting me feel her, or do it to her with impatience; at other times with evident desire to please; but I was so often baulked, and I plagued her so incessantly to meet me somewhere, that at length she did, saying, "Well, it little matters, as I have made my bed, so I must lie on it." I did not know then what she meant by that.

She got a holiday, we had food at a tavern, went to the house to which I first took Charlotte, and into the same room; what a reminiscence! As I got to the door, she looked nervously round and said, "I may as well be hung for a sheep as a lamb." It was a joyous day for me. Once in the house she became gay and amatory, threw off all restraint, and abandoned herself to sexual enjoyment in a way she never did but twice again.

She was simply dressed as was customary with servants in those days. Soon I had her standing naked before me with but boots and stockings on. And what a sight she was. Quite five feet eight high, stout, yet as it seemed to me then, without a single part of her body either flabby or shapeless, her skin was of such dazzling whiteness that her white stockings looked dull by contrast, very light brown hair, which when pulled out nearly hung to her waist, the hair of her cunt and arm-pits in quantity of a lighter golden brown; all looked much darker than their true colour, against the dazzling whiteness of the skin. Ample calves and thighs, breasts firm as ivory, her arms to match in plumpness and whiteness, her hands alone discoloured by work, looked dark against the rest of her glorious person. I recollect this all well, and that at that time I disliked light-haired women: but in her suddenly, the light hair appeared to me lovely.

She changed in manner that day from a condescending matron, to a lover of my own age; had the complacency of a gay woman, tempered with modesty. I had no notion of baudily posturing women which I learned in after life, but had an innate love and perception of all that was beautiful, and began placing her in attitudes favourable to the contemplation of her charms. She complied with all; from belly to side, from side to back I turned her; she smiled as if pleased, curious, and astonished; and when I turned to quench my passion in her, she met me with an ardour less demonstrative, but more stifling and satisfying than Charlotte; it was a worry to think that I had twice fucked her, and seemed to have finished each time before I had began fucking.

The firmness of her flesh impressed me, whether I put my finger between the cheeks of her arse or between her thighs, I could with difficulty get it away; she could have cracked a nut between either. The next wonder was the hair of her cunt, which was long but curly; I now see that she could not have pissed without wetting it, which accounted for her always what we youths used to call mopping it, after she had piddled. The cunt looked twice as big as Charlotte's, but the prick-hole seemed to me smaller; and whether my finger or my prick was in it, seemed to grasp it tightly. My prepuce used to give me then at times pain just before, or when I spent in Charlotte; in Mary I scarcely seemed to feel it, and afterwards a quiet sort of grinding of her cunt, prolonged my pleasure until my penis left it. I was so new to the work, that all those differences impressed me, I compared and thought of them constantly.

She gave no violent writhes, nor twists, nor jerked her arse, nor wriggled as she spent, but just as my short thrusts came on, her belly used gradually to heave up and grow into mine; her cunt almost seemed to be sucking my prick, whilst it throbbed and jetted its sperm into her; my hardest thrusts never hurt; Charlotte used to complain if my prick was too vigorous in her. Then when her pleasure was over; lolling her tongue against mine, and sucking my very breath from me, she quietly subsided; leaving me to lay in her, until with a kiss, she would gently doze off with me in her arms.

A taste had developed as said, which I have retained to the present time. I loved to see a woman piddle, used to make Charlotte do it as often as I could, to place my hand under the stream, and feel its splash on my fingers; and if chance let me hear the rattle in a pot, or see a woman rising up from the attitude, my prick used to stand. I did this with her greatly to her astonishment, she resented it so much that I never repeated it: singular that a woman who would let me lay and kiss her cunt, or put finger and prick up it; should refuse to let me see the water come from it-- but so it was.

Charlotte I loved, and used to feel as if she were part and parcel of me for life, when I was up her, with Mary I thought of thighs, backside, cunt, and her other parts, without much liking her beyond the desire of spending in her. My impression is that I must have fucked that day, as much as I ever did in my life on one day; my mother remarked that I looked ill and worn out when I got home, and again fell on her favourite belief that I was overstudying. How she could have permitted a young man to be so often in the kitchen, and near to female servants, seems to me a marvel of stupidity,--but she did.

Nothing opens a man and woman's heart to each other like fucking. A woman laying satisfied by your side, her cunt bedewed with your spunk, with fingers touching your prick, and mouth fresh from contact with yours; will tell you more than she will at any other time. She did that day. She had thought me a mere boy, getting baudy with coming manhood, and had liked me. My quiet, demure manner, made her imagine that such an attack from me, was among the most improbable things; when I began she made up her mind to leave, but then came the mystery,--

there were circumstances which rendered it needful for her to stay where she was, if possible--what they were she would not say. My assault on her in the bed-room and all that followed upset all her ideas, filled her mind with images of lust and pleasure, and left that undefined sensation and unsatisfied longing which is known as randiness. I suddenly seemed a man to her. My spending in her hand upset her still more. I asked if that had made her let me have her. She replied, "I gave up the self denial of years, abandoned my intentions, and let you do it; when you pushed me into the garden parlour I intended to let you as I went in, I had not quite intended before."

There was the greatest difficulty after that day in getting her, for my mother seemed always in my way, and objected to my being in the kitchen. Mary never helped me as Charlotte used, as cook indeed she could not. She ran no risks, and was never in a hurry, so where I had Charlotte half a dozen times, I could scarcely get Mary once.

She met me out again, and in a fortnight asked for another holiday. It astonished my mother, for more than a year she scarcely had gone out, and never had taken a whole holiday. What another day of ballock-ing it was, in that old, snug, baudy house--but we had a quarrel there.

Even with my inexperience, I knew she was different from Charlotte at the first poke. I used in my mind to compare the differences. Charlotte's curiosity, the manifest novelty of fucking to her, even for a couple of months after her splitting and bleeding; was so different from the steady, quiet, well satisfied way with which Mary copulated. Pondering over this, I wondered if she had been done before, how often, and by how many, or had I been the first? The idea of asking her was always floating through my brain. That day I said to her as her face was towards mine on the pillow, and I was toying with her

119

bubbies, "I wonder who had you before me." She sat up, looked me steadily in the face, and replied, "You have no right to ask me, you are not my husband." "But tell me." "I shall not, it is an impertinence; how can a youth like you know anything about first or second." I blurted out, "Because when first I did it to Char--" the name was almost out of my mouth, but I stopped in time, "when I first had a young woman (correcting myself), I could not easily get into her, it tore my prick, and she bled." "Who was it?" said she. "Oh! a young woman." "But who was it?" I did not reply. "Was it Charlotte?" and she looked me hard and full in the face. "No," said I. "Now was it? Tell me," said she bending over, kissing and coaxing me. "No, it was not." "I believe it was, you once said she was young, and had dark brown hair--it was she." In vain I denied it. "I felt sure it was, and with a youth like you! Is it possible you can have harmed that nice girl! What a wretched, wicked lot you all are, you will be as bad as the others." Then she suddenly said, "Mind, you have sworn solemnly never to mention to any living soul about me; oh! once forget yourself, and it's all up with a woman." Then she laid down, again her manner became quiet and voluptuous--another fuck followed. I again tried the question. She settled me by saying, "If ever you ask me that question again, I will not let you have me afterwards," and I never did ask her that I can recollect until just before she felt us.

But she for some time after asked ME questions about my first woman, "was she tall? were her teeth as good as hers?" and so on. How far she satisfied herself that it was Charlotte, she never said; for I don't recollect that she mentioned her name again, and I gave wrong descriptions; but may have got more information than I meant her to have, as she asked me at odd times when I was off my guard.

A third time, to the still greater surprise of my mother, she took a holiday. We spent it at the house, and she exhausted me and herself. For a day or two afterwards she gave me every chance at home, and we fucked furiously. She took to calling me a dear fellow, when her tongue was not against mine, but which was always the case when our mouths got together; and I imagine now, must have been a greater luxury to her than it was then to me. Soon after she received several letters which I said were from her lover. "I wish they were," said she. Then she took ill, and when better, refused me altogether. I had opportunities, but she would not. I said I wished I had never seen her; she said she wished so too, for she was fond of me, although it was ridiculous at her age and mine. Afterwards when mother was one evening at the bottom of the garden, Eliza gone out to the library. I seized Mary as she closed the shutters; kissing and begging her. She opened her thighs, my fingers were on her clitoris; she kissing me at intervals said: "Oh! no, oh! I can't, dear--I dare not--Walter, Walter, you must not; I am a married woman, and am going home to my husband most likely."

Soon afterwards she told me her history. Married seven years previously, her husband became dissipated and unfaithful; and from being a well-to-do tradesman, brought himself to the condition of a labourer. She forgave him until he gave her a disease, then she left him as she had threatened to do. Nothing he could say would induce her to have anything more to do with him. "Is there anything about me that a man could not be satisfied with for years?" she asked, as if I were a judge.

She went home to her mother. He appears to have been fond of her. Love of women was his great fault; but the disease so set her against him, that all his entreaties were useless. Nevertheless she was his wife, and getting into the mother's house one day, when she was alone

(Mary), he fucked her with violence--and violent it must have been, for she was as strong as a horse. Directly afterwards she left and went to service in London, confiding only her address to her mother, taking a false name, and writing him, that if ever he found her out and annoyed her, she would go abroad. Her husband made the mother a sort of promise to keep steady for three months, but failed in doing so, went to America, had never ceased to write affectionate letters which came to her through her mother, and had recently written to say he had made a large sum of money, and was coming home. He had sent money home to the mother with instructions to settle it on Mary how she liked, provided she would come back to him. Afterwards she showed me his letters; they were well written, and in a style above a man of his position in life.

She had lived in service ever since; with us she had then been a year and a half, and had had but two other places. One she left because a grown up son began to pay her too much attention. At the other the master--a married man-- made love to her, and one day tried to force her. I know the last place, it was about three miles from us.

This news came like a cold bath on me. It suited my taste to have a woman in the house. The idea of losing her was terrible. She refused me my pleasures. I doubted her truth at times, but whenever I did, she would fetch a letter as proof saying, "Now will you believe me?" She refused to say where her home had been, and what her real name was. I used to try to make out the postmark on her letters, but could not. They were negligent in those days in such matters, and postage was dear.

And now I again asked if she had had any other but her husband and me; by all that was holy she declared she had not. "How came you to let me?" "God in heaven knows!" said she, "months ago if anyone had said such a thing was possible, I should have said it was ridiculous; I only thought of you as a tall boy, but that day I felt that my life was passing away without the pleasures of a woman; what you did kneeling down in the kitchen upset me, then I let you; though I thought I should ruin myself by doing so."

She cared but little for her husband, for he had caused her to lead the life of a widow for years. "Suppose I had done anything wrong," said she, "and he had found it out, he would have cast me away; but you men can do what you like, and we poor women have to submit." "But why go back?" "Four months ago I would not have done so, but you have made me find out I am a woman after all; you will understand that better as you grow older. Not many would have kept chaste as I have done until that night. Now I mistrust myself. I am getting fond of you, but what could come of it? And if anything came to the ears of my mother and friends, who are respectable, I should drown myself. I have got plenty of will of my own, although I am quiet."

"You don't care much about poking?"

"I have had my wants, but suppressed them," she replied. "What did you do?" "Oh!" said she in an off hand way, "what other unmarried women do, I suppose." "Frigged yourself." She gave a nod and said, "And not often that." I thought of what Charlotte had told me, but held my tongue.

I tried to get at her at intervals, but it was no use. "It's caprice," said I with my prick out, "you let me when I wanted it three weeks ago, why not now?" "I can't,--I dare not,--it might be certain ruin now." "What does a fellow care about ruin, when his hand is outside a cunt, and his prick is like an iron rod?" Twice as strong as me, she could at all times have escaped me, unless sexual desire was strong on her; desire gives a man force, but it takes away a woman's force. She rose up, nor would she continue talking, until I had buttoned up my prick and promised not to touch her; that done, she said, "Would you wish to ruin me? You might if I let you, I have been very ill as you know, was in the family way, my monthlies stopped, and I have brought them on. When I was in trouble that way, I let you do what you like, now I am going home, what would become of me if I were in the family way then?" This explained all.

I had never given her a present, I never gave Charlotte one; having then so little money. I never thought about it. I had now more, and offered to give her some if she wanted any. She showed me a saving-bank's book. She had got nearly fifty pounds. I bought a pair of gold earrings for her, it was the first present I had even given a woman, and she was much pleased. I had I think some vague notion, that it would induce her to let me have her; but if so, I was deceived.

Mother seemed to be keeping at home to baulk me. My chemicals had been taken back into the garden parlour. I knew she wanted to go to my aunt's; but one morning it was too hot, then it rained, and so on. How I restrained myself from frigging I don't know, for I used to walk up and down my bed-room with my prick out stiff, and looking at it; at length a chance came--my last.

Mother went to aunt's, the ugly housemaid said, "As Master Tom wont be at home, do you mind my going out for a couple of hours?" "No," said my mother, "when the cook is ready." "Please will you tell the cook Mamm," said she, "or she wont let me go." I had then a tutor in mathematics who came on that day, but promised to fetch mother home. I had many times broken my promises to do so, to enable me to get at Mary. Mother said, "I hope you mean what you say, you are getting a man, and should never break your word." Anxious to know when the housemaid would go; I asked her. "I am not going till five o'clock, sir," said she, "unless you particularly want the books," "That will be too late, for I am to fetch mamma home,--never mind."

I finished with my tutor, and out I went. But at about five o'clock came home near to the house, wondering if the housemaid had gone, (Mary I had not spoken a word to), waited in sight of the house, and at last saw a form I guessed to be the housemaid's, going off fast towards the village; five minutes afterwards I knocked, and Mary opened the door. Said she, "What brings you home?" I said I was unwell, had a bad cold, could not go for my mother, would go to bed, would she fetch me a foot-bath, and went to my bed-room. I had been two days planning the thing, an old dodge it was though.

It was hot and quite light, but I drew down the blinds, undressed and put on my nightgown; she brought the bath, we talked. She had not heard from her mother again, it was strange,--was she being played with? It took weeks then to get to America. I kissed and got closer to her, we were on the edge of the bed; I spoke of our meetings and our pleasures, she avoided the subject, said I should take cold, prayed me to have the foot-bath and go to bed. Gradually I got my hand on her thighs, how could she help it?--a woman who had been fucked by me a lot of times. But she was firm in refusing me. I lifted my night-shirt, my prick stood up, the shirt hanging at the back of it like clothes on the hook of a prop. Finding that useless, I threatened to frig myself and began the operation. She said I ought to be ashamed of myself, that she would leave if I did not desist, and turned to go, when I pulled her on to the bed. Soon my fingers were on her slit, her fingers on my prick. "I dare not let you,--oh! pray!" she said, but she was vanquished, silent, and tranquilly laid down on the bed; nature was too strong for her.

I lifted her chemise, had a glimpse of the lovely plump calves, and large, fleshy thighs, as I threw myself impetuously upon her. My belly closed with hers, and pushing my knuckles through the hairs, I guided my prick towards her cunt, but alas! too late. The long abstinence and the excitement were too much for me; just as my fingers opened the cunt-lips, and my prick touched her cunt, throb--throb--gush--gush, and over my fingers, over her thighs, into the thicket of hair, on to the clitoris, on to the smooth, round bum-cheeks below--anywhere--everywhere excepting the right place, my sperm spurted out: and only the last drop remained just as I buried my prick in her. Then instead of meeting her humid tongue with mine, I sank on her breast kissing, yet damning and cursing like a dragoon, at my spoiled pleasure,--I had spent out of sheer copiousness of spunk, and excitement.

Said she, "It is as well as it is, get off." I made no reply, hoping my sexual force would return, for my prick was in her sheath. She moved to release herself. Stronger far than me, she could in any other attitude have easily done so; but the most difficult position for a woman to disengage herself from a man, is when he is on the top of her, well between her thighs, and clasping her backside tightly. As she moved there was no strong will in it; how could it be otherwise? She in the prime of life had been without it for weeks, nature was pleading for me, my prick was in her, my spunk all about her. To gain time I promised to get off in a minute. "Kiss me." Our mouths and tongues met. It was like magic. A voluptuous throb passed through both of us, my prick stiffened to the full, a sympathetic grind of her cunt responded; again we were in the full tide of pleasure, fucking and spending together, the future was forgotten as we sunk quietly down. I had spent twice without uncunting; scarcely was it over than she pushed me off, and washed out her cunt in my foot-bath.

We sat on the side of the bed kissing and feeling each other, it was like the old time, the door wide open to hear the street door knocks. When the housemaid knocked, into bed I got; an hour afterwards home came my mother and into my bed-room. She approved of the hot foot-bath, but insisted on my taking a febrifuge. To keep up the sham, I took it, Mary brought it and stood by, whilst my mother gave it to me; my prick was again standing like a prop at the sight of Mary, and as my mother pulled the bed-clothes over me, she might, if she had had eyes, seen my prick pushing them almost up.

Next morning she gave notice to leave. I never had her again. On one or two occasions I felt her, and if there had been more time might perhaps have had her. At the end of a fortnight she told me that her monthlies were all right. From that day she resolutely refused to even let me feel her. "I don't much care about going back," said she; "I don't think I shall be happy, but I do it for the best; at all events I shall have a home." The day before she went she said, "Goodbye, God bless you, you are a good fellow," but you will play mischief with many a poor girl here before you have done. "I like you very much, and shall always think of you." I never heard of her after, and with her, passed from me the woman who is still in my recollection as one of the most beautiful, and perfect in form; as one who gave me the greatest sexual pleasure,-- but I was of course very young and inexperienced.

My mother remarked that she was the most trustworthy servant she ever had; but that there was a mystery about her. Her boxes were labelled for a place that the coach would not take her to, and her boxes were not like a servant's. "I think she has been crossed in love and ran away," said mother. Said I, "Perhaps she had gone off with a bobby," it was a current joke then, policemen not having been long invented. My mother said in her severe way, "She is a virtuous woman, a youth like you should not utter ignorant jokes about women, especially about the humbler classes, to whom good reputation is everything." I began to see plainer than ever, that I could humbug mother after that.

Many of our conversations are told here in her very words, others as nearly as I can recollect them. I have often wondered at the way this woman behaved to me, talked to me, and all about her. The circumstances as they occurred, even at the time seemed peculiar; I felt as if I was wicked in getting into her, almost as if I was going to poke my mother; but I cannot attempt to analyse motives or sensations, I simply narrate facts. Certain it is, that I never have had a woman who in behaviour resembled Mary, in manner, conversation, and general behaviour,--I always felt as if she were a superior person to me, as if she were obliging me and not herself, and was putting me under an obligation, by letting me fuck her.

Again lonely, I not only wanted cunt, but also the society of a woman, it was so sweet to see and talk, to some one I fucked; to do so secretly, was an additional charm, and I used to feel quite sad. I was then about in my eighteenth year.

CHAPTER VII.

At the Manor house.--Fred's amours.--Sarah and Mary.--What
 drink and money does.--My second virgin.--My first whore.--
 Double fucking.--Gamahucking.--Minette.--A belly up and
 down.

One aunt as said lived in H...shire, a widow; her son, my cousin Fred, was preparing for the Army. I wanted a change, and went by advice to stay there. Fred was a year older than me, wild and baudy to the day of his death, he talked from boyhood incessantly about women. I had not seen him for some time, and he told me of his amours, asking me about mine. I let him know all, without disclosing names; he told me in nearly the words, that it was "a lie," for he had heard my mother say, that I was the steadiest young fellow possible, and she could trust me anywhere. This, coupled with my quiet look, and the care I took not to divulge names, made him disbelieve me; but I disclosed so many facts about women's nature, that he was somewhat astonished. He told me what he had done, about having had the clap, and what to do if I got it; then he had seduced a cottager's daughter on the estate; but his description of the taking, did not accord with my limited experience. One day he pointed the girl out to me at the cottage door, and said he now had her whenever he wanted.

She was a great coarse wench, whom he had seen in my aunt's fields. He had caught her piddling on one side of a hedge; she saw him looking at the operation from a ditch, and abused him roundly for it; it ended in an acquaintance, and his taking her virginity one evening on a hay-cock,--

that was his account of it.

Her father was a labourer on my aunt's estate, the girl lived with him and a younger sister, her name was Sarah; he expatiated on her charm from backside to bubbies, but it was soon evident to me, that with this woman it was no money, no cunt; for he borrowed money of me to give her. I had squeezed money out of my aunt, my guardian and mother, and had about ten pounds,--a very large sum for me then, so I lent him a few shillings.

He had his shove as he called it, and triumphantly gave me again such account of his operations, and the charms of the lady, that I who had been some time without poking, wondered if the girl would let me; arguing to myself, he gives her money--my girls never wanted money,--why should his? He had been dinning into my ears, that all women would let men for money, or presents, or else from lust. "Kiss and grope, and if they don't cry out, show them your prick and go at them." These maxims much impressed me.

"Fred," said my aunt at breakfast, "ride over to Brown about his rent, you will be sure to find him at the corn market," and she gave him other commissions at the market town. I promised to ride with him, but had been tortured with randiness about this great wench of his; so made some excuse, and as soon as he was well off, sauntered towards the cottage, which was about half a mile from the Hall.

It was one of a pair in a lane. Scarcely anyone passed them excepting people on my aunt's lands. One was empty. The girl was sweeping in front of the cottage, the door was wide open. I gave her a nod, she dropped a respectful curtsey. Looking round and seeing no one, I said, "May I come in and rest, for it is hot and I am tired?"

"Yes sir," said she, and in I went, she giving me a chair; then she finished her sweeping. Meanwhile I had determined to try it on. "Father at home?" "No sir, he be working in the Seven-Acre field." "Where is your sister?" "At mill, sir"--meaning a paper mill. I thought of Fred. It was my first offer, and scarcely knew how to make it, but chucking her under the chin said, "I wish you would let me--" "What, sir?" "Do it to you," said I boldly, "and I will give you five shillings," producing the money; I knew it was what Fred gave her usually.

She looked at me and the five shillings, which was then more than her wages for a week's work in the fields, burst into laughter and said, "Why, who would have thought a gentleman from the Hall would say that to a poor girl like me." "Let me do it," said I hurredly, "if you wont I must go--I will give you seven and six pence." "You wont tell the young squire?" said she--meaning Fred. "Of course not." She went to the door, looked both ways, then at the clock, shut the door and bolted it without another word.

The house consisted of a kitchen, a bed-room, leading out of it, and a wash-house. She opened the bedroom door, there were two beds which almost filled the room; at the foot of one was a window, by its side a wash-stand. She got on to the largest bed saying, "Make haste." I pulled up her clothes to her navel and looked. "Oh! make haste," said she. But I could not, it was the third cunt I had seen, and I paused to contemplate her. Before me lay a pair of thick, round thighs, a large belly, and a cunt covered with thick brown hair, a dirty chemise round her waist, coarse woolen blue stockings darned with black, and tied below the knees with list, thick hob-nailed boots. The bed beneath was white and clean, which made her things look dirtier; it was different to what I had been accustomed to. I looked too long, "Better make haste, for father will be home to dinner," said she.

I put my hand to her cunt, she opened her thighs, and I saw the cleft, with a pair of lips on each side like sausages, a dark vermillion strong clitoris sloped down and hid itself between the lips, in the recesses of the cock-trap; the strong light from the window enabled me to see it as plainly as if under a microscope. I pushed my finger up, then my cock knocked against my belly, asking to take the place of my finger, and so up I let it go. No sooner was I lodged in her, than arse, cunt, thighs and belly, all worked energetically, and in a minute I spent. Just as I pulled out, her cunt closed round my prick with a strong muscular action, as if it did not wish the warm pipe withdrawn, a movement of the muscles of the cunt alone, and it drew the last drop of lingering sperm out of me.

I got on my knees, contemplating the sausage lips half open, from which my sperm was oozing, and then got off sorry it had been so quick a business. She laid without moving and looking kindly at me said, "Ye may ha me agin an yer loike." "But your father will be home?" "In half an hour," said she. "I don't think I can," said I. Such coolness in a woman was new to me, I scarcely knew what to make of it. She got hold of my tool, I had not had a woman for some time, soon felt lust entering my rod again, and sought her cunt with my hands. She opened her legs wider in a most condescending manner and I began feeling it. I was soon fit, which she very well knew, for immediately with a broad grin on her face she pulled me on to her and put my prick in her cunt herself, lodging it with a clever jerk of her bum, a squeeze, and a wriggle.

I fucked quietly, but it was now her turn; she heaved and wriggled so that once she threw my prick out of her, but soon had it in again. "Shove, shove," said she suddenly, and I shoved with all my might, she clipped my arse so tightly that she must have left the marks of her fingers on it, then with a close wriggle and a deep sigh, she lay still, her face as red as fire, and left me to finish by my own exertions.

I felt the same squeeze of the cunt as I withdrew, one of those delicious contraction which women of strong muscular power in their privates can give; not all can do it. Those who cannot never can understand it. Those who can, will make a finger sensible of its grip, if put up their cunts.

She got up, and tucked her chemise between her legs to dry her split, she did not wash it. "I am always alone," said she, "between eight and twelve just now," and as any woman just then answered my wants, I made opportunities, and I had her again two or three times, till a rare bit of luck occurred to me.

We were in the bed-room one hot day; to make it cooler I took off trousers and drawers, laid them on a chair, carefully rolled my shirt up round my waist, so as to prevent spunk falling upon it, and thus naked from my boots to waist, laid myself on the top of my rollicking, belly-heaving, rump-wriggling country lass.

I always gave her five shillings before I began; she had taken a letch for me, or else being hot cunted, and not getting it done to her often, dearly liked my poking her; and seeming to want it that day unusually, began her heaving and wriggling energetically. We were well on towards our spend, when with a loud cry of "Oh! my God!" she pushed me off, and wriggled to the bedside. I got off, and saw a sturdy country girl of about fifteen or sixteen years, standing in the bed-room door looking at us with a broad grin, mixed with astonishment, upon her face.

For an instant nobody spoke. Then the girl said with a

malicious grin, "pretty goings on Sarah, if fearther knowed un--" "How dare you stand looking at me?" said Sarah. "It's my room as well as yourn," said Martha, for that was her name; and nothing further was said then. But Martha's eyes fixed on me as I sat naked up to my waist with my prick wet, rigid, red, throbbing, and all but involuntarily jerking out its sperm. I was in that state of lust, that I could have fucked anything in the shape of a cunt, and scarcely knew in the confusion of the moment, where I was, and what it was all about. Sarah saw my state, and began pulling down my shirt. "Go out of the room," said she to her sister. "Damn it I will finish, I will fuck you," said I making a snatch at her cunt again. "Oh! for God's sake, don't sir," said she. With a grin out went young sister Martha into the kitchen, and then Sarah began to blubber, "If she tells fearther, he will turn me out into the streets."

"Don't be a fool," said I, "why should she tell?" "Because we are bad friends." "Has she not done it?" "No, she is not sixteen." "How do you know she has not?" "Why we sleep together and I know." "Who sleeps in the other bed?" "Fearther." "In the same room?" "Yes." "Don't you know anything against her?" "No, last hay-making I seed a young man trying to put his hands up her clothes, that's all; she has only been a woman a few months." If she tells of her, she will tell of me, I thought. It might come to my aunt's ears, Fred would know, and I should get into a scrape.

"It is a pity she has not done it," said I, "for then she would not tell." "I wish she had," she replied. One thing suggested another. "She knows all about what we were doing?" Sarah nodded. "Get her to promise not to tell, and get her to let me do it to her, and I will give you two pounds," said I, taking the money out of my purse.

It was more money than she had ever had in her life at

one time, her eyes glistened; she was silent a minute as if reflecting, then said, "She has always been unkind to me, and she shant get me turned out if I can help it." Then after farther talk, some hesitation, and asking me if I was sure I would give her the money, she said, "I'll try, let's have a jolly good drink, then I'll leave you together," and we went into the kitchen. I saw her dodge.

Martha was leaning, looking out of the window, her bum sticking out, her short petticoats showing a sturdy pair of legs; she turned round to us, it was about eleven o'clock in the day, the old man was at work far off and had taken his dinner with him that day, Sarah had told me.

"You won't tell father," said Sarah in a smooth tone. No reply but a grin. "If you do, I will tell him I saw young Smith's hand up your clothes." "It's a lie."

"Yes, he did, and you know you have seen all he has got to show." "You are a liar," said Martha. Sarah turned to me and said, "Yes, she did, we both saw him leaking, and a dozen more chaps." "She saw their cocks?" said I. "Yes." "You took me to see them, you bitch," said Martha bursting out in a rage. "You did not want much taking, what did you say, and what did you do in bed that night, when we talked about it?" "You are a wicked wretch, to talk like that before a strange young man," said Martha and bounced out of the cottage.

In a short time she came in again, the oldest told me scandals she knew about her sister, and made her so wild, that they nearly fought. I stopped them, they made it up, and I sent off the eldest to fetch shrub, gin and peppermint; it was a good mile to the tavern in the village.

When she had gone I told Martha I hoped she would do no mischief. She was nothing loath to let me kiss her, so there was soon acquaintance between us. She had seen me half naked, how long she had been watching I knew not, but it was certain she had seen me shoving as hard as I could between the naked thighs of her sister, and that was well calculated to make her randy and ready for the advances of a man. "Here is five shillings, don't say anything my dear." "I won't say nothing," said she taking the money. Then I kissed her again, and we talked on.

"How did you like him feeling you?" I asked, "was he stiff?" No reply. "Was it not nice when he got his hand on your thigh?" Still no reply. "You thought it nice when in bed, Sarah says." "Sarah tells a wicked story," she burst out. "What does she tell?" "I don't know." "I will tell you my dear; you talked about Smith's doodle and the other men's you saw pissing." "You are the gentleman from London stopping at the Hall," she replied, "so you had better go back and leave us poor girls alone," and she looked out of the window again.

"I am at the Hall," said I putting my hand round her waist, "and like pretty girls," and I kissed her until she seemed mollified and said, "What can you want in troubling poor girls like us?" "You are as handsome as a duchess, and I want you to do the same as they do." "What is that?" said she innocently. "Fuck," said I boldly. She turned away looking very confused. "You saw me on your sister, between her thighs, that was fucking; and you saw this," at the same time pulling out my prick, "and now I am going to feel your cunt."

I put my hand up her clothes and tried to feel, but she turned round, and after a struggle half squatted on the floor to prevent me. The position was favourable, I pushed her sharply half on to her back on the floor, got my fingers on to her slit, and in a moment we were struggling on the floor, she screaming loudly as we rolled about.

She was nimble, got up and escaped me, but by the time her sister came back, I had felt her bum, pulled her clothes up, and talked enough baudiness; she had hollowed, cried, laughed, abused and forgiven me, for I had promised her a new bonnet, and had given her more silver.

Sarah brought back the liquors, there was but one tumbler and a mug, we did with those; the weather was hot, the liquor nice, the girls drank freely. In a short time they were both frisky, it got slightly into my head; then the girls began quarrelling again, and let out all about each other, the elder's object being to upset the younger one's virtue and make her lewd. I began to get awfully randy, and told Sarah I had felt her sister's cunt whilst she had been out. She laughed and said, "All right, she will have it well felt some day, she's a fool if she don't." We joked about my disappointment in the morning, I asked Sarah to give me my pleasure then. "Aye," said she, "and it is pleasure, when Martha has once tasted it, she will like it again." Martha very much fuddled, laughed aloud saying, "How you two do go on." Then I put my hands up Sarah's clothes. "Lord how stiff my prick is, look," and I pulled it out, Martha saying, "I won't stand this," rushed from the room. I thought she had gone, and wanted to have Sarah; but she thought of the two pounds, and shutting Martha's mouth, "Try her," said she, "she must have it some day, she'll come in soon." When the girl did, we went on drinking. What with mixing gin, peppermint and rum shrub, both got groggy, and Martha the worst. Then out went Sarah saying she must go to the village to buy something, and she winked at me.

She had whilst the girl was outside told me to bolt the front door, and if by any chance her father came home, which was not likely; to get out of the bed-room window,and through a hedge, which would put me out of sight in a minute. Directly she was gone I bolted the door and commenced the assault. Martha was so fuddled, that she could not much resist my feeling her bum and thighs, yet I could not get her to go and lie down; she finished the liquor, staggered, and then I felt her clitoris.

I was not too steady, but sober enough to try craft where force failed. I wanted to piss, and did, holding the pot so that she could see my cock at the door, but she would not come into the bed-room. Then I dropped a sovereign, and pretending I could not find it, asked her to help me; she staggered into the bed-room laughing a drunken laugh. The bed was near, I embraced her, said I would give her two sovereigns if she would get on the bed with me. "Two shiners?" said she. "There they are," said I laying them down. "No--no," but she kept looking at them. I put them into her hand, she clutched them saying, "No--no," and biting one of her fingers, whilst I began again tittillating her clitoris, she letting me. From that moment I knew what money would do with a woman. Then I lifted her up on to the bed, and lay down besides her. All her resistance was over, she was drunk.

I pulled up her clothes, she lay with eyes shut, breathing heavily, holding the gold in her hand. I pulled open her legs, with scarcely any resistance, and saw a mere trifle of hair on the cunt; the novelty so pleased me, that I kissed it; then for the first time in my life I licked a cunt, the spittle from my mouth ran on to it, I pulled open the lips, it looked different from the cunts I had seen, the hole was smaller. "Surely," thought I, "she is a virgin." She seemed fast asleep, and let me do all I wanted.

In after life, I should have revelled in the enjoyment of anticipation before I had destroyed the hymen; but youth, want, liquor, drove me on, and I don't remember thinking much about the virginity, only that the cunt looked different from the two others I had known. The next instant I laid my belly on hers. "Oh! you are heavy, you smother me," said she rousing herself, "you're going to hurt me,--don't sir, it hurts," all in a groggy tone and in one breath. I inserted a finger between the lips of her quim, and tried gently to put it up, but felt an impediment. She had never been opened by man. I then put my prick carefully in the nick, and gave the gentlest possible movement (as far as I can recollect) to it.

Her cunt was wet with spittle, I well wetted my prick, grasped her round her bum, whilst I finally settled the knob of my tool against it, then putting my other hand round her bum, grasped her as if in a vice, nestled my belly to hers, and trembling with lust, gave a hinge,--another,-- and another. I was entering. In another minute it would be all over with me, my sperm was moving. She gave a sharp "oh!" A few more merciless shoves, a loud cry from her, my prick was up her, and her cunt was for the first time wetted with a man's sperm; with short, quiet thrusts I fell into the dreamy pleasure, laying on the top of her.

Soon I rolled over to her side, to my astonishment she lay quite still with mouth open, snoring, and holding the two sovereigns in her hand. I gently moved to look at her; her legs were wide open, her gown and chemise (all the clothing she had on) up to her navel, her cunt showed a red streak, my spunk was slowly oozing out streaked with blood, a little was on her chemise; but I looked in vain for the sanguinary effusion which I saw on Charlotte's chemise, and on my shirt, when I first had her; and from later experience, think that young girls do not bleed as much as full grown women, when they lose their virginity.

Her cunt as I found from ample inspection afterwards, was lipped like her sister's, the hair, about half an inch long, scarcely covered the mons, and only slightly came down the outer lips, her thighs were plump and round, her calves big for her age; she was clean in her flesh, but alas! thick blue stockings with holes and darns, big boots with holes at the sides, a dirty ragged chemise, dark garters below the knees, made an ugly spectacle compared with the clean whiteness of Charlotte's and Mary's linen.

But the sight took effect, my prick had her blood on it, quietly I slid my finger up her cunt, it made her restless, she moved her legs together, shutting my hand in them; she turned on her side, and showed a plump white bum, over one side of which a long streak of bloody sperm had run. I pulled her on to her back, then she awakened struggling and called out loudly, but I was heavy on her, my prick at her cunt's mouth, and I pushed it up until it could go no further, whilst she kept calling out, I was hurting her.

"Be quiet, I can't hurt you, my prick is right up you," said I beginning the exercise. She made no reply, her cunt seemed deliriously small, whenever I pushed deep, she winced as if in pain, I tried to thrust my tongue into her mouth, but she resisted it. Suddenly she said, "Oh! go away, Sarah will be home and find us." I had my second emission, and went to sleep with my prick up her,--I was groggy. She slept also.

I awakened, got up tired with heat, excitement, drink and fucking. She got up, and sat on the side of the bed half sobered, but stupid; dropped a sovereign, and did not attempt to pick it up. I did, and put it back into her hands; she took it without saying a word. When buttoned up, I asked her what she was going to do, but all the reply I could get was, "You go now." I went into the kitchen, banged the door, but held the latch, the door remained ajar, and I peeped through.

She sat perfectly still so long, that I thought she was never going to move; then sat down on the chair and laid her head against the bed, looking at the sovereigns at intervals; then put them down, put her hand up her petticoats carefully feeling her cunt, looked at her fingers, burst into tears, sat crying for a minute or two, then put a basin with water on to the floor, and unsteady, partially upset it, but managed to wash, and got back on to the chair, leaving the basin where it was. Then she pulled up the front of her chemise and looked at it, again put her fingers to her cunt, looked at them, again began crying, and leaned her head against the bed, all in a drowsy, tipsy manner. Whilst so engaged, her sister knocked and I let her in; she looked at me in a funny way; I nodded; she went into the bed-room and closed the door, but I heard most of what was said.

"What are you sitting there for?" No reply. "What's that basin there for?" No reply. "You have been washing your grummit?" No reply. "What have you been washing it for?" "I was hot." "Why, you have been on the bed!" "No, I ain't." "You have, with he." "No, I ain't." "I know he have, and been atop a you, just as he were atop on me this morning." "No, he ain't." Then was a long crying fit. Sarah said, "What's the good of crying you fool, no one ain't going to tell, I shant, and the old man won't know."

Then their voices dropped, they stood together, but I guessed she was asking what I had given her.

Then I went in. "You have done it to my sister," said Sarah. "No," said I. "Yes, you have," and to Martha crying, "Never mind, its better to be done by a gent, than by one of them mill-hands, I can't abear 'em; leave off, don't be a fool." I went out of the room, Sarah followed me, and I gave her the two sovereigns. "You know," she said, "some

141

one would ha done it to her; one of them mill-hands, or Smith would, he's alius after her, and I knows he got his hands upon her."

Fred went up to London next day, and I was at the cottage soon after; the girls were there, the elder grinned, the younger looked queer, and would not go to the bed-room. "Don't be a fool," said the elder, and soon we were alone together there. Half force, half entreaty got her on to the bed, I pulled up her clothes, forced open her legs, and lay for a minute with my belly to hers in all the pleasure of anticipation, then rose on my knees for a close look. My yesterday's letch seized me, I put my mouth to her cunt and licked it, then put my prick up the tight little slit and finished my enjoyment.

Afterwards when I had her she was neat and clean underneath, although with her every day's clothes on. She was frightened to put on her Sunday clothes. She was a nice plump round girl, with a large bum for her size, with pretty young breasts, and a fat-lipped little slit, the lining of it instead of being a full red like Charlotte's, Mary's, and Sarah's cunts, was of a delicate pink. I suppose is was that which attracted me. Certain it is that I had never licked a cunt before, never had heard of such a thing, though "lick my arse" was a frequent and insulting invitation for boys to each other.

I saw her nearly every day for a week, and her modesty was soon broken. Sleeping in the same room with her father, accustomed to being in the fields or at a mill, such girls soon lose it; but she seemed indifferent to my embraces, and all the enjoyment was on my side. "I've not much pleasure in that," said she, "but more when you put your tongue there." I could not believe that was so in a young and healthy lass, but being always in a hurry to get my poking done lest her father came home, used to lick, put up her, spend quickly and leave; but she soon got to rights. I licked so hard and long the next time I had her, at the side of the bed; that all at once I felt her cunt moving, her thighs closed, then relaxed, and she did not answer me. I looked up, she was laying with eyes closed and said, that what I had done was nicer than anything. I had gamahuched her till she spent.

After that she spent like other women, when I had her. I tell this exactly as I recollect it, and can't attempt to explain. She worked at a paper mill, slack work was the reason of her being at home, now she was going back to work; I feared a mill hand would get her, and offered to pay her what she earned; but if she did not go to the mill, her father would make her work in the fields, and she dare not let him see she had money.

Indeed the two sisters did not dare to buy the finery they wanted, because they could not say how they got the money. So back to the mill she went, it being arranged that she should stay away now and then, for me to have her. "Oh! won't she," said Sarah "she takes to ruddling natoral, I can tell you." Sarah said she told her everything I had done to her, including the licking, and I felt quite ashamed of Sarah knowing that I was so green, as I shall tell presently.

Fred returned, and I had difficulty in getting her often. My cousins walked out in the cool of the evening, I with them; often we passed the cottage, and I made signs if I saw the girls. I sometimes then had her upright in a small shed or by a hay-stack in the dark, where the hay pricked my knuckles.

Fred was soon to join his regiment, was always borrowing money of me "for a shove," and never repaid me; but he was a liberal, good-hearted fellow; and when in after life I was without money and he kept a woman, he said, "You get a shove out of ------," meaning his woman, "she likes you, and I shant mind, but don't tell me." I actually did fuck her; nor did he ever ask me,--but that tale will be told hereafter. Nothing till his death pleased him more than referring to our having looked at the backside of his mother and at his sister's quims, he would roar with laughter at it. He was an extraordinary man.

One day we rode to the market-town; and putting up our horses, strolled about. Fred said, "Let's both go and have a shove." "Where are the girls?" said I. "Oh! I know, lend me some money." "I only have ten shillings." "That is more than we shall want." We went down a lane past the Town-Hall, by white-washed little cottages, at which girls were sitting or standing at the doors making a sort of lace. "Do you see a girl you like?" said he. "Why, they are lace-makers." "Yes, but some of them fuck for all that; there is the one I had with the last half-a-crown you lent me." Two girls were standing together; they nodded. "Let's try them," said Fred. We went into the cottage; it was a new experience to me. He took one girl, leaving me the other, I felt so nervous; she laughed as Fred (who had never in his life a spark of modesty), put his hands up her companion's clothes. That girl asked what he was going to give her, and it was settled at half-a-crown each. Fred then went into the back-room with his woman.

I never had had a gay woman. A fear of disease came over me. She made no advances, and at length feeling my quietness was ridiculous, I got my hands up her clothes, pulling them up and looking at her legs. "Lord! I am quite clean, sir," said she in a huff, lifting her clothes well up. That gave me courage, I got her on to an old couch, and looked at her cunt, but my prick refused to stand; her being gay upset me. She laid hold of my prick, but it was of no use. "What is the matter with you?" said she, "don't you like me?" "Yes, I do." "Have you ever had a girl?" I said I had. Fred who had finished, bawled out, "Can't we come in?" This upset me still more, and I gave it up. In Fred and his girl came, and he said, "There is water in the other room." I went in and feigned to wash myself, and hearing them all laughing, felt ashamed to come out, thinking they were laughing about me; though such was not the case, it was because Fred was beginning to pull about my woman.

I had more money than I had told Fred, and when he said he was thirsty, offered to send for drink, thinking my liberality would make amends for my impotence. Gin and ale was got; then I began to feel as if I could do it. "She's got a coal-black cunt," said Fred, and I seemed to fancy his woman; then he said to mine, "What colour is yours?" and began to lift her clothes; "let's change and have them together," and we went at once into the back room, whither the two girls had gone. One was piddling, Fred pulled her up from the pot, shoved her against the side of the bed, bawling out, "You get the other," and pulled out his prick stiff and ready. An electric thrill seemed to go through me at this sight, I pulled the other into the same position by the side of Fred's; then the girls objected, but Fred hoisted up his girl and plunged his prick into her. Mine got on to the bed, leaving me to pull up her clothes. The same fear came over me, and I hesitated; Fred looked and laughed, I pulled up her clothes, saw her cunt; fear vanished, the next moment I was into her, and Fred and I, side by side, were fucking.

All four were fucking away like a mill, then we paused and looked at our pricks, as they alternately were hidden and came into sight from the cunts. Fred put out his hand to my prick, I felt his, but I was coming; my girl said, "Don't hurry." It was too late, I spent, laid my head upon her bosom, and opening my eyes, saw Fred in the short shoves. The next instant he lay his head down.

I believe now that really all four felt ashamed for directly after we were all so quiet, one of the girls remarked, "Blest if I ever heard of such a thing afore, you Lunnon chaps are a bad lot." A long time afterwards I again had the girl for two and sixpence, Fred was then in Canada; she recollected me well, and asked me, whether gals and chaps usually did such things together in London.

Fred and I used to examine our pricks for a few days after, to see if there were any pimples on them. Fred soon forgot his fear and shame, and offered to bet me the fee of the gals, that he would finish first, if we went and repeated the affair, but we did not.

Martha became very curious about me and my doings with Sarah. New to fucking as she was; she got jealous at the idea of anyone sharing my cock with her. She was curious too to know about her sister's pleasure; the elder had I think got all she wanted to know from the younger, and had made but little return for it in information.

Then my amatory knowledge was increased by an event unlooked for, unthought of, unpremeditated; I am quite sure I had neither heard, nor read of such a thing before; and should at that period of my life have scouted the idea, as beastly and abominable, though I had done it. How I came to lick Martha's cunt even then astonished me, I thought that it was the small size, the slight hair, and youthfulness of the article; but I used to lick it very daintily, wiping my mouth, spitting frequently, and never venturing beyond the clitoris. It occurred to me one day instead of kneeling, to lay down and lick; so I laid on the bed, my head between her thighs, my cock not far from her mouth, and indulging her in the luxury; for it was much the idea of pleasing her that made me do it. She played with my cock and wriggled as my tongue played over her clitoris, then grasped my prick hard, which gave me a premonitory throb of pleasure. "Do to me what I am doing to you," said I, "put it in your mouth," scarcely knowing what I said and without any ulterior intention. She with her pleasure getting intense, impelled by curiosity, or by the fascination of the cock, or by impulse, the result of my tongue on her cunt, took it in her mouth instantly. How far my prick went in, whether she sucked, licked, or simply let it enter, I know not, and I expect she did not either; but as she spent I felt a sensation resembling the soft friction of a cunt, and instantly shot my sperm into her mouth and over her face. Up she got, calling me a beast. I was surprised and ashamed of this unlooked for termination, and said so to her.

I had as said arranged signs as I passed the cottage about our meetings, yet had difficulty now in getting at her without being found out, and never should, excepting for the elder sister, to whom I gave every now and then money. She took care of the house, rarely went out, but worked at a coarse of lace, and earned money that way. She used to sit outside the cottage door if fine; working, and curtseying when we, who were called the Hall folks, passed. My aunt said one day, "What a strapping wench that is, don't you think so Walt? you always look at her as you pass." I might have replied, "Yes she is, and her arse is remarkably like yours," but I did not, and was after that more on my guard. Fred had not had the girl for a long time, that freed me a little. Then Martha shammed ill two days to stay from the mill and let me have her, and I spent a good many hours with her. As I turned my head quickly one day, I thought I saw the bed-room door close, and it occurred to me, that the elder had been watching; she looked letcherously at me as I came out.

I went one day soon after, and found Sarah alone. She

147

made some excuse about her sister being obliged to go to work. I was going away angry, when she asked me to look at her new boots and stockings. Amused at her vanity, I looked and she put them on. "Them fits fine," said she, showing her legs amply. I was not excited about it, and was going. "Ain't you never going to ha me agin?" said she. "I've no money." "We are old friends, never mind money, if I hadn't got you Martha we moight ha been good friends still,--ar wish a hadn't." "You did it to save us," said I. "Ah, but yer shouldn't leave old friends, and I ha watched and made yer both comfortable." Well, thought I, this is an invitation to fucking,--she had a wonderful slip in her cunt, and I began to rise. "You have lots of friends," said I. "I take my oath, that no friend has seen me since the day you got my sister; ain't I been allus on watch for yer, did yer ever pass without seeing me?"

A woman who wants fucking is not easy to resist, even if she is ugly and middle-aged. There she sat, the picture of health, her petticoats nearly up to her knees; I had never before seen them excepting in coarse blue woolen stockings. I rolled her clothes up, saw the big thighs, the next instant had my fingers in the slit; up knocked my doodle. She shut the shutter, locked the door, and with a pleased look got on to the bed. Her cunt struck me as quite a novelty, and I got ready for insertion.

"You like her better than me," said she. It was a poser, but a man always likes the woman he is going to poke better than any other, and so I denied it. "Why don't you do to me what you do to she then?" "What is that?" "You knows." "No." "Yes you do." "I feel it like this." "More than that." "What?" "You know." "I don't, tell me." There was a pause. It came into my head that she knew I had licked Martha's quim, and it had such an effect on me, that down went my doodle, and I was almost ashamed to look at her; for as said, until I licked Martha, I had never done such an act, and did it with a sort of belief that I was a great beast, and should have said so of any man who did anything of the sort. Indeed after spending in her mouth, I had felt so very much disgusted with myself, that I left off the licking altogether, and had made the girl promise she would never tell her sister, nor refer to the matter again. So I was silent, standing with one hand on her belly just above her split, and in an uncomfortable state of mind.

She broke the silence. "Do it as you do it to she." "I don't know what you mean," I again stammered. "Yes yer do now." "What has Martha told you?" "Nothing, but I knows." And finding I was about to get on the bed, "Naw, naw, kiss it." So I put my mouth down on to the hair and gave a loud kiss. "Naw," said she, "do it as you do it to she, I am a finer woman than she by long chalks; what is't yer sees to take to her so? you knows you tickles her with yer tongue." The murder was out. I wanted to mount her, she baulked me, and kept repeating in a jockular, playful, manner her request. So I got her to the side of the bed, her large thighs wide open, and legs hanging down in a favourable position, intending to please her; she gave her cunt a dry rub with her chemise.

I began with dislike, but there was something in the novelty which warmed me. What a difference between her and her sister. I could lick the younger one's all but hairless orifice with comfort, and she always laid quiet; but I had to pull open this one's sausage lips and hold back the dark thick fringe, which got into my eyes and tickled my nose. No sooner had my tongue touched her clitoris, than the lips closed round my mouth, and as my saliva worked up on to the cunt-hair by her movement, it wetted my nose and face, she heaved and bounced her arse so much. Then her thighs closed round my head tightly enough to squeeze it off, she buried her hands in the hair of my head, and up went cunt again, bringing my nose into the hole, then with a jerk she got her cunt away from me. I was not at all sorry to desist.

"Oh! do it natural,--do it natural," said she, and her thighs opened and hung down, showing a slobbered cunt. I went into her just as she lay at the side of the bed, and in a minute her cunt was wetter than ever.

I have no doubt that the wench spent almost directly I licked her, but I did not know it. When I asked her if she liked it, she said, "The old fashioned way be the best, but I have done the same as she." I questioned her, but never knew whether her sister had told her or not, or whether she had peeped and seen us together at it.

I made her promise she would never tell her sister what I had done. She hoped I would see her again, but having promised Martha that I would not have Sarah again, told her so. She said she was tired of watching for us. The sisters were often quarrelling, and I believe out of jealousy about me, yet I fucked her again.

I may mention about the risks I ran, that I was once with Martha on the bed, when I heard my cousin's voice asking Sarah who was at the door, if she had seen me pass.

I could not get the younger readily enough, had been long from home, and was about returning. I had spent all my money, and told Sarah one day after I had poked her, that I was going away. Her sister was then at the mill. Said she, "What will Martha do?" I supposed she would get another sweetheart. She shook her head, "Martha be poisoned." "What?" "Don't be afraid," said she, "she be in the family way, we call it poisoned in these parts, when a girl be'nt married." It was true. The girl had only menstruated once or twice before I first had her, and now her courses had stopped. There was no attempt at making a market of me, all needed was to get her right again. The elder took Martha to a fortune-teller, and she got better of her difficulty. I borrowed money of my aunt and giving Martha all I could, went back to London. She left the neighbourhood.

I saw Martha two years afterwards, when visiting again my aunt; she was in house-hold service, and was out for the day. I waylaid her, hoping to have her again; we kissed and fondled, and with difficulty I felt her quim, but could not accomplish my wishes; she was going to be married, and soon after I heard that she was.

Sarah also was going to be married to a farm labourer, and when I joked her about his finding her out, she laughed and said, "Lord, he war my first sweetheart," from which I inferred that cousin Fred was mistaken about taking her virginity.

My first cunt-licking, and cock-sucking took place with Martha; I had never before played such amatory pranks, and all came about by instinct. For a long time I was ashamed of myself, and never breathed a word on such subjects to anyone; I don't think I should have done so even to Fred, but he was then away. Gradually I was learning by instinct the whole art of love. What made me offer money to get Martha I can't say, I don't think that I had ever heard of tempting women's virtue by money, but I never forgot the lesson, and much improved on it as time went on.

I now had had four women. The difficulties in the way of getting at them, were very useful in preventing excesses; and kept me in health. It seems surprising to me now, how little I seemed to have thought of baudy attitudes, and lascivious varieties; for belly-to-belly poking on the bed, was nearly all I did. I had still the modest, demure, demeanour which deceived my mother (coupled with her ignorance of life generally) and relations, and though very proud of my achievements, kept them much to myself, never disclosing the names of my women, and only telling one or two intimate friends of what I had done; who reciprocated by telling me their achievements. Fucking had eased my prepuce. I made a practice of pulling it backward and forward several times a day; in fact whenever I piddled. My prick had grown bigger in the two years, which pleased me much, but about the size of it I had a curious doubt, which will be told of further on.

I was though demure, quite a man in manner and looks, and with women behaved in a way which one or two of my relatives remarked. I used to think to myself when talking to them, "Ah! I know what sort of opening you have at the bottom of your belly." The cousins whose cunts I had had a partial glimpse of, I used to like to dance with, wondering how much the hair had grown on them. I used also to think about my sister's cunt that I had seen when in the cradle, but just then she died. My experience indeed much increased the charm of female society to me.

Chance had given me two virgins out of four women, that was a luxury unthought of, uncared for, and in no way appreciated; the virgins were no more liked by me than the others.

Cousin Fred will appear at less frequent intervals, he was away sometimes for months, then for years, but he is named whenever he played an important part in my adventures,--he was participator in others which will never be written about here.

CHAPTER VIII.

Fanny Hill.--Masturbation.--Friend Henry.--Under street-
gratings at the gunmaker's.--A frigging match.--Sights from
below.--In a back street.--A prick in petticoats.--
Evacuations.--Ladies scared.

I went back to London, and resumed my preparations. Penniless, I tried to get money from my mother, but could not. I tried to feel our ugly housemaid, who threatened to tell. Just then a friend lent me Fanny Hill, how well I recollect that day, it was a sunshiny afternoon, I devoured the book and its luscious pictures, and although I never contemplated masturbation, lost all command of myself, frigged, and spent over a picture as it lay before me. I did not know how to clean the book and the table-cover.

Fascinated although annoyed with myself, I repeated the act till not a drop of sperm would come; and the skin of my prick was sore. The next day I had a splitting headache but read at intervals, and again frigged; and did this for a week, till my eyes were all but dropping into my head. In a fever and worn out; the doctor said I was growing too fast, and ordered strong nourishment; but I used to take the infernal book with me to bed, and lay reading it, twiddling my prick, and fearing to consummate, knowing the state I was in. It was indeed almost impossible to do it, and when emission came, it was accompanied by a fearful aching in my testicles.

My friend had his book back, my erotic excitement ceased, I grew stronger, felt ashamed of myself, and soon found a new excitement.

I had a friend who like me was intended for the Army, his father was a gun manufacturer. The eldest son died, and the old man saying that five thousand a year should not be lost to the family, made his other son--my friend-- go into the business. He resisted, but had no alternative but to consent. Their dwelling-house was just by ours, but the old man now insisted on his son residing largely at the manufactory where he invited me to stay at times with him, which I did.

Several houses adjoining belonged to the old man, at the East-End of London, where the manufactory was. Some faced an important thoroughfare, the rest faced two other streets, and at the back, a place with out a thoroughfare, on one side of which was the manufactory and workmen's entrance; on the other side stables. The whole property formed a large block.

The house faced the better street, the family had for forty years lived in it before they became rich, and it was replete with comfort. The old man had since lived there principally, for his love was in his business, and he had made all arrangements for his convenience. He had a private staircase leading from a sitting-room into the manufactory, and could go into the warehouse, or the back street, or out of the front door of the house unnoticed. The people employed, never knew when to expect him. He was a regular Tartar, but for all that a kind-hearted man.

There now lived in the house an old servant with her sister, who had been many years in the family. One was married to a foreman in whom his master had much confidence; these three were in fact in charge of the premises, although nominally the keyes were given up to my friend whom we will call Henry. The old man wished his son to be happy, allowed friends to visit him, there was good wine, put out by the old man in small quantities from time to time, good food, good attendance, and all to make things comfortable; but the old man resolutely forbade his son to be out later than eleven o'clock, and kept him as my mother kept me, almost without money. I expect that the old servants were told to keep an eye on the doings of Henry.

The basement was used as store-room for muskets, put into wooden boxes which stood in long rows upon each other like coffins. It was a large place and originally only went under the factory, but the old gentleman gradually as he acquired the adjacent houses, let them, but retained most of the basements, so that his stores ran not only under the premises he occupied, but largely under half a dozen other houses of which he only let the shops and upper portions. On four sides this large basement had glimpses of light let into it, by gratings in the footways of the streets.

At one end and on the principal street was a row of windows, beneath what was then a first class linen-draper's shop--first class I mean for the East-End--a large place for those days, and always full. Women used to stand by dozens at a time, looking into the shop windows which were of large plate-glass--a great novelty in those days-- people waiting for omnibusses used also to stand up against the shop.

Henry and I were old school friends, I had seen and felt his cock, he mine; I had not been with him an hour before he said, "When the workmen go to dinner, I will show you more legs than your ever saw in your life." "Girls?" said I. "Yes, I saw up above the garters of a couple of dozen yesterday in an hour." "Could you see their cunts?" "I did not quite, but nearly of one," said he. I thought he was bragging, and was glad when twelve

155

o'clock came.

At that hour down we went, through the basement stored with muskets; it seemed dark as we entered, but soon we saw streams of light coming through the windows at the end; they had not been cleaned for years. We rubbed the glass and looked up. Above us was a flock of women's legs of all sizes and shapes flashing before us, thick and thin in wonderful variety. We could see them by looking up, it being bright above; but dark and dusty below, they could not by looking down see us, through the half cleaned windows; or notice round clean spots on the glass, through which two pairs of young eyes almost devoured the limbs of those who stood over them.

As our only way lay through the work-shop and we did not wish it known that we were there (there was no business done there, unless arms were being stored or taken out), we went back before the workmen returned from their meals; but for several days did we go into the place, gloating over such of the women's charms as we could discern; legs we saw by the hundreds, garters and parts of the thighs we saw by scores: quite enough to make young blood randy to madness, but the shadowy mass between the thighs we could not get a glimpse of.

"There are vaults," said I, "if there, we could see right up, and be at the back of the women." We tried unused keys to find one to open the door, and at length to our intense delight it unclosed. We stepped across the little open space under the gratings into the empty vaults, and there arranging to take our turns of looking up at the most likely spots, we put out our heads and took our fill at gazing. We were right under the women, who as they looked into the shop windows, jutting out their bums in stooping, tilted their petticoats exactly over our heads. If there was no carriage passing, we could at times hear what they said, but that was rarely the case.

In those days even ladies wore no drawers. Their dresses rarely came below their ankles, they wore bustles, and standing over a grating, anyone below them, saw much more, and more easily, than they can in these days of draggling dresses, and cunt swabbing breeches, which the commonest girl wears round her rump. For all that, so close to the thighs, do chemise and petticoats cling, that it was difficult to see the hairy slits, which it was our great desire to look at. Garters and thighs well above the knees, we saw by scores. Every now and then either by reason of scanty clothing, or short dresses, or by a woman's stooping and opening her legs to look more easily low down at the window, we had a glimpse of the cunt; and great was our randiness and delight when we did. On the whole we were well rewarded. Many as the legs and thighs are, that I have since seen, I doubt whether I have seen so many pairs of legs half-way up the thighs, and all but to the split, as I saw in the times we stood under that big linendraper's shop window. Old and young, thin and fat, dirty and clean, ragged and neat, there was every possible variety and number of legs and their coverings.

There were two states of the weather which favoured us: if muddy, women lifted their clothes up high. Having no modern squeamishness, all they cared about was to prevent them getting muddy; and then with the common classes, we got many a glimpse of the split. But a brilliant day was the best. Then the reflected light being strong, we could see higher up if the lady was in a favourable position. We could see if they had clouts round their cunts, and had some strange sights of which I will only tell one or two. One day, quite at the end of the gratings, two women,

neat, clean, plump, and of the poorer classes (for we could soon tell the poorer classes from their legs and under-clothings), stood close together. It was my five minutes. Henry was at my back. They had been standing talking, close together, not seeming to be looking at the shop, in fact they were at the spot where the shop window finished. One put her leg up against a ledge, keeping the other on the grating; it was a bright day, and I saw the dark hair of her cunt as plainly as if she were standing to show it me. The next minute she gathered up her clothes a little high, and squatted down on her heels as if to piddle, her bum came down within four or five inches of the grating, and I saw through the bars, her cunt open just as a woman does when she pisses. I thought she was going to do so, when a plantive cry explained it all; she had a baby, and all the movements were to enable her to do something to it conveniently. At the same time her companion dropped on one knee, pulling her clothes a little up, and arranging them so as to prevent soiling them, she put the other leg out in front, and sat back on the heel of the kneeling leg. Then was another split, younger and lighter-haired, partly visible from below, but not so plainly as the dark-haired one; and they did something in that position for five minutes to the squalling child.

I lost all prudence, whispered to Henry; and together we stood looking, till they moved away. "My prick will burst," said I. "So will mine," said he. The next instant both our pricks were out, and looking up at the legs, stood we two young men, frigging till two jets of spunk spurted across the area. It would have been a fine sight for the women had they looked down, but women rarely did. They stood over the gratings usually with the greatest unconcern, looking at the shop windows, or only glanced below for an instant, at the dark, uninhabited looking area.

This was the beginning of a new state of things. We got reckless; Henry had business to attend to, I none, I ceased to think about what might be said of our being so much in the store-house; and used to go by myself, and stay there two or three hours at a time. Then I gave way to erotic excesses. My prick would stand as I went down the stairs. I used to wait prick in hand, playing with it, looking up and longing for a poke until I saw a pair of thighs plainly, then able to stand it no longer, frigged; hating myself even whilst I did it, and longing to put my spunk in the right place. I used to catch it in one hand, whilst I frigged with the other, then fling the spunk up towards the girls' legs. It was madness; for although the feet of the women were not three feet above my head, yet the smallness of the quantity thrown (after what stuck to my fingers), and the iron bars above, seemed to make it impossible that any of it should reach its intended destination; but I think it did one day. A youngish female was stooping, and showing part of her thighs. I flung up what I had just discharged; suddenly her legs closed, she stepped quickly aside, looked down and went away. I am still under the impression that a drop of my sperm, must have hit her naked legs.

We both also grew more lascivious, having frigged before each other, we took to frigging each other. I went to my home, on going back, found he had taken other young men to see the legs. One night five of us had dinner, we smoked and drank, our talk grew baudier; we had mostly been schoolfellows, and dare say we had all seen each other's doodles, but I cannot assert that positively. We finished by showing them to each other now, betting on their length and size, and finished up by a frigging sweep-stakes for him who spent first.

At a signal, five young men (none I am sure nineteen years old) seated on chairs in the middle of the room began frigging themselves, amidst noise and laughter. The noise soon subsided, the voices grew quiet, then ceased, and was succeeded by convulsive breathing sighs and long-drawn breaths, the legs of some writhed, and stretched out, their backsides wriggled on the chairs, one suddenly stood up. Five hands were frigging as fast as they could, the prick-knobs standing out of a bright vermillion tint looking as if they must burst away from the hands which held them. Suddenly one cried "f-fi-fir-first," as some drops of gruelly fluid flew across the room, and the frigger sunk back in the chair. At the same instant almost the other jets spurted, and all five men were directly sitting down, some with eyes closed, others with eyes wide open, all quiet and palpitating, gently frigging, squeezing, and tittillating their pricks until pleasure had ceased.

Afterwards we were quiet, then came more grog, more allusion to the legs of women, their cunts and pleasures, more baudiness, more showing of pricks and ballocks, another sweep-stakes, another frigging match, and then we separated.

I do not think that excepting to Henry, that baudy evening ever was referred to by me.

I got up I recollect next day ashamed of myself, and felt worse, when he remarked, "What beasts we made ourselves last night." What changes since then. Two of the five found graves in the Crimea, the third is dead also; Henry and I alone alive. He with a big family, with sons nearly as old as he was at the time of the frigging matches. I wonder if he ever thinks of them, wonder if he ever has told his wife.

I spent much time now in this leg inspection and frigging myself, till I could scarcely get semen out of me. I hated myself for it, yet went on doing it, when luckily I lost the exciting sights. Some women happened to look down and saw us. A man without a hat came several times and looked down the gratings. Henry's father came to the manufactory, as he often did, went into the stores, asked who had opened the area-door, locked it up, had a new lock put on, and forbad anyone to go into the stores excepting to get out the guns, and so we lost our game. We never asked a question, nor made a remark on the matter; and came to the conclusion, that some one had complained to the linendraper that persons were looking up the women's legs, and that he had written to Henry's father on the matter.

I went home used up, and in a state of indescribable disgust with myself, entirely ceased masturbation, and in a month went again to visit my friend,--he had found out another grating.

The back of the manufactory as said was in a cul-de-sac. There were but the manufactory and stables in it. The workmen entered that side. There were gratings, and coal-vaults beneath the street similar to those beneath the linendraper's shop. Workmen's wives bringing their husbands' dinners, used to stand and sometimes sit down over the gratings, but their legs when seen were rarely worth the seeing; it was usually but a sight of dingy petticoats, and dirty stockings. We were however content to look up at them, for they belonged to women, but soon tired of doing so.

One night (we had never been there at night before), for some reason or the other which I don't recollect we went down and found two women pissing down the grating, then a man and woman together, and discovered it to be the pissing-place of the gay women, in the main thoroughfare; and where if the nights were dark, couples used to come for a grope, a frig, or even for a fuck at times. The pissing often took place over a grating, we could hear, and feel, but not see.

Then we got a common dark lantern, had the top shade taken off, and a funnel, or short chimney put with a slide, so that when we pushed the slide off, the light shot up through the chimney, and throw a strong light on a circle about one foot across. With this we went down waiting till we heard some one above, then opened the light and saw what was to be seen. Sometimes we waited for hours without seeing anything, but it is astonishing what cunt-loving, baudy young men will go through for the sake of seeing a woman's privates. At other times we saw a good deal. If it were a light night, we saw nothing. No one knew we went down at those hours, the workmen had gone, and the private staircase from the dwelling house at any time let us into the factory; from the factory we could go anywhere on the premises.

When we heard feet, or a rustle of petticoats over the grating, taking up the light we sometimes saw a white bum, a split gaping like a dog with its throat cut, and a stream of water splashing from it. We never used to move, but sooner than not see it all and as well as possible, let the stream come over us. Sometimes two women came together; sometimes we could hear to our mortification that they were pissing on the pavement close by, without coming over the grating. We could often hear their conversation. Now and then a woman shit down the grating, we used to watch the turds squeeze out with a fart or two, with great amusement. Once a man did the same, we saw prick, balls, and turd, all hanging down together, we could not help laughing, and off he shuffled as if he had been shot. He must have heard us.

There was one woman whose face we never saw, but who came and pissed over a grating so regularly every evening, and sometimes twice; that we knew her arse perfectly. We lost sight of her and used to wonder if she had found us out, for she finished one night with such a loud fart, that we laughed out,--and she must have heard us.

One night half a dozen ladies came, we knew they were ladies by their manner and conversation, which we could hear perfectly, there being no carriage traffic in the street. "Can anyone see?" said one. "No," said another, "make haste." We heard the usual leafy rustle, and immediately a tremendous stream was heard; then two more sat down close together. I turned on the light at all risks, there were two pretty white little bums above us, with the gaping cunts, they were of quite young girls, without a hair on them; the women then were scared I suppose, for they moved. One said, "Make haste, don't be foolish, nobody is coming." A rustle again, off went the slide, up went the light; what a big round bum, what a great black-haired open cunt did we see, and a stream of water as if from a fire-engine. "Oh! there is a light down there," said one. Up went the bum, piss still straining down, down went the clothes, and all were off like lightening.

Another night we heard two pairs of feet above us, one was the heavy footstep of a man. "Don't be foolish, he won't know," said a man in a very low tone. "Oh I no,--no, I dare not," said a female voice, and the feet with a little rustling moved to another grating. Henry and I moved on also. "You shall, no one comes here, no one can see us," said the man in a still lower tone. "Oh! I am so frightened," said the female. A little gentle scuffling now took place, and then all seemed quiet but a slight movement of the feet. "Are they there?" whispered Henry from the vault. I nudged him to quiet, and putting the light as high up as I could, pushed aside the slide a little only.

We were well rewarded. Just above our heads were two pairs of feet, one pair wide apart; and hanging only partly at her back the garments of a female; in front the trousers of a man with the knees projecting slightly forward between the female's legs, and higher up a bag of balls were hanging down hiding nearly the belly and channel, which the prick was taking. The distended legs between which the balls moved, enabled us however to get a glimpse of the arse-hole and of a cunt. The movement of the ballocks showed the vigour with which the man was fucking, but there must have been some inequality in height; and either he was very tall, or she very short; for his knees and feet moved out at times into different positions. He then ceased for an instant his shoving, as if to arrange himself in a fresh and more convenient posture, and then the lunges recommenced. He must have had his hands on her naked rump, from the way her clothes hung, showing her legs up to her belly, or to where his breeches hid it, or where the clothes fell down which were over his arm.

Once I imagine, the lady's clothes were in his way, for there was a pause, his prick came quite out, her feet moved, her legs opened wider. He did not need his fingers to find his mark again, his long, stiff, red-tipped article had slidden in the direction of her bum-hole; but no sooner had they readjusted their legs, then it moved backwards, and again it was hidden from sight in her cunt. The balls wagged more vigourously than ever, quicker, quicker; the lady's legs seemed to shake, we heard a sort of mixed cry, like a short groan and cry together, and a female voice say, "Oh! don't make such a noise," then a quiver and a shiver of the legs, and all seemed quiet.

When I first had removed the slide, I did so in a small degree, fearing they might look below and see it; but if the sun had shone from below, I believe now they must have been in that state of excitement, that they would not have noticed it. To see better I opened the slide more, and gradually held the lantern higher and higher, until the chimney through which the light issued was near to the grating. I was holding it by the bottom at arms length; and naturally, so as to best see myself. Henry could not see as well, although standing close to me, and our heads nearly touching. "Hold it more this way," said he in an excited whisper. I did not. Just then the lady said, "Oh! make haste now, I am so frightened." Out slipped the prick,--I saw it. At that very instant, Henry pulled my hand, to get the lantern placed so as to enable him to see better. I was holding it between the very tips of my fingers, just below the feet of the copulating couple. His jerk pulled it over, and down it went with a smash, just as the lady said, "Make haste, I am so frightened." A huge prick as it seemed to me drew out, and flopped down, a hand grasped it, the petticoats were falling round the legs, when the crash of the lantern came. With a loud shriek from the lady, off the couple moved, and I dare say it was many a day before she had her privates moistened up against a wall again, and over a grating.

Henry and I laughing picked up the lantern and got back to the house; I went to my bed-room in a state of indescribable randiness. I had for some time broken myself of frigging, and now resisted the desire, tried to read but could not, undressed and went to bed. My prick would stand. If it went down for a minute and my thoughts were diverted, the very instant my mind recurred to those balls wagging above my head, up it went again. I tried to piss, the piss would not run. At that time when my prick was stiff, I used to pull the prepuce back, so as to loosen it. I laid down on the bed, prick stiff. If it could have spoken, it would have said, "Frig or fuck, you shall, before I give you rest." So I pulled the prepuce slowly back,--only once,--and as the knob came handsomely into view, out shot my spunk all over the bed-clothes.

Getting up to wipe and make things clean, I saw something on the brim of my cap which I had worn; the cap was on the table. I took it up and found a large spot of sperm which had come from the happy couple, it must have followed the withdrawal of the prick; and had my head been a little more turned up, it must have tumbled on my face. I did not mind wiping up my own sperm, but doing so to theirs seemed beastly. Yet what was the difference?

We heard one night some one squat down, and turned up the light; there were petticoats, legs and an arse, but instead of the usual slit, we saw to our astonishment a prick and balls hanging down between the legs, it was a man in woman's clothes, and he was shitting. The sight alarmed us, we talked over it for many a day afterwards, for we did not then know that some men are fond of amusing themselves with other men.

I never saw but that one couple fucking, but we could hear groping and frigging going on close by. We heard women say, "Oh! don't!" Gay women, we heard say, "Here is a good place," but they did not often select the gratings, why? I cannot tell, for they were partly in recesses in the wall which enabled people to get more hidden. The bars were wide apart, and I suppose the regulars did not like that, yet they often used the gratings for pissing down.

These sights did not occur all at once, I went home, stopped, returned, and so on; in the meanwhile not having women, I then frigged, left off, then took to it again, and so time went on. Fewer women came at last up the street, we imagined that with all our care, they had found out that people were beneath the gratings, and avoided them. The favourite place was the recess at the workmen's door to the factory at which were two steps; we could hear but not see when a couple was there, we used then to go up into the factory and listen at the door. Generally, feeling and frigging was only going on, bargaining for money first.

"Give me another shilling. Oh! your nails hurt. What a lot of hair you have. What a big one! Oh! I am coming! Don't spend over my clothes," and so on, we heard at times.

Meanwhile there was either no servant at my home worthy of a stiff one, or those who would not take one; and I had no alternative but to frig. Money my mother again kept from me. What I got, I sent to the poor girl Martha, who then had not got rid of her big belly; gay women I had fear of; devoured by desire to get into a woman again, I even looked longingly at the wife of the foreman who took charge of the house in which Henry lived, although she was fifty. I recollect seeing her making my bed one morning, and getting a cock-stand at the sight of the woman so near a place to lay down on.

CHAPTER IX.

Mrs. Smith.--A brutal husband.--My second adultery.--A chaste servant.--Road harlots.--A poke in the open.--Use for a silk handkerchief.--A shilling a tail.--Clapped.

Henry had now much business to attend to, I had none. I used to wander into the back street just as the men's wives brought them their dinners, so as to look at them. They were not allowed inside, but if the men chose to eat inside they could do so, their wives waiting outside. Six or eight men had their dinners brought, the rest went away. The women most frequently sat on a door-step, or loitered over the gratings up which we used to look at night; or squatted down against the wall. I had once or twice looked up their clothes, but found little inviting, with the exception of a plump little pair of legs which belonged to a Mrs. Smith. She looked about twenty-six years of age, her husband twenty years older, a good workman but a brutal fellow. He bore a bad character among his fellows, and was thought a brute to his wife. Some said his wife drank; there was often a row in the street between them at dinner-time, he used to sit on the door-step and eat his dinner outside, she standing near him, and her legs came at times over a grating. I used to dodge downstairs at times at the workmen's dinner-hour, and have a look up, and that is how I saw, and began to think of the legs of Mrs. Smith.

I took a sort of fancy to her, or rather her legs, so plump and clean. I saw she had a nice clean face with bright brown eyes, and then had a desire to fuck her. I again had desisted from frigging, had sworn to myself not to do so again, and now getting strength wanted a woman badly. Our eyes had often met, I had even got out of her way when passing her, a courtesy not often then shown by gentlemen to workpeople. I used to stare at her so, that she began to look confused when I did. The husband never seemed to notice anything but his dinner, at which he usually swore. Sometimes I spoke to him about gun-making. I wanted to poke Mrs. Smith, but there did not seem to be the remotest chance, nor had I any intention of attempting it, but used to look at her with my cock standing, and wondering what sort of cunt she had. I had been brought up religiously, and the idea of having a married woman seemed shocking. I was shocked when I found that Mary was married. At length I nodded, smiled, and established a sort of intimacy in that way without speaking, managing to meet her as it were, quite casually when going to, or leaving the workshop.

One day the man dined on the step, his wife standing

by his side; down I went to peep up her clothes and heard him rowing. "Why the hell had she not got him beef instead of mutton; God damn her, why were there no potatoes!" That was his style. Angry words passed, the voices grew louder, I heard a loud smack and a strong oath, he had hit his wife and gone back into the workshop.

There was a great gabbling of female voices over the grating round Mrs. Smith. "I would not stand it," said one. "It is a shame," said another. "He ought to be proud of such a wife, an old beast," said another. The husband came out again. "I have done my best," said she, "you are not a man anyhow, or anywhere, for two pins I would run away from you." A loud oath, and another smack followed.

I heard Mrs. Smith sobbing. "I have had a little drink," said she, "I told him so. He makes me so unhappy, I must; but I spend scarce a trifle and it's what I earns myself. Ain't I clean? don't I bring him good meals?" "You do, you do," said they. "It's a shame," she went on, "he is not a man, not in bed, not anywhere, not anyhow, I don't aggravate him, I put up with everything, it's full six months since he's been a husband to me, although we sleeps in the same bed," she added in a significant way, "yes, six months full." "Lor," said half a dozen voices together, then said one, "Don't he do anything to you then?" Things quieted, off went Mrs. Smith with some of the women, two remained waiting for their husbands' platters, they squatted down on the step.

"They're a miserable couple," said one. "Yes, and likely, he is never at home, no wonder she do take a drop of comfort." "No, it ain't." "She is a nice little woman, and no man gets his meals nicer." "No, that they don't." "He's too old for her, but he ain't jealous." "No, in course not." "Why he ain't done it to her for six months," said one.

They both chuckled then. "Why, my old man don't forget me like that, and he is ten years older than Smith," said the other. "Ah!" said the first, "he's a bad 'up altogether, men be a bad lot, the best on 'em." The time-bell rang, their husbands brought out their dinner-cans, and off the women went.

I can scarcely tell what followed exactly or how it came about, for even now to me it seems astonishing. I was but between eighteen and nineteen, and had not had the remotest idea of getting Mrs. Smith, though I longed for her lewdly when my cock stood. I was timid with women until I knew them well, I could never begin with our own servants until they had been in the house a few days; yet directly I heard this conversation, a chance seemed in my way, and without meaning it I followed it up.

With but little idea of married life or habits, I saw that not only were they a wretched couple, but that for months Smith had never touched his wife. I imagined then that married people were always doing it, that women were randier than men,--a common belief of young people. I thought: how she must want a poke! how she would enjoy it! Out I went to see if Mrs. Smith was about, and saw her walking off with a group of sympathizers, who dropped off gradually, until she was left with one, with whom she went into a public-house. In a few minutes they came out and parted. On she went alone, and went into another public-house, and then wiping her eyes as she came out, went her way alone; I after her, lewd and thinking to myself, "she has not had it for six months," and so on. She went into a public-house now by herself. I waited till she came out, and saw she had been taking too many drops of comfort.

Without any definite intention as far as I can remember, but simply for lewd gratification, I went up to, and addressed her. She recognized me and stood stock still. She had a small bottle of what I found afterwards to be gin in her hand, which she put into her husband's dinner can. I told her I was sorry for her, having heard the row and all she had said. The reference to her wrongs roused her, and she said vehemently, "He is not a man anyhow or anywhere," and then was silent. I did not know what to say more, and walked on by her side. After a time she said, "Why are you walking with me sir?" The only reply I made was that I liked it, and was sorry she had such a bad husband. She said she would rather be alone, but I walked on with her she carrying the little tin can with a cover. I not knowing what to do, offered to carry it for her, but she would not let me.

Then she remarked, "You are very good, but don't come any further, it won't look well for a poor woman to be walking with a gentleman; neighbors make mischief, and God knows, I have enough to bear already." My boldness having quite left me, I shook hands with her, which seemed to astonish her, and off she went. I followed her at a distance, to her house, which was one of a row of small cottages fronting a ditch, and a field, on which carpets were beaten, and boys played, a scrubby poor place as you may be sure.

I turned back hesitating. One moment wondering at my boldness, and wickedness in thinking of a married woman; the next, thinking I was a fool for not having asked her to let me; when I saw in the path, the top of the tin can she had been carrying. Here was a chance. I walked about for half an hour before I mustered up courage to go to the house. She opened her eyes wide when she saw me. "What do you want?" "Here is the top of the dinner-can," said I innocently. "Oh!" said she, "I am so glad, he would have hit me if I had lost it." As she took it I entered and closed the door.

She had finished the gin, for the empty bottle was on the table. She may have been more than fuddled, I cannot say; for I was so excited that I recollect only the most prominent circumstances. I was in a funk, but my cock was stiff, and that overcame all scruples. The house had but two rooms: a kitchen I was standing in, the street-door opened on to it. An open door showed a neat bed in a clean white-washed bed-room. How I began I know not, but recollect telling what I had heard, and that for months he had not been a husband to her. That set her off talking wildly, and she said it all over again. She was sure he was spending his money on some dolly, hoped she might catch her, then cried, wiped her eyes and said, "Well, that is no business of yours, I am a fool for talking to a young gentleman like you, I don't know what you are doing here."

"Let me do it to you," said I, "I have seen up your clothes, let me,--you are so nice, and I want you so badly; why should you not, he is no husband to you, and you such a nice woman." That was my artless beginning, or something like it. Fright at my impudence was struggling against my cock-stand. For a second she seemed speechless, then replied, "Well sir, you ought to be ashamed,--a married woman like me." "He is no husband to you, he never does it to you, you know,--I heard you tell the women so; they laughed, and said he had some hussy whom he did it to." "That's no business of yours, but he is a bad one," and she began crying again. "Now go sir go,--if he came home, he would murder me, if he found you here."

I don't know how the next came off, but I know I was kissing her, that I got my hand up her clothes, on to her cunt, that I pulled out my prick, that the struggling ceased, that I edged her to the bed-room, and that up against the bed she made a stand. "Oh! my God sir, I am a married woman, pray don't." Paying no heed, I got her clothes up and as she stood, was bending and trying to get my cock up her; but she was little, and I could not; it shoved up against her navel, and motte. That I suppose stirring her lust, overcame her, for she got on the bed, I got on her, and up her in a second.

I was in a bursting state of randiness, and she must have been the same. I was ready to spend, she readier; for I had no sooner entered her than her breath shortened, she clasped me tight, quivered and wriggled, and we both spent. I lay up her, cock ready for further work. Up to that time I had not properly felt her, nor seen her body. I began fumbling about, put my hand down feeling cautiously round the stem of my cock and my ballocks. All was wet, I slid my finger below her cunt (feeling even near to an arse-hole was then beyond me), there it felt wetter; that stimulated me, and on I went grinding. She lay with her eyes closed without speaking. Soon we both went again, I had fucked her twice without uncunting.

The quiet dreamy enjoyment had barely began, when she pushed me off and sat up saying, "What have I done? what have I done? I am a married woman!" Then comes tears, then a kiss from me, then talk, then tears, and at intervals she told me a story of a bad, brutal, morose husband, who had not fucked her for months. Half frightened, half hysterical, it seemed as much pleasure to her to tell me her misery, as it had been to have me doing her husband's work. We moved off the bed. "Oh! my God," said she, "look at the bed." I saw one wet patch as large as a tea-cup, and another as large as a crown at the spot where her bum had laid on the counterpaine. "What shall I do?" "Wash it." "But I have no other." It was a bore no doubt. I left without being able to get permission to see her again, but only tears, and an expression of her conviction that she was a wicked woman.

Although she had not asked me not to tell anyone, which women so often do who commit these little slips, I did not mention it to Henry. For three or four days afterwards she did not come to the factory. I went to her cottage. She was out. At length at the dinner-hour I met her face to face by the factory. She looked ready to drop. An hour afterwards seeing her burly husband at work, off to her house I went, and gave a single knock. She opened the door, nearly fell back with surprise, and before she could recover herself I was indoors. I had an altercation, a refusal, almost a fight, but I conquered. Again she was fucked on the bed, and now for the first time I had a look at her charms, her cunt unwashed.

She was a plump little woman, dark-haired on head and tail, her quim was neither large or small, her thighs round and white, she was an ordinary person, neither handsome nor plain, and my curiosity was soon satisfied. She kept exclaiming, "Oh! if he should come home!" I fell to work again with vigour, and soon again spent. As I got off I observed under her bum again a large wet place, but now on her chemise. "What a lot of spending you have done," said I. "I can't help it," said she. My experience was small, but I knew that from no other woman whom I had stroked, had such an effusion taken place. Before I had spent I had felt her wetness on my fingers. I had her on another occasion, and the same thing occurred. I notice this because I only recollect meeting one other such case since; Mrs. Smith, like the other to whom I refer, used after a few pushes up her to squeeze her cunt, shiver, and discharge quite copiously, to be followed with a second pleasure and discharge when I spent. I only reflected on Mrs. Smith's peculiarity some years afterwards.

In about a week I had her again at her cottage. Then

she said if I came any more she would have trouble, for neighbors had already remarked a gentlemen at the house. I disregarded this, went and knocked. She opened the door cautiously with the chain up, and seeing me, shut it in my face. I was then about going to my own home, and feared I should not have her again, but found out that the husband spent his evenings at a tavern (I had a strange pleasure in looking at him after I had had his wife), that he was to be at some workman's carousal, watched him go to the public-house, then ran to his cottage, gave a single loud knock at the door, which was this time opened unsuspiciously, and in I pushed before she could scarcely see who it was.

I had difficulty in persuading her to let me, she was more timid than ever, but promised that I would never come again.

Then she got on to the bed. The crisis was just over when we heard a knock. With a shriek she pushed me off and got up. "He will murder me, he will murder me," said she. I stood blank with bewilderment, relieved by another knock and a voice crying "beer." She fell on the floor fainting, and so alarmed me, that I nearly called in the neighbours. I put a pillow under her head. I don't know what induced me, for not three minutes before I was frightened out of my life, but as she laid there close by the fire (at the knock we had rushed into the kitchen), I pulled up her clothes. The flickering of the fire showed her thighs and cunt in a strange light to me. As I pulled her legs asunder, I felt ashamed, but lust was strong. I looked at the cunt, the novelty of an insensible woman on the floor excited me, the next instant in spite of her, for she recovered just as I laid on her, my prick was up her, and my knuckles on the hard bit of dingy carpet, and as I grasped her bum, it seemed that my poke was most delicious. So much for novelty and imagination. I left immediately afterwards.

Then I went home to my mother. In about three weeks, went to see Henry, again as I said, but really to get to Mrs. Smith, and found her husband had been discharged. I went off to the cottage, it was empty. They had gone no one knew where, and he had half murdered his wife. I wondered if it had been about me. Then my conscience upbraided me with having committed adultery. I took to going to church more regularly, and repeated the commandments emphatically.

I was now approaching nineteen years, was at home doing nothing but study, and with scarcely a farthing of money. I tried to get into one of our servant's unsuccessfully, she was a plain lass, but had a cunt, which was all I wanted. I began to kiss and fondle her, which she submitted to demurely. Then by surprise one day got my hand up her clothes, and between her cunt-lips. She loudly screamed, which luckily was unheard, for my mother was out. Her cunt felt wet, and I found from my fingers afterwards that she was poorly built. She rushed downstairs crying violently, the next day gave warning and left, much to my relief. She never I am sure told my mother, but I was in a fright until she had left.

I restrained myself from frigging, although sorely tempted to do so, and luckily found cheaper and better relief. Having had but one gay woman, and having a dread of them, neverthless, my mind involuntarily turned to them, especially as I now defied my mother, stopped out of nights latish, and consequently saw more of them. But I had no money.

Between London and our suburb, there were some lengths of road bounded by fields, and only lighted by oil-lamps. At places small houses were being built in side-roads, which were altogether without light. Gay women of a poor class, were then of an evening about the darkest parts, or they used to walk where the roads were lighter. They were of that class who go with labouring men, and were not attractive, although cleaner and better-looking than the same class now is.

One evening I worried an aunt out of two pounds, which I had with a solitary shilling besides; and was returning, when a woman accosted me. She walked by my side and talked, but I could not afford a sovereign, which was a much larger sum then than it now is, and a shilling seemed to me a ridiculous sum, so I determined to run, for fear I should be fool enough to let her have a sovereign. "I can't," said, "good night, I only have a shilling." "Make it two," said she. "I have not got more." "Give it me then." I stopped in astonishment at the idea of her taking such a trifle. "She is going to take it and go off," thought I, for I had known such a thing, but I gave her the shilling and then stood still. "Well, are you not going to have it?" said she, "make haste." It was a dark night, but I saw from a white gleam that her clothes were up, felt where the nick was, and in much agitation thrust my tool up it.

Having a woman in the open up against a field fence, and without seeing her cunt, or even her face, was a novelty to me. For a long time I had been bottling up my sperm. All fear left me, and it seemed the most delicious fuck I ever had had. In a few pushes I spent, and kept my belly up against hers in silent delight, till I felt sperm trickling down over my balls. Telling me to take care of my shirt she drew her bum back. Scarcely recovered from my pleasure and still wondering how I had such pleasure with so poor a woman, I suppose I must have said something of the sort, for she remarked, "Why not? we are all made the same way, and if some of us had more cheek, we might have as good clothes as the best, but there are plenty of real gents glad enough to have us," and so we talked for a minute. I had not felt her and now longed to do so, but was too timid to ask her. She turned away. I had been wiping my cock with a silk pocket-handkerchief, to prevent any sperm getting on to my shirt. A happy idea came. "Let me feel you, and do it again and I will give you this silk handkerchief, for I have no more money." Laughing and saying, "I suppose it is silk," she accepted it. I think now of the exquisite delight, with which I felt the thighs and bum of that poor woman, who might for all I could see, have had the great, or the small pox, or have been as ugly as the devil; but I stroked her belly, twiddled her wet cunt-hair (she had pissed), plunged my fingers into her wet cunt, and at length spent again in it, with more delight, than I have had with some of the most dashing women since that time.

After funking about pox and clap, for a few days, out I sped one evening to try to get her again, delighted at the economical rate at which I found it now possible to have women. But I always was liberal, and gave her three or four shillings. Several times I had had her afterwards and never saw her face. At length I insisted on going when I could see her. She refused until tempted by an offer, then agreed to meet me at a place which she named; saying, "And I will put on a clean chemise and stockings." I met her, and found her to be about thirty-five years old, and one of the ugliest women I ever saw.

She was so plain that all desire left me. I looked her all over, to which she made no objection, remarking as she pulled up her clothes, "Ah, you may look, I am as clean as any woman although I am what I am." I went on looking at, and fiddling her about, but no erection came. She gave an uneasy motion with her bum and said, "Oh! you are tickling me so, why don't you get on?" I said I did not want it yet, which so astonished her, that she sat upright, and looked at me and at my tool. Then she made me lay down on the poor bed, and mutual feeling soon brought me to a proper state. "Don't you be quick or you will spoil me," said she. Her manner was quite different from what it had been on the high road, it was amorous. I forgot her ugliness, and fucking with all my heart, spent when her hard breathing, tightening cunt, and clasping arms, told me she enjoyed it also.

Then the miserable room, and her ugliness revolted me. I moved to get off, but she retained me, asking me to talk. Somewhat against my inclination I did. She laid hold of my prick, pinching it. The gentle pleasure returned, and it ended in my doing her again, as much to her delight as mine. She said so. Instead of feeling pleased, it made her seem to me ugly. I went away, and although I argued with myself, especially when I only had a shilling or two, yet I never could bring myself to have her again. When I saw her on the road, I went the other side of the way, and soon lost sight of her.

Finding that I had not suffered by my indiscretion, I got bolder, took the run of the road, and must have had a dozen girls at a shilling a tail. One night as I fumbled a girl, she frigged me vigourously. "I will do it this way," said she, "you will like it so." But I refused. "I will give you such pleasure," said she again, "all the gents say I do it better than any girl." But again I refused. "I am afraid my monthlies are just coming on," said she. But up I put it, and went home satisfied. Two or three mornings afterwards I felt a slight itching at the tip of my prick, but took no notice of it; the next morning piddling, to my horror I saw a little yellowish fluid oozing, and sat down in consternation. I had got a clap.

This laid me up for weeks, I went to a strange doctor and managed to keep it from my mother, but was in anxiety as to how I was to pay the doctor. Fortune and misfortune often follow each other. My long promised appointment came from the W... Office just as I was getting well. With overwhelming joy I saw some chance of a little money, beyond what I got by begging from relatives; and then also my mother, at the advice of an uncle, who pointed out that in a year and a half I could not be kept out of my property, allowed me a fair monthly stipend.

I now found out that women of a superior class, were to be had much cheaper, than my great friends used to talk of; but at the time I write of, a sovereign would get any woman, and ten shillings as nice a one as you needed. Two good furnished rooms near the Clubs, could be had by women for from fifteen to twenty shillings per week, a handsome silk dress for five or ten pounds, and other things in proportion. So cunt was a more reasonable article than it is now is, and I got quite nice girls at from five to ten shillings a poke, and had several in their own rooms, but sometimes paying half-a-crown extra for a room elsewhere.

When with but little money, I used to take out my best silk handkerchiefs, and give them with money, and once or twice I gave nothing else. One night to a nice-looking girl I said I could give her nothing but a handkerchief. "All right," said she without a murmur. When I had fucked her, she laid still on the bed and before she washed her cunt examined the handkerchief very carefully. "It's a rare good new one, it will pop for half-a-crown where I am known, where did you prig it?" looking at me as she spoke, and then added, "Yet you look like a gentleman too." I recollect it as well as if it were yesterday. I at that time used to take pleasure in laying as long as I could after I had spent, then getting up and kneeling between the girl's legs opening her cunt and watching the spunk at the mouth, or the big drops rolling down between the cheeks of her bum. I was kneeling so then, and was not a little shocked at her remark. That girl was young, handsome, well made, and in the Hay-market would now get anything from one to five pounds, yet I had her several times for three and four shillings a time.

CHAPTER X.

A big cunted one.--Sister Mary.--A wet dream.--Charlotte

reappears.--Consequences.--My first child.--Cook Brown, and

housemaid Harriet.--Masturbation and foolscap.--A deaf

relative.--An uncomfortable pudendum.--A lacerated penis.--

Sudden dismissals.

Just at this time the following incident occurred. Going one Saturday night up Granby street, Waterloo road, then full of women who used to sit at the windows half naked; two or three together at times in the same room on the ground-floor, with the bed visible from the street, and which street I often walked in for the pleasure of looking at the women. A woman standing at a door seized my hand, asking me in, and at the same time pulling me quite violently into the little passage. I had barely seen her, and upon her saying, "Come and have me," replied that I had scarcely any money. "Never mind," said she, "we will have a fuck for all that." She shut the door, closed rapidly the outer wooden shutters, which all the ground-floor windows had in that street, and began to kiss me and feel my prick. I then saw she was half drunk. Quickly she pulled me towards the bed, threw herself on it, pulled up her clothes to her navel, and cried aloud, "Fuck me,--fuck me,--fuck me.--oh! how I want a fuck, make haste." She was a tall woman with dark hair on her cunt, neither very long nor thick. As I looked at it, I saw the inner lips hanging out a full inch, I put my finger, two, then three fingers up her cunt easily. It was enormous. It shocked me, having never seen such a cunt before I am quite sure. She meanwhile did nothing but jerk, and wriggle her arse about, shouting out, "Fuck me,--put your prick in,--fuck me,--fuck me."

The look of her thing, its size, and her manner so shocked me, that my prick refused its work, and I told her so. She jumped off of the bed, fell on her knees, and began sucking my prick violently, made it stiff in spite of me, got on to the bed again, and recommenced crying out for me to do it to her. With a feeling of disgust I got on her, slipped my prick up and began, but it felt nowhere. I could not make out that it was up a cunt at all, so loose was it. If it had been in a wet bladder, it could not have felt looser, and it shrunk up again to nothing. "I can't do it," said I in a fright, for her manner was so lewd, and became so ferocious, that it quite upset me. "What! a fine young man like you can't do it," said she. "No" (and as an apology), "I often can't do it." Again she got it stiff by sucking it. That quite disgusted me, but on to the bed and into her again I got. My doodle in a minute began to shrink, but whilst in her, she wriggled and jerked away so hard, that I think she must have got a pleasure, for she laid quiet for a time. I was very glad to get off; but was not to be let off so easy. "I will give you a pleasure," said she, "I can if anyone can," and although it disgusted me, for such a thing had never been done to me before, and I tried to stop her, she dropped upon her knees saying, "You will come to see me again I know, for a man can always do it one way or another," put my prick in her mouth and sucked and palated it. I was too young and too full not to feel it. Spite of myself I spent, and just as I did, grasping my balls with one hand and frigging the stem with the other, she drew back her mouth about two inches, kept it wide open, went on frigging, and the sperm squirted out into her mouth and on to her face; then she resumed sucking it until every drop was out of me.

That over, she rose and said, "You will come to me again, won't you? I will always do that to you, and anything else you like." I gave her a shilling and promised, but never felt so sick and disgusted with a woman before. Everything about the woman was repulsive. I have since met four or five woman with very large cunt-holes, but hers was the largest. I am perfectly certain I could have put my fist up it. I avoided the street for some months, which was a great loss to me, for I often used to go through it, to gloat on the charms of the women as they lolled out of the windows. When I thought of my prick being sucked, it used to disgust me awfully, and it was many years before I knew what pleasure it was to a man, at times; but it never has been done to me again, in the manner that woman did it.

Then I saw the woman in taking whose virtue I lost my own,--Charlotte.

Our cook married. A new cook and housemaid came, the latter a pretty dark-eyed girl of about eighteen years of age, named Mary. Directly I set eyes upon her I liked her, and thought I would try to get her. My clap and cheap pokes, had not made me much in love with gay women; whose free-and-easy ways somewhat shocked my timidity. Some time had elapsed since I had had any others, and my mind naturally reverted to the nice pokes I had had with servants. My chances were fewer than ever. One of my sisters was now frequently at home, Tom no longer needed a servant to be with him, and the housemaid was less frequently away from the kitchen. But I felt myself more a man, my good fortunes made me feel more sure of success, more prompt and determined in attack.

At first I watched her closely and thought I must have seen her before. A resemblance struck me, and I remarked to my mother, "How like that girl is to Charlotte, who lived with us." "She is her sister," said she. I was startled, for a feeling came over me that I ought not to try her.

But it brought my liason with Charlotte vividly to my recollection. The first meeting, the glimpse of her cunt as she got down from the cart, my first grope, our first poke, were now constantly before me; and I longed with all my heart to have her again, though I knew it was hopeless.

Gradually my mind centered itself on Mary, and as I saw the resemblance to her sister, I used to wonder how far the resemblance extended. Whether her haunches were as large, her thighs as round, her cunt so made, fringed, and dark, and so on; until I desired to have her, as much for her resemblance to Charlotte, as for herself. Yet I had fear and reluctance to make advances, because she was Charlotte's sister.

Meanwhile I was chaste, was in good health and wanted a woman awfully. Then I had a wet dream; dreamed I had Charlotte in my arms, that she ran away and left me with Mary, who pulled up her clothes, and invited me to fuck her. Before I could get in to her, I awakened, found that I was on my back and was spending on my night-gown.

I had heard much of these dreams, had had one

partially, and now had experienced a complete one. It threw me into a state of irritation, but seemed to fix the hidden charms of Mary strongly in my imagination. Desire so carried me away, that from gently rubbing and titillating myself, I passed to frigging a discharge, whilst thinking of Mary's cunt.

In the morning I had the enervation I have always since felt after these dreams, and my usual disgust at having frigged myself; a feeling which was not allayed when I looked at my night-shirt. I had a dread of letting it be seen, but left things as they were. Mary and the cook made my bed, and must have seen it. Servants see funny things on beds often. I wonder what they say, and what they think about it. It can't be easy for a young woman to see sheets, and night-gowns, spunk-stained; without its effecting her imagination baudily, and paving the way for somebody to stain sheets and linen with herself.

I gave up all idea of attacking Mary, but "cock and cunt will try to get together." There is no use in resisting it. So again with no fixed intention, but simply from pleasure for the time being, and impelled by desire (all my silk handkerchiefs were gone and I was again without money), and by opportunity, I got to courting, and we soon kissed. I had pressed her belly against mine, got my hand on to the calf of her leg, and was on the high road to the snatch at her cunt, which my experience now told me was the right thing to do, when all came to an end.

I went daily to the W---- Office returning about half-past four. One day when about half-a-mile from home, a lady in black silk and with a dark veil approached me; but as if she had made a mistake, when close to me, turned on one side and passed on. I looked back and saw she was standing still, then on she went, and so did I, and had nearly forgotten her, when I heard quick footsteps in the rear, and some one saying, "Mister Walter, don't you know me?" I turned round, stopped and tried to see who it was, but the veil prevented it. She hesitated an instant, then lifted it, and I saw Charlotte.

With flushed face, bright eyes and a gentle smile, she looked exquisite. My heart beat tumultuously, my love returned in an instant. I put my arm round her, and regardless of the publicity of the place, gave a kiss. There was it is true scarcely anyone about, but she as well as me when I had done it, saw the impropriety. "Don't, for God's sake," said she, "what will people think?" "Let us walk," said I, and pulling her arm through mine, on we went; I looking into her face all the way, noticing how much the time which had passed had improved her, and overwhelming her with questions. I felt overjoyed, as if again I should possess her, and old times had returned. She for a few minutes seemed to give way to similar elation. Just then I saw a gentleman named Courtauld approaching, he was our next-door neighbour. We nodded as we passed, but the incident altered the current of our thoughts. I led her down a turning where there were scarcely any people, and saying, "I am so glad old Courtauld did not see me, for his brother lives just by us, and his old servant is often there and knows me." She relapsed into silence. I went on chatting of the happy times we had had, and the pleasures we had tasted together. She remarked, "Oh! pray don't talk of that any more, recollect I am married, let me say what I have come to say, and then I must go."

"To say to me?" said I. "Pray don't misunderstand me, I thought you would excuse it," said she getting confused, "besides it is my duty, and of course knowing what I do about you, I was so afraid of something." "What do you mean?" "Well if I had known where she was going to I would have made mother stop it, now I come at once to ask you not to hurt her." I proposed going into a small half-country ale-house close by, but she refused saying, that if seen to do so, and it became known to her husband, it might cause much harm. "Oh! no," said she in a hurry again, "I must go, I must get back, I came to ask you not to hurt her, promise you won't for my sake." All this time I was in a fog. "Who--who,--what do you mean?" said I. "Oh you know,--Mary, I mean Mary, she is my favourite sister, pray don't harm her." The whole affair was clear to me at once. "Is that what you came about?" I asked disappointed. "Yes, I have been coming for a fortnight, but could not make up my mind; her last letter made me determine at any risk to do so, and now dear, promise me not to hurt her, and I will go."

I was annoyed and wounded in vanity, for I had almost brought myself to think she had come for the pleasure of meeting me. I had no intention of quitting her so soon, felt as if I could not, so chaffed her, "What do you mean by hurting her?" "Don't talk nonsense, you know what I mean." "Another case of cock and cunt coming together." "If you talk like that, you insult me, and I did not think you would." "Well, I love you and would not like to hurt your feelings, what you really mean is, that I am not to try to do it to her." "Why of course, don't ruin her, that is what I mean."

We had walked without any intention on my part to the outskirts of our village, where the pew-opener's house was in which Charlotte and I had spent many an hour in love's frolics. The house was in sight, the hope of again having her came to my mind. In her excitement, which was as great if not greater than mine, she had not noticed where we were, until quite at the angle. The pew-opener was at the door, gave me a nod, and thinking it possible I might be coming in I suppose, left the door ajar. "Come in," said I. "Never! oh! no, you have brought me here purposely." I saw there would be difficulty. "Here is that old Courtauld's house-maid, damn her," said I. "Where,--where,--which way?" said she looking in alarm in all directions, but unable to see clearly through her veil. "There,--there," "just step inside the door till she has past." She stepped in quickly, the next instant I half pulled, half hustled her through the little door into the bed-room, slammed the door, locked it, and stood still, half afraid of my own boldness. She went to the window and began to peer through the blinds to see the old housemaid.

"I can't see her," said she, "she must have passed, tell me which way she went, and let me go." "Not yet. What do you want about Mary?" "Promise for my sake, you won't try to ruin her." "Well, let us have a longer talk, how do you know I want to do so?" "I know you do." "Sit down." "I cannot." "Then I won't promise, why should I?" "Oh! don't be a blackguard, don't oh! don't,--you shant have her, I will take care," and then she burst out crying.

I loved her so that I felt I would do anything to please her; but wanted her so much, that I could be cruel enough to do or say anything to have her again. Desire was the stronger. The sofa, the bed, the room, her beauty, all made me feel savage with lust, so I temporized. "I am so excited," said I, "I scarcely know what to say, what to do, tell me more, what you know, what you want, for all this stems so strange to me,--sit down." "No." "Sit down only while you tell me." "No." But I laid hold of her and pushed her on to the sofa, and there I held her, and after beseeching her to be quiet and kiss me, she did so. Then she sat for a minute, drying her tears, and began her tale and her request.

"Mary is my favourite sister, she lived with us for a year after I married, but mother wanted her and she went home. She grew tired of being at home, went to service, did not like it and went home again; again grew weary; and to my astonishment, the last time I went to see the old people, found she had gone to live with your mother. I was frightened for her sake, for I love her dearly." "Why frightened?" I asked. "Why frightened? don't I know you, do you think I have forgotten all?" "I never thought of doing her harm." "Perhaps not," she replied, "but I would not trust my sister near you, if she had the least liking for you, or you for her." I protested I was indifferent to her. "Why kiss her and squeeze her so?" I began denying it, and she stopped me saying vehemently, "Now don't tell stories, you never did to me, I know all, I know you do, you mean her harm, or if you don't, harm will come of it. Look, here is her letter," and she put it into my hands. To my astonishment I found Mary had told her sister all, mixed with warm encomiums of me. I was shut up, and could only say I meant no harm. "Perhaps! but harm must come of it. It nearly brought me to ruin, for I would have done anything, lived anyhow to keep near you; but I have escaped it. Poor Mary may not, for you are older now and may do more harm! she is a different temper from me, and in despair will go wrong altogether; so I pray you if you loved me, not to injure her for my sake. If she came to harm, I should break my heart," and she broke again into tears, getting up at the same time to go.

I pulled her back and kissed her tears away. "Charlotte, we cannot meet and part like this, I love you still, I have never ceased to love and think of you, oh! let me." I could say no more, for in my eyes then there was a sanctity about a married woman which stilled my tongue. "Oh! let me," was all I could say.

She understood what I wanted, and replied, "I am married and cannot, let me go." At my entreaties she kissed me freely, yet all the time struggled to get up.

I thought to myself, "You have had her. She loves you

still. Think of the pleasure you have had with her. Here she is in your power, and cannot escape without a riot, which she will fear." Kissing her fiercely, stifling her voice with my mouth, "I must, I will have you again," I pulled her violently back on the sofa, and had my hand on her thighs in an instant.

"Oh! don't, for the love of God, think I am married, don't make me afraid of myself; oh! take care, you crush my bonnet, what shall I do, how shall I get home?" Holding her tight, I dragged the bonnet off her head, and recommenced. We made such a noise, that the old pew-opener knocked at the door and asked if anything was the matter.

"By God," said I, "either I will have you, or you shant go out of this house this night," and so I struggled on through tears and entreaties, threats, kissings and promises, till with broken voice her head sunk back, her struggles ceased, her legs opened, my hand slipped over her smooth thighs, and nestled in the warm moist slit it had so often toyed with in time gone by. It is nigh fifteen years since that delicious afternoon, but I recollect my sensations as I touched her cunt, as well as if it had been but yesterday.

Resistance had ceased, for a moment in silent enjoyment I laid with my fingers in their warm lodging, then too impatient to get to the bed, or take the full luxury of my fortune, I arranged her on the sofa as well as its size permitted, with her petticoats up in a heap, and with my trousers half unbuttoned, flung myself upon her, and entered the smooth channel in which I first had spent my virginity. Frantic with excitement, the pleasure came on ere I was in full up her. She, excited and loving, clutched me tightly in her arms, whilst her cunt and belly moved sympathetically. In too short a time we spent together.

My position was a fatiguing one, I was half on, half off the sofa; hers was but little less so, yet as long as our privates would keep together, we kept them so. I poured out my love to her, and joyed to hear from her that she loved me still. But our position could not last for ever; gradually I slipped off. My prolonged embrace, my sensuous imagination, and my love for her had told so upon me; that I was already contemplating the pleasure of another poke, a desire to see her charms came over me, I went on to my knees and had a glimpse between the open thighs, of the half open cunt, from which a love-drop was rolling. She pushed down her clothes, and sat up, looking at me, and blushing like the most modest of maidens.

It is extraordinary what objection so many women have to a man's looking closely at their cunts. A woman will stand naked, lay naked on her belly, or bum, stand with one leg on a chair, kneel with one leg on the bed, be looked at frontways, backways, sideways, and be pleased with the admiration. You may lay and kiss the outside, put your fingers up and probe it, rub your knuckles into it, tickle or frig it; but directly you want to pull the lips open, to see the hole which lays hidden by the hairy outer lips, to see where your prick is longing to hide its head; they object, put their thighs together, say, "No, it is not to be looked at." Or if angrily pressed, reluctantly half yield, throw themselves down, so as to put their back to the light, lifting one leg so as to hide the light, and using every manoeuvre to prevent you looking closely at it; and if you desire to look when it's laden with the efforts of your love, they will struggle to prevent you. Gay or modest, it is the same among the English; although a gay lady will yield to please her friend. With the French the objection is less, a French gay woman will pull open her cunt with her own hands, and let you pull open her arse-hole if you can and like it. I have known a few women of other nations and even of my own as free and easy, but the rule is as I say. This cannot be modesty. I rather imagine it results from a fear that some discharge will show itself, and sicken the man's appetite.

Up jumped Charlotte, and went into the adjoining room. I heard her splashing away a long time at her cunt, and went to her. I had no desire to wash away from my person, anything which had come from hers. She pushed me back. I had a glimpse of her, naked to her waist, washing something. She said, "My linen is in such a mess I have been obliged to wash it." She had found much spunk upon it, and washed it for fear of being found out. She put a petticoat over her neck to hide her charms, the chemise was so wet that it was almost impossible for her to put it on, and she did not know what to do.

"Good God, you will catch your death of cold." I rang the bell and gave it to the old woman to dry. "Now," said I, "you cannot go, it is of no use, I must have you again, and will see all your charms, I had you first, I have had you again, and again I will have you; don't be foolish, all harm is done."

Crying, entreating and saying she was married, I got her on to the bed, and stripping myself was soon folded in her arms. My prick was ready, she had struggled hard, now saw it was useless, and lay in all her beauty before me, her head on the pillow and her eyes closed, leaving me to work my will.

I saw her as leisurely as my throbbing prick would let me from head to foot, that she had grown stouter, taller, and was now a splendid woman. Her breasts were full and hard, her buttock large and solid, her thighs more rounded, the hair of her cunt thicker. Curiously I opened its lips and put my finger in, to see if marriage had made any difference, but was far too young and inexperienced to find it out, if there had been any. It seemed the dear old split which had so often given me pleasure before; that look and feel finished me, in another second my ballocks were bang-iny away against her bum, and she met my embraces with fervour which too soon came to an end. Repose followed, the luscious tongue-kisses ceased, our sighs stopped, and we fell asleep.

But not for long. The wet chemise was brought back. That off her mind into bed I got with her. The coach by which she now could go home did not leave until eight o'clock, hurry was of no use; with my finger in her quim, side by side, mouth to mouth, we laid and talked.

Her anxiety was about her sister, whom I swore I never would attempt. That settled her. She wanted to know all about me, that was soon told. I never mentioned Mary's name, although she asked after her. Then I was curious about her married life, how she got over her marriage night, how often he poked her, and so on. I got but little out of her, beyond that he had not discovered that she had been fucked before, and that he was a good husband to her; my other questions she said were disgraceful. I felt mad to think that another man should put his prick where my fingers then were, so I asked if she enjoyed it with him, whereupon she burst into a passionate flood of tears, and it closed with her saying, "Whether I love him or not, he is a good fellow to me, and if I am found out and disgraced it will serve me right." Would she meet me again? "Never, never, I love you still, but never again." It ended in another fuck.

And so it went on till the time for going. Never in my life up to that time had desire been so strong in me. When I knew she must go I insisted on again doing it, but could not come up to the scratch, until with a sharp frig it stiffened and again it was put up her. What a long hard poke it was, what a test of my manhood, how proud was I when with a sharp and sudden pleasure I felt my spunk squirting up her dear quim, and a spasmodic clutch, a sharp sob and "dear Walter," escaping from her told me she had spent with me.

She washed, I dressed, swearing I would never wash my prick again till I saw her. "I have poked you darling, five times," said I in triumph. It was the first time I think I ever had done so, but am not sure, and proud enough I felt. We soon relapsed into sadness and tears, and telling our love to each other, parted at the coach-stand.

I was mad again for her; had now money, and twice went down to the place to get a glimpse at her and failed, but saw her husband in the shop. We stared at each other. I wonder if he felt that I should have liked-to throttle him, for so I did. I wrote and got no reply. I pumped her sister, to see if I could learn where she walked or went, and got no information; indeed soon lost opportunity for suddenly her sister left us. Her father came to ask my mother to excuse her on account of his wife's illness, and she never came back. I have but little doubt it was only to get her away from our house, and that it was Charlotte's doings. I never saw Charlotte again, though I still may do so; but to this day I have an affection for her, and although she must be forty, should like to poke her.

Next year, one day my mother opened a letter, it was from the E------ family; and read aloud little scraps of it to me, and my sisters who were in the room. "That family is all doing very well," said she; "Mary who was with us but three months last year is married." She went on reading, "And Charlotte's husband has taken a large shop and is making money.--Ah! I am very glad of it, for she was a nice respectable girl. Oh! here,--and has just been confined with a fine boy.--I am very glad," said mother. I looked and found it was nine months after Tom's birthday, and that that day nine months some one had fucked Charlotte five times. I was delighted.

My appointment now made it needful to dine late, so we reverted to a six o'clock dinner. This neither suited the cook nor housemaid; both left, and two new servants came. I was about nineteen years old.

The cook whose name was Brown was clean, fat, and wholesome to look at, and I should say forty-five years old. She must have weighed sixteen stone. The width across her arse as I eyed it outside her dress, looked greater than that of Mary the cook; there was a roguish twinkle in her eye, which made her look like a good-tempered monthly nurse, her eyes were blue and her hair brown.

Harriet the housemaid was very tall, and very sallow, had jet-black hair and black eyes, with the expression of a serpent in them. She showed splendid teeth when she laughed, and then looked half cat, half hyena. She never looked you in the face long, was so quiet in her movements that the cat moved less noiselessly; she startled you by being close to you when you did not know she was near, and had a sneering laugh. After a day or two my mother remarked she did not like the pair, and was sorry she had engaged them.

Up to this time I had only poked two servants, Charlotte and Mary. Others had not been to my taste. With one I tried it on and failed, and when randy now could not help thinking of the couple in the house. I tried it on with Harriet, but she so snubbed me, that I set her down as an impregnable virgin. Then I turned my eyes to Brown, though it seemed absurd to think of such a fat middle-aged woman; but I one day chanced to see that she had a very fat pair of calves, and I knew she must have a big arse; and as fat legs had an irresistible attraction for me, I tried to see more of them, but without the thought of taking liberties with their owner.

I saw her legs again, from thinking of them and her rump, my mind naturally went to her cunt, which I pictured must be very thick-lipped and hairy like that of Sarah's, whose cunt had made a great impression on me. Her age then seemed to fade from my mind, and I used to follow her when going upstairs, trying to see her legs, and flattering myself she did not see what I was after, but she knew it as well as I did.

One day going upstairs she stumbled upon her dress, and as if to prevent doing it again, held it up, so as to show nearly to her knees. When she got on the top stair she turned round, and as if she had only just seen me, dropped her dress quickly. Another time she stooped and jutted out her bum, so that I saw a good deal up the clothes, whilst she pretended to be doing something to her boot. It seemed to me accidental, but it was all intentional.

Then my prick used to stand when I saw her. About nine o'clock one morning she came into the garden when I was there, and gathered some herbs. Her stooping posture gave me a cock-stand, and under its influence I joked her about her legs and my seeing them. She gave a suppressed laugh and saying, "Lawd! did you sir?" went down into the kitchen. What made me go down I do not know, but five minutes afterwards I did so; and just by the kitchen door, saw her with one leg on a chair, putting up her garter.

I stood stock still and silent. She adjusted one garter neatly, then put up her other leg, unrolled the garter, pulled up the stocking and put on the garter quite deliberately. I saw the flesh of her large thighs, for her garters were tied above the knees, and she pulled up her petticoats freely. Putting down her clothes she turned round, saw me, then with a grin said, "Lawd sir, how you startled me."

Bursting with randiness I lost all prudence. Mother, sister, Tom, and the other servant were about the house, but up to the cook I went, whispering, "I saw your legs, what jolly ones, what thighs, what a cunt you must have, let's have a feel," and got one hand up her clothes. She pushed me away saying, "Hish! here is missis." It was a lie, but it frightened me away.

The same evening I went downstairs after our dinner. The housemaid had been sent to the circulating library. Mother, sister and Tom were, as they usually were after dinner, when the weather was warm; sitting in the summer-house at the bottom of the garden. I usually sat with them, but slinked into the house, and down into the kitchen; which being underground was darkish, although then it was light until eight o'clock. Cook when she saw me, grinned and became familiar, for she was a regular old stager, and knew well, that when a man wanted to take liberties with her, she might safely take them with him. "What do you want?" "To feel your cunt," said I, "see your legs, feel that crummy rump of yours, cookey." "Then you won't," said she laughing, and lifting a heavy saucepan off the fire with both hands, she carried it towards the sink in the back kitchen. Randy and ready, I saw my opportunity; and as she neared the sink, thrust both hands up her clothes, grasped her arse, and was fumbling for her slit; when putting down the saucepan with a bang, she flung round, and hit me such a slap on the head as knocked me over, saying, "Why, you young devilskin, it would serve you right to tell your mother of your capers," and then she stood and laughed at me.

I persisted, kissed the old party, and told her how I

wanted her, for indeed at that moment I would have fucked her, if she had been eighty. She repulsed me saying in a whisper, "Harriet is upstairs." "She is going out," said I. "Wait till she has, if she hears you, she will make mischief." As I felt this might be true, I desisted.

I went back to the garden thinking, and hoping mother and sister would not go indoors. When Harriet had gone oft, I went back into the garden parlour quite leisurely (for mother could see me do that), then down to the cook. It was nearly dark. In a minute I had pushed her up against the dresser, was groping her, and she was feeling my prick and ballocks with seemingly hearty enjoyment. She opened her legs to give me every facility. I attempted to get into her, but her clothes and big belly prevented me. She held my prick against her cunt, so that it pushed against her orifice, but did not go up it; and such was my state, that I spent against it. She kept hold of the prick, rubbing it, and gently squeezing it, until not a drop of sperm was left in it. Then for fear of being found out, upstairs I went again. The whole business, had not occupied five minutes.

I had once spent by accident in Mary's hand, and had fear lest it should disgust her. There was something about this affair, which seemed quite different. I could scarcely make out how, with a cunt close to my prick, I had spent as I had done. The next night came, I tried it on at the same hour with the same result. She not only let me feel her, but put my fingers to her cunt, at a place where she wished me to rub her, she meanwhile frigging away at my prick. But I wanted more than this, and just as it was too late, she let me put my prick in. At the first spurt of my spunk, she by a twist threw my prick out, and caught hold of it with her fingers, letting me spend over her thighs and linen, but squeezing and frigging at my doodle until it had shrunk thoroughly down.

For a month the same thing occasionally happened. She would let me finger, feel, rub her (in the nearly darkened kitchen), putting one leg on a chair, or stooping down, or any way to let me feel both inside and outside well. When I got my prick out, she immediately began to frig it. I used to have quiet rows with her, for not letting me put it into her; and when at length she did, I was always near spending; and do not think that more than once, I spent up her completely, so did she manage to throw me out just as my sperm began to flow. All was done standing up.

She treated me like some one she had known for years, did everything before me, talked both baudily, and beastly, called my balls, my cods, and used to say, "Hish! let me piss first." Then she would sit down on a pail in the back kitchen and piss, sometimes farting, and saying, "oh!" with a laugh, when she did so. She would belch without ceremony, blow her nose through her fingers, and I noticed she never washed her hands (whilst I was present at all events), when I had spent upon them. She would say, "How are your cods off for starch to-night?" She was complaisant enough in letting me feel, would turn her backside round and let me fumble about it anyhow, but although want made me do what I did, it never seemed quite pleasant to me, and I disliked her. I never got a glimpse of her belly or cunt. If the front-kitchen was not dark enough, she moved to the back, before we began our pranks, and scrupulously avoided light. Her cunt I felt was a large one, but so far from having the quantity of hair I expected, she seemed scarcely to have any. One thing she did which annoyed me. After feeling my cock, she would slide her hands under the balls to my arse-hole which she would press hard with her middle-finger, giving a "tchick" with her tongue, at the same time.

All this took place in about six weeks. "Hush!" said she

one night, "some one is listening." I could hear nothing, but she whispered, "Go up to the garden." I did. It was dusk, and I thought I saw a figure enter the garden parlour, just as I got up the garden stairs. All were out but me and the two servants. Cook at the same time went up the kitchen-stairs, calling out loudly, "Harriet, is Master at home, do you know?"

A few days afterwards when at our fun, we stood in the door jamb; Harriet was at the top of the house. Said cook, "If I push you hard by the shoulders, go out into the garden at once, without saying a word." It was nearly dark. The kitchen garden-door was shut, but she opened it wide, before we went to work. I had my prick against her cunt, when a push came; off I went buttoning up, and after a time across the garden, into the parlor. Afterwards Harriet brought up lights, her eyes cast down as usual. The next day the cook whispered to me, "It was that bitch Harriet watching, I found her coming downstairs with her shoes off, saying she wanted a candle;--but I will be even with her."

I never had the cook but once after that. She would not let me. The two servants quarrelled so, that my mother threatened to dismiss both. When I tried it on with Brown, she said, "Why don't you ask Harriet, you young devilskin?" I told her there was no chance. She said she was quite sure that I should not be the first. Another day she repeated it saying, "I bet she will let you, the baker has had her I believe." Then she put me up to watching the baker with Harriet. The man came in the afternoon. Just when I returned one afternoon, I posted myself at the garden entrance-gate from the fore-court, from which door ajar, I could see the street-door. The baker after giving her a kiss, made a poke at her quim outside her clothes, which she returned by knocking a loaf against his trousers just by his tool, and laughing. This I told the cook, who said, "She will let you, if you try, young devilskin, she has seen you and your cods naked." "Seen me naked?" "Both of us have," and then she told me how.

Opposite my bed-room door at the end of the room, was a cheval-glass, between it and the door was my sponging bath, then a big tub. Any one looking through the key-hole could see me naked, when I was in it. I took the bath directly I was up, which was at about the time the servants went down. Many a time have I looked at myself naked in the glass, making my prick stand, to see how I looked in that condition. Both servants had seen me so. They had sometimes arranged the key so as to leave the hole clear. Never had it occurred to me that I should be so looked at, although I had often looked through a key-hole myself, at women. The cook made this clear to me, by standing in the tub and requesting me to look at her through the keyhole.

We arranged that I should bathe the next morning and suddenly open the door. "Pull your cods about well, and I warrant Harriet will look as long as she can," she said. I did so, heard the servants door carefully open, and then frigged my cock, till it was as stiff as a poker. Stepping out of the bath with a towel, as if to dry myself, I opened the door suddenly, and found Harriet just rising from a stooping position. She rushed downstairs but quietly for fear of awaking my mother. For all that I could not make up my mind to try Harriet, but tried to get Brown again. "No thank you, young devilskin," said she "not with that bitch of Harriet about."

Then I had a strange erotic fancy. Randy with abstinence and fearful of Harriet, I took to frigging and spending against a piece of paper pinned against the wall of my room, opposite to the glass, and when standing in the tub.

Autumn was coming. As I could not then get leave of absence, my mother with my sister from school, and little brother, went without me on a visit to my aunt in H--f--shire, leaving an old female relative who was very deaf, to take charge in her absence. Cautioning her especially to make me comfortable, and look sharp after the servants, she said that she could not bear them and would perhaps dismiss them on her return; for she had heard them using foul language to each other. I heard this.

Cook gave me unasked her opinion, that Harriet would let me sleep with her. Instigated by her, I asked Harriet how I looked naked. She did not reply, and went downstairs. I overheard them quarrelling. Afterwards asked her before the cook. She did not know what I meant, she said. I then asked the cook if she had not been looking at me through the key-hole. Cook laughed saying, "He caught you, Harriet once, he caught you." "You are a liar," said Harriet. "Oh! if it comes to that," said cook, "we have both seen you naked a dozen times." There was a row interrupted by my deaf relative coming home. The same afternoon cook whispered to me, "Come to our room when we are both in bed."

That night with candle in my hand and in my nightshirt I crept stealthily into their room; both were awake, Harriet sat up in bed staring at me. When I entered cook asked me what I wanted. I replied, "To see as much of them as they had seen of me," and pulled up my night-gown to my waist. Cook laughed, Harriet said, "Now leave the room." "If you are a fool and make a row," said cook, "we shall be both sent off." Just then we did hear some sort of noise, cook sat up and listened. "It is nothing," said she, and with a grin laid down. I drew off my night-shirt, standing then naked, and Harriet laying down with a modest look; I felt encouraged, extinguished the light, and jumped into bed by the side of Harriet. The bed was so small I was obliged to hold on to her, to prevent myself falling out. She turned round her bum towards me and got close to the cook, which gave me more room; and for a minute we all three lay as close as three herrings in a barrel.

Darkness encourages baudiness. Harriet had tucked her clothes tight round her, but I could feel her bum outside, and there did not seem much of it. I tried to push my fingers between its cheeks, and there was much struggling and quiet complaining on her part, and joking on mine. Harriet appealed to the cook to help her, but she only chaffed and chuckled. At length putting my hand towards the bottom of the bed, I got hold of her night-gown end, gave it a pull, and it came clean up, the next moment my naked body met hers from her heels to her waist. She gave a howl, cook said, "I'll go into young devilskin's room, and leave you to take care of him," got up and went across to my room, and into my bed; and there was Harriet and I in bed alone.

She seemed furious, I felt her over, she was powerless, I dared her to call out, and at last in one of her writhings to escape my fingers, getting on her back; I rolled on to her and pinned her under me with my weight; but her legs were tightly closed, and so for a moment I laid my stiff prick between the shelving of her thighs, the tip just laying buried in the hair of her cunt.

"I can feel your cunt with my prick, I am on it, let me do it," said I, and struggled to force her limbs open with my knees.

"No," said she. Again I asked and got a request to get off. "Not if I lay here all night," said I. I did lay for some minutes, she complaining of my being heavy, and hot; I every minute trying to wriggle my prick between her legs, coaxing and kissing, and begging. "What made you think of coming here with both of us in bed?" said she at length. "Wanting you." "It's funny," said she, "and Mrs. ------ downstairs." "You know," said I, "that unless you bawl she cannot hear." At length I told her that if I did not do it inside, I must do it outside, and began shoving my prick up and down, which made her restless. She asked me if I would tell the cook. "No." Gradually her thighs opened, I slipped down between them, and felt my prick at the portals of her cunt.

The rest was quick enough. I felt my way through a mass of hair to a low-down slit, a hole which seemed tight, and as I guided my tool, fancied for an instant I was again going to have a virgin. I was mistaken, but the entry needed a hard, sharp, and painful push to me, and a comparatively easy passage followed. No sooner did I feel up, than all came to an end, spending copiously I sunk on her, long before the strokes could have told on her sensations, for in a savage voice she said, "Now, get off, I hope you are satisfied, and that beast Brown has got me as she thinks. Now, I suppose you are going."

I rolled off, but let her know I meant to stay. There seemed something odd about her which awakened my curiosity. The knob of my tool seemed to catch as it came out and hurt me, so I began feeling, which I had not done before, nor did she want much solicitation to feel me, and as she did so, it struck me she was not unaccustomed to the feel; but her cunt was a wonder, it was so small and tight on the outside. The feeling had a good effect, and in half-an-hour I got up her again. And what a difference! After a few thrusts she gripped me like a vice, she did not heave, but writhed and wriggled in a way which in my young experience I never had noticed before; she threw her long legs round me and with her equally long arms tried to feel my balls from behind. Then a certain feeling of constriction in her cunt seemed to hurt, but it brought me to the crisis just as with a last wriggle and sigh her limbs relaxed, and she became quiet. I laid for some time in her, but although gradually reducing, my prick did not come out. I attempted to withdraw it, and it seemed sore and as if something caught the knob and kept it back. At length out it came, and we both fell asleep.

Some one pushed me. It was the cook. "Now young devilskin," said she, "be off, or you will be found out." It was broad daylight. She pulled the clothes off us. I was on my back with my privates visible. There lay Harriet on her back also, with everything visible from her knees to her breasts, and I saw for the first time her black cunt-fringe. The cook grined and awakened her. Up she got, off I went to my room, and found my prepuce torn at the top, raw and all but bleeding.

When I saw them the next day Harriet was savage, for the cook was chaffing her. The next night I again turned the cook out and had Harriet. On the third night the cook was restive. "You may do what you like together, I shant take any notice of you," said she, "but I am not going to be turned out of my own bed." When I began to fumble about her, with the view to annoy her into leaving, she struck out right at my ballocks saying, "If you annoy me, I will soon settle you for the night," and it ended in Harriet coming into my bed-room.

I examined every part of her body much against her will, nor did she fail when she warmed under my overhauling to look at me. But a woman is soon satisfied, and when she has squeezed the balls, and looked at the tip, she has done. Some men--and I am one--are insatiable and could look at a cunt without taking their eyes off for a month. So I satisfied myself well, and at times afterwards,-- for she was a peculiar, and an unpleasant woman in every way, one of the out-of-the-way ones not often met with, and one I never want to meet again.

She was quite five feet ten high, her face was sallow and nearly white, her eyes sloe black, but with the look of a dull serpent in them, her mouth large, long, and straight, teeth white and large, and the whole were shown when she laughed, and then she had half the look of a wild beast. Whenever she smiled baudily, her look was still more unpleasant; when thoroughly lewd, her eyes opened on you with a still worse stare; often just before she spent I have seen them, and they startled me.

Her hair was jet black and magnificent, it fell nearly to her waist; her shoulders were broad, but there was scarcely more breast than on a girl of fourteen, and seen sideways she looked more like a man than a woman. Her ribs you could count as she lay; she was very wide across her hips, but she had almost as little flesh on her buttocks, as on her shoulders; her belly was flat, and as she laid down seemed to fall in, and the sides rose to the two projecting hip-bones; in fact she seemed to want filling up all over, and yet she was not like a skeleton.

Her legs were thin, her thighs seemed closer than in other women's. I used to say when fucking her, "Open your thighs." "They are open," she'd reply, "they are the same as other women's." She had a huge conceit of herself, and if I said other women's seem to open more, used to reply, "What do you know about it?"

Her cunt was set in a quantity of longish black hair, strong but not very curly. I didn't much like the look of that. The slit quite hidden by the hair was long and the lips thin; of inner lips she had none, and the first idea as I pulled aside the hair was that the cunt was large; instead of that, low down, and near to her arse-hole was a hole not bigger than that of a girl's of ten years; you saw both holes quite close together. Her cunt was in fact a study. Something seemed to bar the passage; for about an inch further up it seemed smaller. The whole thing seemed out of proportion, yet I could not say how, or where that deformity was, with the experience I then had.

Her arse being so flat, her cunt-hole so low, and her thighs so close, my prick as it entered seemed to bend under in some way and hurt me; my tight prepuce was often torn rudely down, and frequently bled. When I probed her cunt with my finger it never seemed to have the soft buttery feel I had been accustomed to, but to be harsh; so I found it best to wet my prick copiously with spittle when I had her. Then off we used to go; she raising her long legs until her heels were above my buttocks, writhing and wriggling under me and finishing her pleasure with a sort of snort. Then my prick would be up her until quite small, when with pain at the knob, I pulled it out, making a sucking noise as it came away; nor do I think till pulled out, that any spunk left her, such a fit it was at the mouth.

I had much opportunity with her for a few weeks, and she took good care that she would have her fill of me. She took sleeping with me as a matter of course. I used to awaken and find her twiddling it up. If I went up to my room in the middle of the day and Mrs. ------ was out, she came up directly, and I had her, for I felt ashamed to say I did not want it. I am not sure, and at that time did not know much about the thing, and how little a woman really lascivious will stop at, but believe that in the night when I was asleep, she used to suck me up; for I have awakened and found her with her face upon my doodle kissing it. She asked me to kiss her black pussy, and now think she must have wanted me to lick it, but did not then see what she wanted. There was one thing I did with her which I had not done before, and which the flatness of her backside favored doing, fuck her from behind, both laying on our sides, and it became my favourite way. I used to go to sleep after my spend with my prick up her in that fashion; she with her long arm put between her thighs clutching by balls.

I was constantly at her, and more by her randiness than mine. The cook used to grin and say, "Well young devilskin, you seem jolly well knocked up," and made Harriet savage by saying, "Have a little mercy on him." The cook now took no notice of me, she was a coarse beast, would go to the servants' closet leaving the door wide open, and begin to talk with me as I passed; Harriet called her a beast one day for doing so.

I found that the cook after going to her room used to go down again. Harriet would let her out and she stayed out all night, Harriet letting her in in the morning. One night Harriet did the same, saying her mother was ill. I spoke to the cook about it; she said, "Her mother! pugh-- she goes to see the baker." I began to feel very uncomfortable about these tricks in case it came to my mother's ears, and that I knew of them.

The cook asked me to look carefully at Harriet's belly, and explained to me that I should find certain marks of her having had a child, and to tell her (cook) if I did. I could not find them. "I am sure she has had one for all that," said cook. I never told Harriet what I had looked for. The cook one day said, "If you tell Harriet what we have done together I will split on you both and tell your mother. I don't care a dam for the place and am tired of service," so I held my tongue. Harriet always declared she was a virgin until she had me, and that the cook had had two or three children. I did not tell Brown that, for fear of a row between them. Another night that Harriet stopped out, the cook said, "You may come to me if you are frightened to sleep alone." I went. She undressed, pissed and farted; but seeing her fat form, into the bed I got. When I was stiff she said if I would tell all about my doings with Harriet I might poke her as I liked. I told her most that she asked me; but she threw my prick out just as I spent for all that.

Things were now uncomfortable, they quarreled so. One night I asked Harriet who was frigging me up, whether the baker did not do it enough to her. She dropped my tool, rushed across to the cook, said that she had been telling about her, and made such a row, that even my deaf relative was awakened, and came out of her bed-room asking from below if anything was the matter. I was on the landing when I saw the light and hopped across to my own room in a fright. Up came the old lady, the cook came out and said, "Harriet is very unwell Maam, can you give her a little brandy?" I had no fuck that night. The next night she began about the baker. I would answer nothing. She said, "If I have had him it's my affair; at all events it's an insult to a woman whom you never gave the slightest present to yet."

I was struck with that. My allowance was due, and I took her home some article of jewelry. She made me for the ensuing week fuck her till I was as dry as a bone, and my very arse-hole ached the last time I did it,--it was the day before my mother returned. She sat on the side of my bed and frigged me for a quarter of an hour before she got it stiff, saying that I did not seem to like her as I used to.

My mother and sister came back. I never got a poke for a fortnight. When mother returned nothing would get it out of her head, that I had not been out late of night; it never could be got out of her head that it was late at night that did the harm. Not being able to get Harriet now, I waited for her one night as she went to the library. As I got

209

near a wall by our house, I saw a man and a woman standing close up against it together; the man went away directly I approached, and I saw Harriet. "There was a man with you?" said I. "Yes," said she, "it was the baker, whom you have heard such stories about, I am going to marry him." I pulled up her clothes, and to my surprise she resisted, for the first time saying, "I want to piddle," which she did, and then I had her. Her height made an uprighter easy, her quim did not seem to need so much wetting as usual.

A day or two after this event I came home, my deaf relative opened the door. Finding that she was laying the cloth, I asked, "Where is the servant?" My mother said, she had turned both the hussies away, and the people who gave their characters ought to be prosecuted. With heart beating I asked what was the matter. "It's not needful for you to know," she replied, "they are a bad couple." I saw at once I was not implicated, so asked no more, nor did I ever see them again; though about ten years after, I met in the streets a tall gaunt haggard woman who stared at me, and I think it was Harriet.

For some years this episode seemed a funny one, especially the cook's uncunting me just as I began to spend, but of course I know now why she did it, or fancy I do.

Her inciting me to get Harriet also astonished me, but I have since found girls anxious to get others into the same way as themselves. Many I am sure like doing that, and all girls who have been fucked illicitly like other girls to do the same.

Harriet was a lewd bitch. I never liked her, and her cunt always gave me pain as well as pleasure, but she was at hand, and so I got into her of course. I can't even now make out what was the matter with her cunt; for though she would let me look at it at times, she always hindered a quiet inspection, besides I could not at that time of life look at a cunt for a minute without my cock standing. Then I rushed it up the machine and had done for a time. I had seen one virginity, but that was but for a minute, for I pricked it directly. All I recollect afterwards was that it did not look as open as other cunts, I could not describe it. I did not care about virginities and never thought about them. I liked best a good, large, fat-lipped, hairy hole into which my prick glided easily. When Harriet said I took her virginity, somehow I felt sure she was lying, but had it been true I should not have noticed it, as far as my pleasure was concerned.

CHAPTER XI.

Charwoman and daughter.--At a key-hole.--Cutting corns.--A
shower and a barn.--A fat rumped Devonian.--Suggestive
pictures.--A bum-hole offered.--Erotic madness.--Remorse.

We could not get servants for some time. A middle-aged charwoman came to assist, and one of her daughters came from time to time, stopping generally the night. Their cottage was not far off, I had seen the girl from an infant, she was then about eighteen years old. I had often smiled when I met her, of course I smiled now. She was quite a slim little girl, there was nothing of her, but I was at an age when anything having a cunt attracted me.

Profiting by experience, I now used key-holes; fortune favored me, for some reason instead of one large bed, two small ones were put into the servant's room; between them a wash-stand and a chair on each side of it were nearly opposite the key-hole. How I chuckled at this, for unless the key-hole was covered, I could see nearly all one bed and both chairs and wash-stand. I saw the old woman wash and use the pot, put on her stockings and other things, the other bed was a little out of range. I could not so often see the girl, but did at times.

One evening the girl only stopped. So soon as I heard mother's door closed, out I went in my nightshirt, and through the key-hole saw the girl naked. She put the light on the floor, one leg on the chair, and with a small hand-glass looked at her quim, her bum was towards me. Not satisfied she turned round, sat down facing me, putting the candle on the floor and with legs so wide open as she could went on with her investigation. I had a reasonably good look at her, and her cunt. As said; she was nothing to look at, but I got in a fearfully excited state and made some noise at the door which alarmed her, for up she got and stood still listening. I went to my room, looking through the half-closed door, hers opened and out came her head. I nodded and back she went.

The next day she was going home, and as I now (although having rows with mother about it) went out when I liked, just before she left I went out and walked. It was dark. In two or three minutes out she came. After walking by her side for a time I asked her point blank how she liked the look of it last night. "What do you mean?" I told her all I had done. "Oh!" she said with intense surprise, "what a mean thing to do." I told her how one of our former servants used to look at me naked. After a minute she did not appear to be at all disconcerted at having been seen naked; from my description she could have had no doubt what ever that I had seen all. "What did you look at your quim for?" asked I. "Ah! that's my business; what did you look at me for?" "To see your cunt." Being at a dark part of the road I began kissing her, and got my fingers on to her belly. She made no row, but crossed her legs; and small and seemingly weak as she was, succeeded in preventing me feeling. I was out with her an hour, kissing, coaxing, attempting; I got my fingers and hand over her bum and belly, but not on to her slit. At each failure she laughed and said, "done again." I swore I would some day. "No you won't, you're not the first that has tried," said she, and I went home without having felt her quim properly.

I attempted it the next day and at every opportunity in the house and out of it, till new servants came. She felt my prick, would look at it, squeeze the balls, talk about fucking and baudiness to any extent, tell me what she had seen, and what she had heard about such matters. She at length scarcely resisted my feeling her bum, belly and legs, yet I never got my finger on to her slit, so as to feel the moisture; for she closed her little legs and wriggled, or got away from me somehow. Once or twice when I got a little rough, she set up a squeal, and I desisted. I offered her money. She replied, "No thank you, I am not going to spoil my chance that way." Our conversation used to begin by my saying, "How is your duff?" "Oh! nicely, thank you; how is your jock?" "All right and stiff, waiting for your duff." "Then it will wait a long time," and so on. It always ending in my trying to feel her, and getting no further. At length they left, new servants coming.

I frequently saw her afterwards, and always began the same game. My mother was told I had been seen talking to her, so after that I only spoke to her at dusk. Some time afterwards she married a gardener, and I occasionally saw her, but recognition came to a knowing nod and smile, which she always returned. Meanwhile I had got my fortune, as I shall tell; had no end of women, and had forgotten her, when walking across a field not far from our house, I overtook a short woman with a little child, and it was she. A shower came on, and we went into a barn, no one was in it. She told me I was said to be a "dreadful chap after the gals." "You know all about that now," said I. "Yes," she replied with a grin, and gradually talking baudier, we went on, until in a few minutes I had laid her down and fucked her on the hay. "I told you I would do it," said I. "But you didn't when you said you would,--now it won't matter." That was her notion. The rain continuing, she said she must go, whether wet or dry. Neither of us had an umbrella. She pulled her gown over her head, and saying, "You won't tell anyone, will you," took the child by the hand and was going, when my appetite came again. I pulled her back, and with little persuasion, again went up her. She enjoyed the fuck greatly. As I lay on the top of her we heard a bang, and the barn grew dark; a man was shutting the door. "Ulloh!" said he, "I didn't know any one was there; I hope I ain't disturbed you." We made no reply, but out we went. "You will have a boy out of this," said I. "I hope I shall," said she. That was the end of my adventure, for I never had her again, and she soon left the neighborhood. It was her own little child that was with her.

Though I have (as I shall in other cases) told all I had to do with her consecutively, yet between the time when she was in our house, and the time of meeting her at the barn, three or four years must have elapsed; and didn't we talk baudy in the barn before I got into her. That may have warmed her up, yet I believe she wanted me, as soon as she found herself alone with me. Her little child witnessed the business.

Just at this time or a little later, an adventure of a serious kind occurred to me.

The streets leading out of the Waterloo road were then occupied much by gay women. Some were absolutely full of them; they were mostly of a class to be had for a few shillings if they could not get more (my Granby street adventure has been already told), but many a swell I have noticed lingering about there. My mother now took nearly all my money for my board, but with the little remaining, I had a knock off occasionally. It was one of my pleasures to walk up those streets when dark and talk with the women at the windows, which were always open whatever the weather, unless some one as within engaged with the ladies.

Each woman had generally but one room, but two or three used to sit together in the front room in their chemises. There was the bed, wash-stand, chamberpot and all complete. Perhaps one lolled out of the window, showing her breasts, and if you gave such a one a shilling, she would stoop so that you could see right down past her belly to her knees, and have a glimpse of her cunt-fringe. Sometimes one would pull up her garter, or another sit down and piddle, or pretend to do so, or have recourse to other exciting devices when men peeped in.

I used to look in and long. Sometimes had a shilling peep, and then bashfully asked for a feel of the cunt for it. I so often succeeded, that ever since then I wanted that amusement, have offered a shilling for a feel, and met with but few refusals in any part of London. Sometimes it ended in a fuck. Once or twice to my astonishment they took mere trifles, and as I think of it, there is wonderfully little difference between the woman you have for five shillings, and the one you pay five pounds, excepting in the silk, linen, and manners.

One night I saw a woman with very fat breasts looking out of the window (I was then fond of stout women); and after talking a minute, asked her if she would let me feel her cunt for a shilling. "Yes," said she. In I went, down she shut the window, and in another minute I was groping her. She did not let me feel her long. I had not felt such a bum since Mary's (already told of), and it so wetted my appetite, that I struck a bargain for a fuck. She was soon stripped, and all I now recollect about her is, that her cunt was large and covered with hair of a brownish colour; that her eyes were dark; and that she seemed full twenty-five years of age. I fucked her on a sofa.

When I had buttoned up she produced a book full of baudy pictures of which I then had seen but few; and I went a second time to see the book, rather than her. Looking over it, she pointed out to me with a laugh, several pictures of men putting their pricks into women's arse-holes, and into the rumps of other men. Having never before seen such pictures, and having no idea of the operation, I felt modest, and turned to others; but she so regularly as we turned over the leaves pointed out this class, that my sense of shame gave way to curiosity; and not believing, asked if it was possible to do it so. "Lord yes," said she. "Does it not hurt?" said I. "Not if properly done," she replied, and went on to say it was delicious some men thought; and she talked altogether in a very knowing way about it; told me how it was best to grease the hole first, then the prick, and to shove gently, and went on so, that I said on a sudden, "Why, you have done it, I think." "Yes, but only with a particular friend of mine who is very fond of it,--and so am I; it is better than the other."

I felt shocked, bewildered, and excited. The subject dropped, but she sat feeling me, slipping her finger under my balls, and pressing my arse-hole with her finger. I prepared to fuck. She suggested she should kneel with her buttocks towards me, so that she could feel my balls when my prick was up her. I assented, and her bum-cheeks were presented to me. Excited by her conversation and her hints, I looked curiously at her large slit, and then at her bum-hole; I touched the latter, and she drove her bum back upon my finger with a laugh. I did not take her hint, but drove my prick into her quim and pushed in the regular fashion. Thinking of the pictures excited me and without knowing what I said, I suddenly pulled it out saying, "Let me put it into the other." "Not tonight," said she, "put your thumb a little way in, your nail is quite short" (she had noticed that I used to bite my thumbnails short). I instantly did, the next moment spent, and dropped over her back, waiting for the last drop of sperm to run off into her.

Her hints, her pictures, of which she had actually scores, stirred my curiosity, her manner disgusted me, yet my brain seemed affected. Is it possible, thought I, that a man's prick can go in there?--impossible. And yet she says she has had it done to her, and my thumb went in easily enough. The more I thought, and the more I reflected how a hard turd hurt me sometimes in passing it, the more I was puzzled about the intense pleasure which she said the operation gave! To solve my doubts (although I had determined not), I went to her again, and saw the pictures. She again talked about them, until scarcely knowing what I was doing, "Will you let me?" I asked. "Don't talk loud," said she, "it will never do to let any one know what we are at." Our voices dropped to a whisper, whilst by her advice I pulled off trousers and drawers, and she stripped stark naked.

Then she carefully greased my prick with pomatum, and put some on her arse-hole; it was the work of a minute, not a word was said. She then stark naked, sat by the side of me on the sofa, began fondling and kissing me, took my hand in hers and rubbed my fingers on her clitoris, half frigged herself with my fingers, I let her do what she liked. Then she turned round. "Put it in," she said when her rump was towards me, "then give me your hand, and don't push till I tell you." Her arse-hole was at the level of my prick as I stood by the side of the sofa, my machine was like a rod of iron, my brains seemed on fire, I felt I was going to do something wrong, dreaded it, yet determined to do it. "Put it in, slowly," said she in a whisper. The hole opened, felt tight, but to my astonishment almost directly my whole prick was hidden in it without pain to me or any difficulty. "Give me your hand." I did. Again she began frigging herself with my fingers. "Rub, rub, push gently," she said, and I tried, but was getting past myself. "Now," said she with a spasmodic sort of half cry, half grunt. I felt my prick squeezed as in a vice, I shoved or rather scarcely began to do so when I discharged a week's reserve up her rectum. My brain whirled with excitement, whilst she leaning over the pillows on the sofa, kept breathing hard and half snorting like a pig, still frigging herself with my fingers.

As my sense returned, I could scarcely believe where my prick was, excitement still kept it stiff, but desire had left me. I pulled it out with an indescribable horror of myself.

"Wasn't it delicious?" said she. "I like it, don't you? You may always do it so." What I replied I know not; I washed, dressed and got out of the house as soon as I could. When in the street, I was sick. I ran off fearing some one would see me, got into a Hackney-coach and drove in the wrong direction; then got out and went a round-about way home, fearing some one was following to upbraid or expose me. I scarcely slept that night for horror of myself, never went up the street again for years, and never passed its end without shuddering, have no recollection of having had pleasure, or of any sensation whatever; all was dread to me. And so ended that debauch; one I was deliberately let into by that woman, having never thought of such doings before as possible, or at all, as far as I can recollect.

CHAPTER XII.

Sarah and Susan.--At the key-hole.--A village fair.--Up against a wall.--An unknown woman.--Clapped again.--My deaf relative.--Some weeks felicity.--Sarah's secret.--Susan's history.--Sarah with child.--Amidst black-berries.--Susan's virginity.--Susan with child.--Sisters' disclosures.--A row.--A child born.--Emigration.

I had now passed my twentieth year. The new servants were sisters (how many times have sisters fallen to me!); the eldest who was cook was named Sarah; the youngest, Susan. Sarah was about twenty-six, Susan nineteen or twenty. I carefully arranged the key in the key-hole of their door the first night, but saw nothing for two or three nights. Then oh! fortune again. They rose later than my mother liked; she came up to their room one morning and found them locked in, so she took away the key. Now I had as far as the key-hole permitted, a fair field, but then clothes hanging upon pegs on the door were often in my way; yet I was so persistent in looking when they went to bed, and arose, that I saw a great deal. How cunning I had got; I had filed and oiled the lock and hinges of my door and theirs, so that I could close and open them noiselessly, used to stoop daily with my eye to their key-hole, stepping from my room with naked feet. I was nearly caught several times, but never quite. It now seems wonderful that I was not.

I was so demure and quiet in talk about women always, and had kept myself so circumspectly, that my mother never had the least suspicion of me,--but in all matters of love and intrigue, mother always seemed to me as innocent as the babe unborn.

For all that, my mother just then, and to my dismay, seeing that my little games would be much interfered with, said I better change my room, and have one on the first floor. Mrs. ------ had remarked, that being a man now I ought not to sleep on the servants' floor. "As you please,-- it's one flight of stairs less for me, but Mrs. ------ is a fool," I cried. "And which room?" "Your sister's. Annie will always be with her aunt adopted, and Jane is only at home in the holidays." But I would not be pushed into a small room; where was my tub to stand? Where my books? I must have the spare room. There was much altercation, I made my mother cry by saying that when of age I would get chambers away from her, and into the spare room I moved.

It was next to my mother's. Installed there I did nothing but complain of its inconvenience. I smoked incessantly in it. The smell got into mother's bedroom, and she could not bear tobacco smoke. I made a noise when she was in bed,--that annoyed her. I did all in a quiet way to make her as uncomfortable as possible. An uncle and aunt who stopped with us when in town, just then came from the country; and not liking my sister's room, went to an hotel, which wounded mother considerably, so she said I had better go upstairs again. I refused point blank; being down there I would remain, and so managed, that she thought I went back as a favour to her, and much against my will; but was I not glad!--and got to my spying immediately.

Within a month I had seen them both stark naked, for being sisters they had not hesitated to strip. I had seen the cook piddle, wash her cunt, and put on her napkin. Susan's bed was not on the right side for me, but nevertheless I saw enough of her to compare her with her sister. Sarah was demure in manner, stout, with a splendid bum, and with little hair of a lightish brown at the bottom of her belly; she wore black stockings of which I then had a horror. Susan had a wicked, merry face, and a splendid bunch of dark hair on her motte which attracted me largely. It struck me that I should have a better chance with her than with her sister, and began making approaches; when one Saturday night seeing Sarah wash herself from head to foot, I got such glimpses of her round fine haunches, and the split between them, that I fell into a fit of randy adoration, which settled the direction of my attentions to her instead of Susan.

I feared to go on with either, because they were sisters, but lust got the better of my fears. I began kissing cook Sarah; who returned it saying, she would not have her sister know it on any account. Shortly after I kissed Susan, who made nearly the same remark; and I found that each was careful not to tell the other; which was just what had occurred with two sisters, of whom I have already written. This was very jolly. Meanwhile I once or twice had a cheap poke on the road, but always with fear of disease.

I had but little chance of the cook having now no pretext for going into the kitchen, and the sisters were not much separated; but I looked up my chances indefatigably, and finding Sunday favourable, to the horror of my mother, left off going to church in the morning because the cook was then alone. After our early Sunday dinner, I used to go to my bed-room nominally to lay down, but really to look through the key-hole at the cook who on that day only, dressed and washed herself in the middle of the day, her sister being downstairs. I got on but slowly; in two months only having taken outside liberties; till meeting Susan coming away from the privy one day, I saw her press her clothes against her belly to dry her cunt, and she saw me. Whenever I met her afterwards I used to tuck my frock-coat between my legs and smile at her. It was an old dodge.

I had then bought a Fanny Hill which I kept in my bed-room locked up. One morning I forgot to put it by, thought of it and rushed upstairs, entered the room where the servants had been making the bed, and saw Sarah intently looking at the book. I had feared that my mother had entered my room, and seen the book. I stood for an instant motionless, she turned round, gave a cry, dropped the book, and rushed out of the room, her face like blood. I locked the book up feeling somewhat uneasy, but afterwards joked her about it and the smutty pictures, and this took effect.

There was a fair held not far from us at that time, the girls were to go there each on separate evenings. Before Sarah went out, I went out, she had agreed to meet me at the fair; it was dusk, she had a female friend with her. We went into a dancing booth and had drink, then into the long room of stalls in which was a dance mob, shouting, crying, pushing each other, scratching backs, blowing trumpets, and speaking baudily to the women. As it got later, the men used to feel outside the women's cunts, and many a so-called modest girl felt a man's prick outside, and passing in the mob without being found out. Many a grab have I had at my prick which could only have been done by a woman, who looked quite demure whilst she did it. I got excited, put Sarah in front of me, and in the first rush, put my hand round and gave her cunt outside her clothes a grab. She upbraided me, rushing out of the crowd at the side to escape me, I after her, into a dark passage, between the backs of the booths, where men were pissing. They hailed her with laughter, asking her if she had come to piddle. Back into the crowd she rushed, I with her, and did the same thing, talking baudily, and kept this up until it was time for her to go home.

I said I should walk home with her. The village-road had but occasional oil-lamps; at places it was quite dark, loving couples were walking or turning off into dark bye-places by hedges and fences to satisfy their amatory wants. This I pointed out to her, and talked of the prints she had seen in Fanny Hill that morning. Altogether she had gone through enough that day and night to make a female randy. Suddenly a girl in the dark squealed, and a masculine voice in the dark shouted up, "That's right, shove your prick well up her, old boy." I tried it on with Sarah on the way home, but it was no go. I felt her bum and thighs, got her hand on to my prick, but she would not let me have her.

Next night I was at the fair, and met her sister Susan there by chance. I got excited and tried the same dodge with her, she had also a female friend with her. I pressed their bellies and pinched their bums when in the crowd; her friend went off with her young man, then I had Susan alone and tried pushing my hand against her belly, more than ever; she took no notice. Her friend and we then met again face to face in the mob. I had an impression that a feel at my balls must have come from her friend. We all went to a public-house and had drink; there suddenly she bid me good-bye, saying it was late, and she must get home, set off running and was out of sight in a minute.

I had no intention of going home, but after thinking an instant ran after her, saw a woman squatting who got up as I neared her; it was she. "You have been piddling," said I. There was some joking on this. The same sort of couples were to be seen cuddling about as on the previous night; the same whispering, squealing ad scuffling a little way off in the dark lanes. She was more frisky than her sister, and more talkative. "Ain't they larking!" said she as a girl gave a half giggle, half cry in the dark. Said I, "They are fucking." She stood stock still for a minute, and then walked on quietly without saying another word. I had not before said a baudy word to her.

Having got the word fuck out, I was game for anything, rattled on baudily; at last after a long silence, something I said made her laugh. I began kissing her, at length she returned it, and next instant I thrust her up against a wall, pushed my hand up her clothes, and my fingers on to her slit, which was as wet as a slop-pail. She cried, "Oh! you vagabond," got my hand away, took to her Heels, and ran off. I after her, till we both stopped breathless.

I tried again, her resistance grew feebler, she was silent, I had her against a wall, one hand holding her cunt, with the other I was guiding my prick to it, it was sliding in, in an instant it would have been up her, when putting down both hands she pushed it away saying, "Oh! gracious God, what am I about again," ran off, and never stopped until she had rang our house-bell.

I went back to the fair and later on met outside it a very short girl, who seemed too respectable to be by herself and had her veil down. I spoke with her, found she was going my way, and walked with her. She knew my name, and where I lived. Two nights scrambling had not got me a poke, that I suppose made me bold enough to make advances to this modest, quiet girl; I stole a kiss, then another, then a hug, then a feel, and finally with scarcely any hindrance fucked her. We walked and talked when it was over, she would not tell me her name or address, nor give me a glimpse of her face; I fucked her again up against our own garden-wall, insisted on knowing where she lived, said I would walk till I saw, and did walk with her for about an hour. She said, "If you walk about all night you shall never know where I live, but you may do it again if you like, or I will meet you to-morrow, but I dare not let you see where I go." I feared I could not poke again, so stopped to piss. She modestly walked on a little; I frigged my prick until the steam was up, then in her well moistened cunt consummated, and parted, promising to meet her the next night.

I looked at Sarah and Susan the next morning, took opportunity of reminding each of them that I had felt their cunts, bragged to each, that a young lady who lived close by had let me do it to her. The next night came, the unknown girl did not keep her appointment, and the following morning found I had the clap. I never saw or heard of her again, nor know who the young lady who gave it to me. She was not a common domestic, I am sure.

This stopped me for a month, but the time was not all lost, for I indulged in baudy talk, and familiarized both servants with it, and the fact that they had felt me, and I them. The eldest used to look uncomfortable, Susan used to brazen it out with a bright roguish eye, that I then almost turned to her, especially as Sarah still wore black stockings; but then Sarah had such fat white thighs, and a larger bum.

When better and I was again alone with Sarah on a Sunday morning, I got her on to a chair, pulled up her clothes all round, exposed her legs, showed her my prick, showed her the pictures in Fanny Hill, got her excited, but did nothing more. Another Sunday I tried it on unsuccessfully. The third Sunday going upstairs just after mother and Tom had gone to church, she said she was not going to be worried with me, and Susan would be at home. Susan had not I found gone to church as usual. Baulked, I was going out, but catching her in the hall, tried to pull up her clothes. She cried, "For God's sake don't, I would not let Susan hear for the world." This confirmed me in what I had felt nearly certain of; the sisters did not tell each other of my games. I heard Susan say to her sister who had gone to the top of the house, "I shan't lose my outing, there is nothing the matter with you," and out she went. The next minute down came Sarah; I stopped her on the landing, by my mother's room.

"Now don't," she began in a coaxing way, but I had not spent for weeks, and as I looked into her bright eyes and flushed face, meant that day to do so if I could. She must herself have wanted it, there was such a soft look about her. My reply was to try to pull up her clothes. We struggled, pushed against the door of mother's bed-room, and we staggered into the room together. Nothing could have been more favourable. I got her up against the bed, her clothes up, my prick against her belly, and there for a minute we struggled.

Opposite my mother's was a small low sort of bedstead called a child's, I don't know why. It was covered with a large skin on a mattress. Mother used it as a sofa. My prick was actually up against Sarah's belly, my balls nestling in the hair of her cunt, my hands tightly round her bum, but her legs were so close together, that I could not get into her; I put one hand down to open the road to her cunt, but could not manage it, though her resistance was growing less. She ceased praying me to leave off, but tried by putting her hands down, to dislodge me from her belly, withdrawing her hands as they touched my prick. The blinds were down, no one but us in the house, I saw the child's bed, pulled her towards it, I going backwards. We fell on it together, she more than half on the top of me; another struggle, and her petticoats were flung up as I rolled her round on to her back. She tried to pull them down, bringing her knees half up to meet them; I saw her buttocks beneath and recklessly pushing with my hand, a finger went half-way up her cunt. Down went her legs quite straight, the next instant I was on the top of her.

I weighted her down, she lay panting. "Now do Sarah dear, be quiet." She said not a word, nor looked at me. I pressed my knees, and with difficulty opened her thighs, and we were belly to belly; with one or two vigourous shoves, in went my prick without difficulty and spending as it entered. So did abstinence, desire, and excitement tell on me. It has often behaved in the same way.

I was now at a time of life when I could do more fucking, and after long abstinence if I liked a woman, could sometimes do it twice before withdrawing. The first words she uttered were, "Oh! let me go downstairs, the dinner will be spoiled." But what did that matter to a man whose prick was stiff up a cunt! So I waited my second enjoyment; and if I know anything about the matter, you my dear Sarah, brought your liquor out to mix with mine.

Scarcely was my prick out of her, before the street bell rang; downstairs she ran, I went upstairs. I recollect how wet my hair and my balls were as I ran, wrapping them up. It was her sister. Directly afterwards home came mother. Dinner was served, what a row there was, the meat was not done, the vegetables smashed. "It is disgraceful," said mother, "has she been upstairs Walter?" How queer I felt at that question, and wonder my confusion was not noticed. I said I did not know. "I will be bound she has,"

227

said mother, "and been trying on her finery before going out to-night, Sundays and dress are the ruin of servants now-a-days." "I have been out," said I to mother. "You would have done yourself more good had you been to church," said she.

After dinner mother went up to her bed-room as was her custom, to doze on the small bed; the next minute her bell rang violently. "Send up Sarah," said she angrily to Susan, and up she went, I went into the hall listening in a funk. "Why don't you keep my bed-room door closed?" said she, "as I tell you." "I am almost sure it was closed when I went out." "Have you been in here?" "No m'am," stammered the poor woman, "the nasty cat has been up here on this bed (luckily the cat had done that once before), and been scratching up the skins." "You must have opened the door,--and oh! the beast has made some mess upon it." Mother told Sarah to wipe up the place, it was only marks of what Sarah's overflowing cunt and my prick had dropped in our hurry. A little more blowing up, and mothers' anger was over. Sarah came down, looking more dead than alive, when I saw her in the hall.

In the evening Sarah went out, and I to church,--so mother thought,--but in reality to meet Sarah. For an hour we walked about, then as it grew dark began kissing. What a difference the morning had made. No resistance now, my hand roved over the smooth bum and belly, a slight objection on the part of the thighs as my hand touched the hairy covering, but for an instant only, then as of a right the fingers felt the moist lapels, which were soon opened by my prick, as I fucked her up against the wall of the garden, at the very spot where some weeks previously I had fucked the unknown lady, and caught the clap.

Good and bad luck come in heaps. I was now in for the good. Next Sunday and others afterwards, we had a nice half-hour on her bed, or my bed, or on the sofa in the parlour; but we left no signs of the cat anywhere.

My mother then went on a long visit to my aunt in H--tf--dshire, wanted me to go, but I could not get away, so she took my sister from my aunt's and Tom, and to my delight took Susan. Sarah was left as servant, the deaf female relative came again to take charge of the house, and we three were alone in it. My mother's last words were, "Give as little trouble as you can, and I hope Walter, you will keep out of bad society, and not be out late." I was mostly to dine with my guardian's executor, an old family friend.

That night and for several weeks, Sarah and I slept together, it was a honey-moon. My old relative, deaf and timid, used to lock her door; I used to go across to Sarah's and lock it, mother having put back the key. We had fear of being found out, but not much. In those weeks we gave way so to our passions, that we were worn out. I taught her all I knew; she was willing, docile, and did all I told her: love's amusements in every variety which I then knew of did we try; never had I had such continuous fucking. The first thing mother on her return noticed, was that I was pale, and then great was her astonishment when told by my old deaf relative, that I had scarcely been out one night after seven o'clock, and up early most days; so my mother put it down to close attention to my studies, for I was preparing.

I told Sarah in confidence I had had a virgin, and that there had been difficulty with her, but none in getting into Sarah. She swore by all that was solemn that she never had had a man, that although she had been kissed and tried, no man had put his hands on her naked thighs until I had. From what she had heard of girl's virginities, she thought she must have been different from them; she could always easily put a finger up her cunt, and I believed her. She spent the second time I did it to her.

Talking excitedly about her virginity and her not having bled when first pierced, she remarked, "Susan told me that when she--" Then she stopped and turned the conversation, but my curiosity was whetted. I pressed her to tell more, she got confused, said it was her cousin Susan, would not go on to say what Susan had said, at last refused to say more. I did not forget it, and one night as I lay kissing her and fingering her clitoris, she told me under promise of the greatest secrecy, that her sister Susan bled when her young man first put it up her, and with this, that Susan had been seduced and had a child; so her father had sent her to service in London, and the better to get her taken care of, had arranged that her sister Sarah should always take service in the same house with her; hence at my mothers. "And, oh!" she concluded, "if Susan or father should ever know what I have done, I should die." The family trusted her.

This accounted for the somewhat forward manner of Susan, for her exclamation when I got up against her belly on the night of the fair, "Gracious God, what am I about again!" Sarah believed Susan could have had no one else but her first sweetheart, and that was more than a year before. All this set me thinking, and more than once when twiddling Sarah's cunt, I thought of Susan's with the thicker and darker hair, and wondered in what other respects it differed from that of her sister.

Now came trouble. Sarah said she was two months gone with child; she had kept it to herself hoping her courses might come on. She got with child she thought the first day I fucked her. We were both in great anxiety, but did nothing to help it. Sunday morning usually passed this way. Directly they had all gone to church, up came Sarah to mother's room or into the garden parlour, there I looked at her belly to see if it was bigger, then she had a crying fit, then we fucked, then she went down to see after the meat roasting, then generally we had another fuck, and all was over for that day; for my prick usually came out of her not long before Susan rang the bell to be let in.

At length her state began to show, her mother just then was very ill and wrote to her, she made this an excuse for asking to go home, intending to try when there to get rid of her encumbrance. My mother with great objection let her go, for she liked her. For one or two weeks before she left someone or other had stopped at home on Sundays, so I was balked in getting at her, and only did it once to her in nearly a month. I gave her what money I could to help her; a charwoman came to work in her absence; it was arranged that her sister should do most of her work as well as her own, as far as she could.

My mind reverted to what Sarah had told me about her sister. Would she not like a doodle up her again, how she must long for a man I used to think. She nearly let me coming from the fair, what if I tried again. Then I thought how wrong it was, seeing what I had done to her sister. But back again the desire came, I grew randier. "I won't try her on account of her sister," thought I, "but there will be no harm in larking with her."

So I began and reminded her of the night of the fair, told her I knew that the hair of her motte was dark, by degrees got her to kiss me, to leave off chaffing her, felt her outside, but went no further. About the fourth day after her sister had left, I got my hands on her thigh. On Sunday when all were at church: to blind my mother I had gone out, but went home directly, and into the kitchen to resume my baudy chaff, I forgot all about her sister, got to kissing and trying to feel her. I was long in the kitchen with my prick out, sometimes hanging, sometimes standing stiff, trying to induce her to let me, but it was of no use. Her cap was off, her hair dishevelled. I had got her clothes once up to her hips, had seen her motte, felt it, got my prick up against it, knocked it about all over her belly, but no more; time was short, and at last with a sort of guilty fear I went out before church was over, and came back in time for our early dinner, telling my mother I had been to ------ church. Then I reflected and thought it was as well I had not done it to Susan.

When mother returned she left my sister and little brother in the country. My old deaf relative remained with us and slept in the room adjoining my mother's. That same Sunday night, I waited until Susan came up to bed, pounced upon her on the top landing and tried to feel her; she dropped her candle-stick and made such a noise, that back I sneaked to bed, and was asleep, when I heard the bell ringing violently in the servants' room. Out I rushed saw Susan on the landing with but a petticoat over her night-dress, and old Mrs. ------ going into my mother's room who was taken very ill.

Down to the kitchen went Susan and I to get boiling water, I heaped wood and coals on the fire, she blew it with the bellows, old Mrs. ------ was upstairs getting brandy and other things ready. What followed I recollect as well as if it were yesterday. Susan was half squatting, half kneeling and blowing the fire furiously. Standing by her my randiness came on, I pulled out my prick, and pushed it right in her face. "For shame!" said she, "I will hit you with the bellows, think of your mother." It did shame me for a moment, I hid my prick, and knelt by her side stirring the blazing wood. But just then I saw her breasts through the half-tied night-gown; it was too much for me; that and the attitude she was in together; losing all prudence, I pushed one hand on to her breast, and the other up her clothes, between her legs,--which were very conveniently opened quite wide,--and on the slit of her cunt. With a suppressed cry she dropped the bellows, attempted to rise, and repulse my hand, and in doing so we both rolled backwards (for I had stooped) on to the floor among the black-beetles of which there were dozens about. "You wretch," she cried in a suppressed voice, "oh! don't,--and your poor mother so ill,--oh! don't,--you shant!--and wanting hot water,--you shant!" in a still louder tone as I got my hand full on her cunt. "Oh! my God, here is Mrs. ------."

Had Mrs. ------ not been as deaf as a post, she must have heard our scuffling, as she neared the kitchen. In an hour or so my mother was better, and Mrs. ------ stopped in the room with her for the night. My mother was asleep when I left, Mrs. ------ had had a good dose of brandy and water, and I knew she would sleep well enough. I went to my room excited by the continual trying it on with Susan; Mrs. ------ had given her a glass of brandy and water, "to keep the cold out," as she said, and she went to her room. I listened, heard her moving about longer than I expected. I had come up some minutes before to deceive all, and was shivering in my night-shirt. I thought how unfair it was to her sister who was in the family way by me, of the risk I ran with my mother in the house; but a standing prick stifles all conscience. I crossed the landing, opened her door, shut it rapidly, and there I was in the room with her, both of us in our night-dresses. She was doing up her hair as I entered, she wore a night-cap.

"I won't let you come in here." "Hush! mother will hear you," said I. Her voice dropped to a whining, "Pray go, I shall lose my character, if any one supposes anything of this; it's very hard on me." Such was my state, that I believe if my mother had come in just then, I should have tried Susan. My reply was to strip my night-gown right off and stand naked; then I caught her in my arms and forced her into a sitting posture on the bed-side, sitting myself down beside her. "Let me do it,--let us fuck, I have felt your cunt,--seen it;--look at my prick,--let me put it in,--let me do it,--you did nearly once,--let me now." "For God's sake go." "I won't." "Oh! don't,--oh I go,--if Misses should hear us, what will become of me." "Don't make a noise then, or she will." "Well go, there is a dear,--not now,-- perhaps some other day I will." She was defenceless, I hitched up her nightgown, saw a pair of nice white thighs. "You shant,--you shant," she cried in a louder tone, pushing down her night-gown. I gave it a violent tug, and pulled it up to her belly, saw thighs, navel, and dark brown hair between her thighs, that I had looked at in glimpses through the key-hole. There was my thigh close to hers, my stiff prick within a few inches of her cunt; considering all she had gone through that day with me, it was a position which would have upset the frigidity of an angel, had she not frigged away some of her passion in the interim.

But her passions were conquering on my behalf, for she was a woman who had known love's pleasures; her voice was quiet as she said, "Oh! pray don't, oh I pray now." I pulled her back and slid my naked limbs between her thighs, then in a moment I was on her, but in an uncomfortable position; two of our legs on the bed, two off, my belly touched hers and pressed her down; with my right hand I guided my prick to her slit. Her hour had come, "Oh! for God's sake, leave me, I will let you another day,--I will,--not now,--oh! if you knew!--oh! now!--oh!..."

It was all but over, my fingers were feeling their way, my prick between them, every motion she made to help herself, helped me; I held her down with force until I felt my penis was on the notch, but as it touched the slippery sides of the red orifice, the first pang of pleasure came and my sperm spat on to it. With a furious thrust I plunged up her and threw my whole body over her, grasping her bum, quivering, wriggling, and pushing. The deed was done, she knew it, and was as quiet as the grave.

The position was painful to both of us, I felt it in both my legs; she moved uneasily saying, "I hope you will go." I had no such intention, kept her down, and my prick in her as long as I could; then got up quickly, hoping to see her spunk-trap whilst her thighs were open. A woman seems always up to this, how quickly they shut them. She did, but the light though feeble was close by, and I saw sperm outside; then she sat at the side of the bed with her limbs uncovered, I stood naked with doodle wet, flabby and shrunken, not a pretty picture at all. She begged me to go, was tranquil, sat twisting up her hair, scarcely made attempt to hide her limbs, all her anxiety was about her mistress finding me in her room; but after a few minutes altercation, I was in bed with her cuddling, and promising to leave directly I had fucked again.

I got into bed without my night-gown, hers was rolled up so that she was all but naked, our naked bodies touched at all points, my hands were free to rove everywhere. How she must have wanted it, only a woman with twelve months abstinence from cock can tell; and when after feeling her cunt well, and putting her unresisting hands round my pego, I pushed her on to her back; there was no difficulty about her thighs, they opened at once as I turned on to her, her frame thrilled, her tongue sought mine, her hand clutched my naked back; she spent I verily believe before I had began, and finished again with me a few minutes afterwards. About day-break neither of us having closed our eyes, I went back to my room, tired out.

My mother kept her bed the next day, so Susan and I had time to talk. "I don't know what to do," said she, "we have made the sheet in such a dreadful mess"; and that night before she went to bed, she took it down and did something to it. I fucked her that day on the kitchen table.

Her sister did not return for a fortnight, and during that time we had plenty of fucking; a few nights after I first had her, she was excessively quiet; on questioning her she said, "I think I got in the family way last night." "Nonsense," but she told me she had heard that women sometimes had a sort of consciousness of getting with child, and added, "I somehow feel certain that I shall have a child from last Sunday." This will be a pretty go, thought I, and asked, "Did you ever have your belly up before, for I don't think you were a virgin when I had you." She denied it, and there the matter ended, but I never could get to see the lower part of her belly; she would let me see up to her cunt, and down to her navel, but never more. My experience might not have taught me much if I had, but I guessed something from what old Brown had told me, and knew that woman had marks of some sort on their-bellies after child-birth.

As the time came for Sarah's return I felt trouble could come with her. The day before she did, Susan cried, said she was certain she was in the family way, and expressed great dread of her sister knowing it. "Surely you don't mind your own sister." "Oh! you don't know how hard she is upon poor girls who get into trouble," she replied. "Here is a mess!" I thought.

Sarah returned, had tried to get a miscarriage and failed, she grew bigger, all her fear was lest Susan should find it out before she left, and on plea of her mother's health, she gave notice. Both girls were afraid of each other, both seemed determined to get as much fucking as possible. Sarah got hers on Sundays, and sometimes on week days. Susan who was more about and could often get five minutes with me slyly, threw herself in my way, got it when and where she could, and had it once or twice daily. I was not loth. The excitement of two cunts and a certain pungency in the position stimulated me. I have seen the two standing side by side, each at the same moment with my spunk in them, yet neither knowing the other's condition. At times before I had washed my prick after one sister, I was wetting it in the cunt of the other, which delighted me.

Things got desperate. Sarah said I ought to marry her, spoke of committing suicide, and at length unable to hide her belly, left. I was anxious to do what I could to help her, so disclosed my case to a friend; who advised me to borrow, as I was so near coming into my property. I borrowed fifty pounds of a Jew, promising to pay him a hundred pounds for it six months afterwards; and got her lodgings a few miles from our house. Susan also got bigger, and made no disguise of her intention of getting abortion.

No disclosure of the sisters to each other had yet taken place, yet I felt it would be done. One morning Susan's eyes followed me whilst waiting at table in a most unpleasant manner. I felt all was found out, so to face it, and get the worst over, threw myself in her way. "You wretch, you scoundrel, you blackguard," she whispered to me on the staircase, "it is you who have seduced my poor sister." Soon a better opportunity was found, and we had a scene; it took place in my bed-room, when the other servant who had replaced Sarah, and my mother were out. I could only say I was sorry. She blazed out worse than ever then, and spoke so violently about my behaviour to herself, that I told her, whatever her sister had to complain of, I thought she had but little, for that mine was not the first prick which had been up her, I was sure. My words and manner staggered and quieted her and after making me take a solemn oath (which I did holding a Bible) I would never tell her sister that she was in the family way by me, she got tranquil, and I fucked her before she left the room.

Susan was dreadfully ill a few days afterwards, she had got a miscarriage; my mother attended to her, thinking she had inflammation of her bowels. I went to see Sarah, who told me some fellow had got her sister Susan in the family way, she could not tell who, for Susan quite refused to say. She was soon after confined with a fine child. Troubles then came apace, the mother of the two women died, Susan left my mother at once to take charge of the old man's house, and never let me have her again after her miscarriage. Then the father came to grief, failed and was sold up. Sarah went home with her child, and after a time, acting on the advice of a friend, I advanced money out of my property which I had then come into, and sent the whole lot to Canada. After a year my child died, and Susan got married. What became of Sarah, I don't know, for all letters soon after ceased; but to the last I believe that Sarah never knew that I had had her sister as well as herself, although Susan knew I had had both of them and was father of both children, or what would have been both children.

This ended my intrigues with servants for some time, for my fucking took quite another direction. Harlots of small degrees amused me till I came into what was a pretty fortune in those days.

CHAPTER XIII.

Of age.--Camille my first French woman.--
Lascivious
delights.--Harlots by the dozen.--Baudy books.--
Tribades.--
A grey-haired cunt.

I came into my property, and to the great horror of my
mother and family, soon gave up my post at the ------ and
my intended career and determined to live and enjoy
myself. I had been all but posted to a regiment, that
commission I resigned, though all my youth desiring it. I
lost much money by doing so. What I did between the
time that I had the two sisters, until I went regularly to the
town, is not worth telling of more than already done. Frig
myself, I did not, gay women since my last clap I was shy
of, but I used to shag a servant of a family close by, and
rather think one of our own servants; but if so, all
circumstances made small impression on me, and nearly
escaped my mind, excepting those of a comely woman of
about thirty with black curls, of a wall not far from a
church, and of fucking her up against it, of her being so
anxious to get indoors by nine o'clock, and scuffling off
with her wetted cunt directly she had finished with me.
Her name or who she was I quite forget.

This I know, that I had no other woman at home, and
had no liking for gay women, nor is it to be wondered at,
since my experience with them was confined to one I had
with my cousin Fred, women by the roadside who would
take a shilling, and others of a queer class in the confines
of the Waterloo road (two debauches there told of) then
filled me with horror, and three claps; yet I was to leave off
giving my passion to quiet women, and bestow all my
attention for a time on gay women.

Walking up Waterloo place one evening, with plenty of money in my purse, and lust in my body, I met a fine, clear complexioned woman, full twenty-five years of age, who addressed me in French, and then in broken English. She had an eye, and manner which fascinated me, her dress was quite elegant, as unlike the French women of Regen street of the present day, as a duchess is to a milkmaid; but she was the ordinary French whore of the day, of whom there were but few in London (there was no railway to Paris); and who were exclusively supported by gentlemen at the West-End. I went home with her to a house at the corner of G-l-n square, after fearing and hesitating.

As I got to the door my fear returned, and but for shame I would not have gone in. "I have but little money," said I, "Have you not a Victoria?" said she. "No." "You will find one, I am sure." By that time the door was opened, and in I went. "You will find one Victoria," said she in broken English as she closed the room-door, "but if not, shall you not give me what you shall find." The room was nicely furnished, out of it was a nice large bed-room and a smaller one (she paid twenty shillings a week for all, as you will soon hear). Four wax candles were lighted, down she sat, so did I, and we looked at each other. I could say nothing.

"Shall I undress?" said she at length. "Yes," I replied, and she began. Never had I seen a woman take off such fine linen before, never such legs in handsome silk stockings, and beautiful boots. I had had the cleanest, nicest women, but they were servants, with the dress and manners of servants. This woman seemed elegance itself to them. A nice pair of arms were disclosed, a big pair of breasts flashed out, a glimpse of a fine thigh was shown, and as her things dropped off, and she stopped to pick them up, with her face towards me; her laced chemise dropped, opened, and I saw darkness at the end of the vista between her two breasts.

A pull up of the stockings and garters, disclosed other glimpses of the thighs and surroundings. Then she sat on the pot, pissed and looked at me, whilst I sat in fear, saying nothing, doing nothing, my cock shrivelled to the size of a gooseberry, and longing to go away. The whole affair was unlike anything I had seen or dreamed of, a quiet business-like, yet voluptuous air was about it, which confused me; it affected my senses deliciously in one way, but all the horrors about gay women were conjured up in my imagination at the same time. I was intensely nervous.

She seeing me so quiet, sat herself on my knee, and began unbuttoning my trousers. I declined it. "Are you ill?" said she. I told her no, scarcely knowing what she meant. Then she unbuttoned me in spite of my objection, laid hold of my little doodle, and satisfied herself that it was all right I suppose; for she hurt me; I could not tell why she squeezed it, for I did not know then the ways of gay women. The squeeze gave me a voluptuous sensation, although fear had still hold of me; then she kissed, and fondled me, but it was useless. Then she said, "You have never had a woman before I see." My pride was wounded, and I told her I had many.

"Are always you like this with them?" she asked. "No, but I really did not want it." "Oh! yes you shall. Come to the bed." She got off my knee, went to the bed, laid down on one side, one leg on, one dropping down to the floor, drew up her chemise above her navel, and lay with beautiful large limbs clad in stainless stockings and boots, her thighs of the slightly brown colour seen in Southern women, between them a wide thicket of jet-black hair, through which a carmine streak just showed. She raised one of her naked arms above her head, and under a laced chemise showed the jet-black hair in the arm-pit. I had never seen such a luscious sight, nor any woman put herself unasked into such a seductive attitude.

"Come," she said. I obeyed and went to the side of the bed, my prick not yet standing. She took my hand and put the finger on to her clitoris, pulled my prick towards her and kissed it, and at the double touch up it rose like a horn. "Ah!" said she moving on to the middle of the bed, "take off your clothes." I was on to her without uttering a word and had plugged her almost before I had said "no," which I had meant to say.

What a cunt! what movement! what manner! I had till then never known what a high-class, well practised professional fucker could do. How well they understand the nature and wants of the man who is up them; hers was the manner of a quiet woman, who had been some time without a prick, it was so like baudy nature in a lady, that I was in the seventh Heaven, "don't hurry"; but the wriggle and heave, and the tightening of the cunt kept hurrying me, as well she knew.

I had scarcely finished my spend, when curiosity took possession of me. She yielded in the way a French woman does to all a man wishes; almost anticipating them. The black hair under her arm-pits first came in for my admiration, then her eyes, her bubbies came in for their share, as raising myself on an elbow, my prick still up her, I looked and felt all over her, I even opened her mouth and felt her teeth which were splendid. Then rising on my knees, I looked between her legs, at the splendid thicket of black hair. Far from attempting to get up, or prevent me, she opened her thighs wider, I pulled aside the cunt-lips, there rolling out from a dark carmine orifice was my essence. At the sight of it, up came my prick, still dripping, and up it went into the sperm-lined passage.

My second fuck over, she washed. No sooner was that done, than I wanted to see it all over again. "You are very fond of women," she said, "I thought you had never had a woman before." Then I explained, gave her the Victoria, and scarcely daring said (for she was dressed again), "How I should like to do it again." "You take up much time of me, but you may, if you like, at side of de bed." Out came my prick, up it went, her duff and belly in sight now, till I spent in her, and promising to see her again I left. One does not get silk stockings, laced chemise, four wax lights and three fucks for a pound now, if rooms be well furnished, or not.

I saw her the next day, then saw her almost daily. Little by little I took to calling at all times, and sleeping with her. The more I had her, the more I liked her. She was a very nice woman in most ways, I scarcely ever found her untidy, dirty, or slammerkin. If not dressed, she had a clean wrapper on, had nearly always silk stockings on, and a clean chemise; and therefore call when I might she was ready to be fucked at a minute's notice. She was a good cook, and would cook omelettes and nice things in her room. I used to fuck, get out of bed, eat, and fuck again with the food almost in my mouth. I used to have little dinners in her room, sent in by a French cook, which were excellent, and then with stomach full and with nice wine, would spend the evening in baudy joys.

What astonished and delighted me at the same time, was the freedom and the way she lent herself to all my voluptuous inclinations. The gay women I had had, I had fucked so fast, and got away from them as soon as I could; my spend even scarcely finished at times. With my mother's servants (my first love Charlotte excepted, and for a time with Susan), my enjoyments were mostly hurried, a fingerstink, a frig on their cunt, and a hurried look were all my amatory preliminaries for the most part; because I was too impatient for the spend, was mostly obliged to seize opportunities in a hurry, or because the girls were impatient at being pulled about. When I had tried with them, some of the little amatory amusements, which were beginning to suggest themselves to my voluptuous imagination, they resisted, or only half lent themselves to my will. With Susan I had tried the most, because I knew she had had a bumbasting before, and she had been more willing; she liked pulling my prick about, but even she made a fuss one night, when I wanted to fuck her with her bum towards my belly, and never let me look at her belly. Thus my baudy longings had never been satisfied. With Charlotte I did a little variety, from curiosity; now I began to want it from voluptuousness. The natural impatience of my age, and my few opportunities, had led me to bring my women to the bed, throw up their clothes, pull open their legs, give a rapid glance at their thighs, belly and cunt-fringe, by which time my prick was nodding and throbbing. Then followed a grope, and the next minute I was fucking as hard as I could.

With Camille all came like new to me. She even anticipated me. If I pushed her to the side of the bed, she fell on her back and opened her legs gently, disclosing her slit in the most voluptuous manner, without speaking. If I strove to open her thighs, open they went as wide as she could make them, leaving me to open, and shut, pinch, frig, or probe her cunt, as I listed. At a hint, she with two fingers would spread open the lips to enable the fullest inspection. If I turned her round, she would fall on the bed arse upwards, like a tumbler. If I cocked up a leg, there she kept it till I pulled it down. I scarcely ever said what I wanted, she guessed my desires from the way I turned her about. It was only at a later time when my baudiness grew whimsical, and invented strange attitudes, or singular caprices of love, that I had to tell her what I wanted; but at first I was too timid for that. She once said to me laughing, "I am a born whore, for I like it, and like to see a man amuse himself with me."

Her every movement, even when I was tranquil, was exciting. If she sat down, her limbs were in some position which by contemplation stirred my lust, and made me rush to stroke her, and was gratified in any form and manner I liked. With her all forms of copulation were wholesome and natural, so that I had enough variety.

I was constantly with her until pretty well fucked out, then I stayed away a while. When I recommenced she I expect thought I was weary of her, and set to work to keep me, by putting into my head things I had not heard, or thought of, asking if I would like to sate my lust in such, and such ways; and then procuring for me what she had suggested.

I was indeed worth treating so, for though I only gave her a sovereign at first, my money quickly began to go into her pocket from mine. The more variety I had, the more I paid, which was but natural, and fair.

She had a book full of the baudiest French pictures; there was not an attitude depicted in it that I did not fuck her in. That done, she asked me one day if I would like another woman to feel whilst I had her. She came, and I fucked Camille feeling the other's cunt, longing to fuck it, but fearing to propose it. Camille guessed what I wanted, and proposed it herself. With what joy my prick entered the stranger's split, Camille looking on, holding her cunt open for inspection at the same time, and going through the motions of frigging herself whilst I was shoving. Then came endless variety. I had two other French ladies, and fingered their cunts whilst I fucked a third, then two more, laying cunt upwards, legs in the air, and arses meeting over Camille's head. At last I had six altogether at once, and spent the evening with them naked, fucking, frigging, spending up or over them, making them feel each other's cunts, shove up dildoes, and play the devil's delight with their organs of generation, as they are modestly called.

Then came other suggestions. "I know such a little girl, not above this high," she said. I ballocked that little girl. Then she knew one six feet high. She also I had. Then she knew one with an immense duff of hair on her cunt. Of course I had her. Then one with none at all; and mightily pleased was I, as my doodle rubbed in and out of that hairless cunt, the owner laying at the side of the bed, I standing up, and Camille holding a candle over the hairless quim, to enable me fully to see and enjoy the novelty, I was pushing up.

At intervals when worn out with spending, or disinclined to find the money needed for this endless variety of women and cunt-hunting, I frequently spent evenings quietly in Camille's society. I got from her information about habits of women, in a way which is not often given to young men by gay women; learned that women thrust sponges up their cunts, to prevent men finding out they had their courses on. For the first time with her, I understood that women could, and did frig themselves; and on her own cunt, placing herself my finger there, I first knew the exact spot where a women rubs for her solitary pleasure. She told me of women rubbing their clitoris together so as to spend,--what the French call tribadism,--and two women of her acquaintance did this. All of us half spoony with champagne after a jolly little supper; she set the two girls rubbing their cunts together. The two girls on the top of each other, I thought a baudy amusement, and did not believe until after years, that flat fucking was practicable, and practised, with sexual pleasure.

Then should I like to see a man? Now it was not many years since I had frigged two or three, and declined it. Yet one night she expatiated so much about the wonderful size of a young man's prick, and what a lot he spent, and how respectable he was, and what gentlemen had him, etc.; that I who had a dislike to men being near me, consented, and a fine young Frenchman came. I could not for half-an-hour go near him, but my temptress meant I should, and I frigged one of the largest pricks I have ever seen, and saw his spunk squirt over Camille's arse, which the Frenchman requested her to turn upwards for him to spend on; indeed he said he could not make his cock stand until he saw her arse. Directly afterwards I had the most ineffable disgust at him, myself and all, and never saw him again.

I would not again be in the room with a man, but she arranged to let me see through a hole made in the door, herself fucked by another man, which I immensely enjoyed, but had not the sight repeated. I even used to hate the idea of her being fucked by any one but myself; not that I had anything in the way of love or liking for her, which might have been termed affection.

So time went on, I paying handsomely, trying to see and do anything she suggested, and glorifying myself at being in the lucky way of doing and knowing everything. I told much to some special friends, some of whom wanted to find out my sources of such enjoyments; others thought I was a mere braggart.

Nearly a year ran away, and four thousand pounds, leaving me with infinite knowledge and a frame pretty well worn; but I never had a love ailment, nor have I ever taken one from a French woman yet.

She never suggested arse-hole work. In her book were pictures of buggering, and she asked me if I would like such a thing. I frightened at what I knew, which seemed like a horrible dream, said, "certainly not," and asked if it was possible. She told me it was, but was "villaine," and the matter was never again referred to.

With much fucking I got done up, and one night could get no cock-stand. She asked me if I had ever played at minette. I did not know what it meant. She told me it was having my prick sucked. I told her no. I have already narrated my licking the slightly haired cunt of young Martha, and how when doing so, she having my prick in her hand close to her mouth, and was playing with it, when scarce thinking of consequences, "Kiss it," I said, "put it in your mouth"; and that the young girl randy with my licking, put it to her mouth or tongue, and that I immediately shot out my spunk without meaning it. That remained in my recollection as a nasty subject. The big-cunted woman also sucked me against my will. So when Camille suggested it I refused. There was another French woman with her; they were both naked on the bed, and I had been fumbling both, and baudily amusing myself, with no cock-stiff or fucking desire about me. After a while I laid down on the bed with them, the other French woman told me, that some men never did anything else, and that she would like doing it to me. She had found out I was pretty liberal, and I dare say counted on my being so now, if I could get by her a new sensation; but I declined. The two women were laying in the reverse direction to me on the bed, so that I could see and play with both their cunts, a favourite posture with me then. After extolling the sensation of minette, she without my consent turned over me, and getting me between her knees back up, and so that her bum-hole and cunt were within a few inches of my nose, she began; whilst Camille who knew what would fetch me better than I knew myself, moved up her backside, so that I might grope her more freely. The double cunt feeling, the suction and sight generally, was too much for me, and the mouth soon drew my sperm with long lingering and half painful pleasure. My tender-tipped prick suffered, as it often did indeed when not in the proper receptacle.

The act made some impression on me, for I soon after had it repeated by the same woman, and she did it that time so that I saw the prick in her mouth. I expect it upset me instead of giving me pleasure, for I stopped her, and my doodle dropped; but I permitted her to recommence; then I felt something press my arse-hole, it tickled and hurt me, I called out, "What are you doing?" at the same instant spent. "What have you done?" said I. "Nothing," said she winking at me, for Camille was in the room. I did not like the business; she had shoved her finger or thumb up my bum-hole. I was too young to appreciate that luxury, took a horror at her, and never would have her again, nor would I have my prick sucked any more. Many years elapsed before I either had my arse-hole felt or felt a woman's, after that night.

Then I had an old woman. Those she had brought me had mostly dark-haired cunts, and her own was black. As cunt was an inexhaustable subject with me, we were always talking about it. She said she knew a woman whose hair was quite grey. "Is she very old?" "No not above fifty." That was older than my mother, and I could not think of it; but the conversation was renewed. "She has got as much hair as me, but quite grey, nearly white, and she is a nice clean woman; have us both, and you can see the black and white together." So a fattish middle-aged woman certainly fifty and who seemed to me sixty, came; her hair was nearly white, Camille lent her stockings and chemise to make her decent I suppose, and the old woman who spoke scarcely a word, but drank furiously, turned up to me. She made some objection to showing her grummit, remarking she did not know it was to such a young man, but being told if she did not, she might go without pay, the sight came off; the cunt-fringe was nearly white. She was an English woman. Camille suggested I should have her; the old woman demurred, but Camille settled (and I really used to do almost what she advised), that I should have her and look at the grey cunt at the same time. So it came about; but when half up to spunking time, Camille said, "Take it out of me and put it into her." When a prick stands and novelty is in the way it rushes at it. Out I pulled my prick, and put it up the grey cunt, spent in it, and pulled it out almost before I had finished. I never saw the old lady again.

CHAPTER XIV.

Piddlings.--Posturings.--Breast and arm-pit.--A turn over.--

Used up.--Wanting a virgin.--Camille departs.--The Major's

opinion.--Camille returns.--Louise.

I have told the most novel fucking bouts I had with, or through Camille, excepting the final one; but should say that whatever women she got me I turned to her with pleasure again. Sometimes when I had one or two to amuse me, I used to give her the preference for the fuck, and she always had one of the gruellings, for she was very handsome, understood everything, was sensuousness itself, but not vulgar. When I had a fit of extra lewdness she got me other women. Of course she got profit out of all, a thing I knew nothing about then. Often I had no want but for her, and she used to strip herself, or dress just as I wished, put her body into some attitude, then lay and read the paper whilst I used to sit and read as well, looking up from time to time at her. Then I would put her in a new attitude, and go on so for a time; then would make her piss, catch it in the pot, piss at the same time in it, stick a dildo up her cunt, and have every variety of amusement I could think of. She was always willing, never in a hurry, never refused. A charming harlot.

Making her piss was a favourite amusement with me, I would keep her a whole day without doing it, so that I might have a good long stream out of her when looking on.

I was most curious about the way a cunt opened and shut in squatting. It was the subject of my earnest investigation. I used to put two chairs so that they would not slip, nearly close together, and lay down with my head between them. Then Camille naked all but boots and stockings would stand up on the chairs, one foot on each; the legs naturally a little open as the chairs were a little apart, just disclosed the cunt. Then she would sit down slowly, so that I could gradually see the gap widen, the red nymphoe show, the clitoris jut out, and at length the whole cunt-gape ready for the piss. Then she would rise slowly and repeat it till I was tired; then still laying down I used to hold a large basin on my breast and belly, and squatting above my head she would piss into the basin. I would feel the cunt, and if very wet, dry it. In all this she was obedience itself; she never moved from one posture till I told her to get to another, would answer any question with frankness.

I have never lost this pleasure in seeing a woman piss, but at that time was too impatient to vary the amusements which a man and a woman can have with their piddle. It was reserved to me with other women, notably a French woman named Gabriell, and Sarah F--r, to have the fullest variety and enjoyment in that particular.

I had fucked Camille in every way excepting her arse-hole, I had spent between her bum-cheeks, but without the slightest intention of invading the bum-hole between them,--indeed then had a great dislike to looking at a woman's arse-hole. At last fucked her arm-pits; she had a splendid arm, and an unusually large quantity of black hair beneath it which I much admired. One day she was poorly, I began fucking between her breasts, she suggested another woman, I would not have one; from her breasts I got to shoving between her arm and her breasts; then she wetted her arm-pit with Castile soap, which is of a soft slimy nature, and I fucked and spent between it. After a time we improved on this; she would lie in a convenient posture, I would lay a sheet of clean white paper on the bed, and just as I was coming, protrude the tip of my prick so as to free the pit, and shoot my spunk on to the sheet of white paper; or would catch the spunk in my own hand, and before my frensy of pleasure was over rub it on her cunt, then fling myself on the bed and go to sleep.

I used to have her at the side of the bed with her bum towards me; then she would gradually twist herself round, and cocking one leg over my head, get herself with her back on the bed without uncunting my prick. This had to be done very gradually, for a jerk, and my prick used to slip out. I used to bet with her about this, and she generally managed to twist round and win. "Now push,--keep it well in,--hold on, I am going to lift my leg," she would cry at the difficult point, which was when she had got her bum sideways to me, and was about to lift her leg; then putting my hands well on her hips, I used to draw my belly to her, and prick into her, as tightly as I could, whilst she gradually raised a leg, and pressing her bum up to meet my pressure, gradually got on to her back, with her limbs in a natural easy posture on either side of my hips. By that time I had got steam well up, and a shove or two usually let me off.

At last having done as great a variety of ballocking, and learn more baudiness than most men of my age, I was knocked up, fucked out. My mother with whom I still nominally lived, was in despair. My guardian alarmed at the rate I was spending my money remonstrated, so I left Camille and her bevy of women, and went to the sea-side. There I renovated, and then spent my time on the sands, trying to see the women in the water. As I grew better my randiness returned, I got hold of gay women, but my old timidity clung to me, I used to pay them to piss, and had a grope up them; but do not recollect having anything more. I came back to London, and for two or three days afterwards Camille's cunt had no rest. Then I temporarily got into another servant, and ceased to see Camille much. She tried all sorts of inducements to continue it on the old footing.

Then although she knew every incident of my life, she took to asking if I had ever had a virgin, saying, "Are you sure, did you see her cunt before you had her? Would you not like one again, if I can get you one, a young virgin French girl, one sure to be a virgin?"--and so on until she made me doubt if I had ever had one. At last I thought that I should like to have another. Well, she could get me a young French girl, but would have to go to France, it would cost a large sum of money. This talk went on for some time, and little by little I agreed to give her fifty pounds to pay her journey, and also to keep her lodgings on. She postponed the journey for a long time, but at length she went. She made me promise to do something for the girl besides paying her,--which meant something or nothing,--but I promised to pay the journey of the virgin back to France, should she want to go; and also whenever I had the girl, to pay Camille a "Victoria," "because," said she, "you will have my rooms and prevent my bringing friends home."

So I came down with fifty pounds. Off she went in quiet dress, and looked a quiet lady or middle-class woman. She advised me to keep myself steady, and the very moment before she left, whilst the cab was at the door, I turned her with bonnet and travelling dress on, bum outwards, and fucked her; she hurrying me all the time for fear she should lose the coach, she had not time to piss, or wipe or wash. "It will give me good fortune perhaps," said she laughing, "or make you wish me back, it is lucky for me."

There was but a slow rail to Dover then, nothing but tidal boats, and to Paris, the way I thought she was going, no rail at all, and it was a long journey. Whether she went to Paris or not I don't know, but from later experience think not, that she was a Southern woman, and went straight home. She was to be back in a month. It came, but not she; another week, another, and I began to think I had been sold; another, and I gave her up altogether, and experienced a little relief, for the habit of seeing her had so got hold of me, that I could not shake it off, and yet I was tired of her, but I wanted the virgin.

There was a middle-aged man with whom I chummed much at my Club, a major retired, and a most debauched individual. He borrowed money of me, and did not repay it. His freedom of talk about women made him much liked by the younger men; the older said it was discreditable to help younger men to ruin. Ordinarily very careful how I spoke about women (for my loves having lain much in my mother's house, caution had become habitual to me). I one night talked about virgins and of getting them. He said such things were done; that Harridans got a young lass, if well paid for it, but that they generally sold the girls half-a-dozen times over, "and," said he, "they train the young bitches so, there is no finding them out; you may pay for one who was first fucked by a butcher boy, and then her virginity sold to a dandy; you may pay for it my boy, and not find out you have been done." I pondered much over this, and the next night returned to the subject. His opinion was that an old stager like him was not to be done; but that any randy young beggar would go up the girl, and flatter himself he had had a virgin, if the girl was cunning. "When you see the tight covered hole with your eye, find it tight to your little finger, and then tight to your cock, my boy; when you have satisfied your eye, your finger, and your cucumber, and seen blood on it, you may be sure you have had one,--and not otherwise."

Thought I, "I am going to be humbugged." Another week, no letter, I went to her lodgings, and found she had taken away everything she had with her. That night I told a little of my hopes to the Major, not telling him who the kind lady was, or where she was gone; but it made him laugh. "You are done brown my boy, done brown; that woman will never turn up again." He joked me so, that I avoided him, and kept the subject to myself afterwards.

Again to the lodgings; the landlady could not keep them vacant any longer; I paid the rent, but she got no parquisites, I increased the allowance. Then again I went; the landlady said she did not expect to see her again. I had now set my heart on having this virgin; ten weeks nearly had gone; I said if Camille was not back next week she might let the rooms. It passed; a bill was put up in the window, and the next morning calling as a forlorn hope, there was a letter for me,--she would be back in a week. I was in a state of excitement that week, and kept myself chaste, with the idea of the virgin cunt, and Camille's well paced roger-ing in anticipation.

The day came. I was so impatient, that I was there quite early; she arrived some hours earlier than she had said, and seemed surprised at finding me; my impression is that she did not want me to be there when she came back. She came in a hackney-coach; a stoutish full-sized young woman with a funny bonnet and long cloak on, got out of the coach with her, and in a free-and-easy way helped the things upstairs. She called her Louise. The wench put down a big box, and on my turning round after giving Camille a kiss, I saw she had seated herself on it, and hands on her knees was looking at me. "Uncord the box," said Camille. Said the girl, "I am tired." She uncorded it, again sitting down, and looking at me said, "Is that your young man?--he's a good-looking fellow." Camille told her to hold her tongue, to go on unpacking, and that I understood French, eying her at the same time in a savage way, and looking at me at times very uneasily. She was a rough sort of girl, she said, a relative of a friend of hers, had come as her servant, and in a short time would understand her place; smiling at me in a knowing way as she said that. Camille always addressed her servant in French, me in English; but I understood French tolerably well.

Louise did as she was told, but bounced about in an independent way, threw off her cloak and bonnet, and putting her hands on her hips stared at me again. I stared at her, thinking of the virginity I was destined to break up. Certainly she was appetizing; her cloak off showed a thick woolen dress of dark brown striped with blue, a fine big figure, a couple of big breasts; her arms naked nearly to her shoulders, as French peasants usually wore them, were large, fleshy, and brown; the petticoats were half-way up to her knees, and showed the thickest woolen black stockings on a stout pair of legs, and feet in thick shoes with brass

buckles; she had immense gilt earrings, and was in fact in
the dress of a Bordeaux peasant woman.

I did nothing but stare at her, Camille nothing but
scold her, talking to me at intervals. The girl got the boxes
ready for opening, then walked about, taking up poker and
tongs, chimney ornaments and everything in the room
with curiosity. Camille and I had so much to say, that we
took little notice of her; then she threw up the window and
looked out. As she bent forward her short petticoats
showed her legs up to her knee-backs; Camille was about
to stop her looking out, when I winked, and stooping saw
a thick roll of stockings just beneath the knees, and the
flesh just above. Camille understood. "Madame, madame,"
said the girl, "come here, here is fun." I heard Punch
squeaking in the streets; she was delighted; her mistress
went to the window giving me a knowing look, and
looking out of the window with the girl, put her hands
over the girl's petticoats and lifted them slightly. Louise
took no heed of this being so engrossed with Punch; I
dropped on my knees and saw half-way up the girl's thighs.
I had been chaste for a few weeks, or nearly so, the sight
of Camille had fired me, the thighs finished me; I shoved
my hands up Camille's petticoats on to her arse, got her
into her bed-room, and with her clothes in a lump on her
belly, drove up my prick, spending directly I got up her
cunt.

With half my spendings outside, half inside I lay with
throbbing prick, which only came out when it had spent
again. Camille vowed she had not had a man for weeks,
and took it out of me, perhaps fearing if I went away with
stiffening left, some other cunt would take it out. The
ballocking over I went home.

I was early there the next day; Louise had been installed
in the little room leading out of the sitting-room. Camille

told me a great deal about the distance she had gone, and the trouble and expense she had been put to in getting the girl's relatives to let her come; she hoped I would pay the additional expenses; and that I did at a cost of about twenty pounds. What with that and paying for her journey, and for lodgings while absent, Louise had cost me nearly ninety pounds already. Then I undertook to pay for the additional room, in which a bed having been put, an extra was charged; cooking now being done downstairs. Then Louise must have a new gown; then Camille thought I ought to give her something for herself, because whilst away for me she had made no money. That I refused and blazed up about it; for all that agreed to pay for a new silk dress for her, and a lot of little odds and ends on the second day of Camille's return, for all of which outlays I had only had a peep up the girl's petticoats.

Then I had a talk about her. The girl was the daughter of a small grape-grower, a friend of Camille's; they thought Camille was in London as a dressmaker, making a lot of money, because she sent money home to her father. Camille offered to take her, saying she would be sure to get on, if not in one way, then in another; that good-looking girls always did well in London. The girl was mad to come, and persuaded her parents to let her do so; believing that Camille got her living honestly; she was to be her servant until she could be put in the way of doing well.

"What are you going to tell her now? what are you going to do with her? what will she say when she finds out?" I asked.

Camille did not know. The girl would find out, and then she must excuse herself as well as she could, would say it was better, and jollier, and more money making than to make dresses. Besides, the girl could not help herself, and would have to make the best of it.

When was I to have her? I asked. As soon as I could get her; there she was, and I might try when and how I liked; help me more she could not, she could not insist on Louise letting me; but no doubt she would in time, no one else should have her.

I was not so sure of that. Camille was gay, and although I had for more than a year excluded most men from the house, yet she did have other men there, and I knew they would see the girl, might like her, might pay Camille; all the remarks of the retired major came strongly before me, and I thought I was going to be sold, and said so.

She replied that I was not; she would leave me with the girl when I liked; if the girl spoke to her she would advise her to let me, but would have nothing to do with influencing her beyond that; and when the event came off, she meant to be out, so that Louise's friends could not say anything. If she went gay it was no fault of hers, young women would have it done to them, it was natural. That was the game she meant to play.

I saw that I had paid her only for bringing a girl, and must take my chance of getting into her; all she would do was to keep the coast clear. I don't know what I really did expect Camille to do, but think I imagined that she would have got the girl in bed with her some night, let me get into bed with them, and helped to make her fuck, if she would not. This was dissipated, I was to have the chance I should have had with a servant in my mother's house, or less, for this girl I should not see so often, and could not be sure she would be so well looked after.

So Camille went out, leaving me alone with the servant whenever I wished. I expect she went with other men at houses of friends, and so got her time paid for twice over, and made a good thing of it; perhaps she thought, the longer this lasted the better it would be for her. I think now that that was her game.

FINIS VOLUME ONE

~PROVIDING EVERYTHING THAT MAKES LIFE PLEASANT ~

M.G.V.T

FOR THE BEST YET TO BE;
PURVEYORS OF INTENSE PLEASURE &
SECOND TO NONE FOR OVER 100 YEARS WITH
ROOTS GOING BACK TO THE FIRST FINE
TAILORS STORE BY WILLIAM TYSON.